Mr. Campbell was born in Edinburgh in 1912, and was educated at Edinburgh University. He worked as an editorial writer on a Scottish newspaper until 1937, when he moved to South Africa. *The Heart of Africa* (1954) was his first book to be published in this country, although six others had appeared in England and South Africa. He is now the head of the Tokyo bureau of *Time* and *Life*. He is married, and the father of three children.

THE HEART OF INDIA

THE
Heart
OF
INDIA

Alexander Campbell

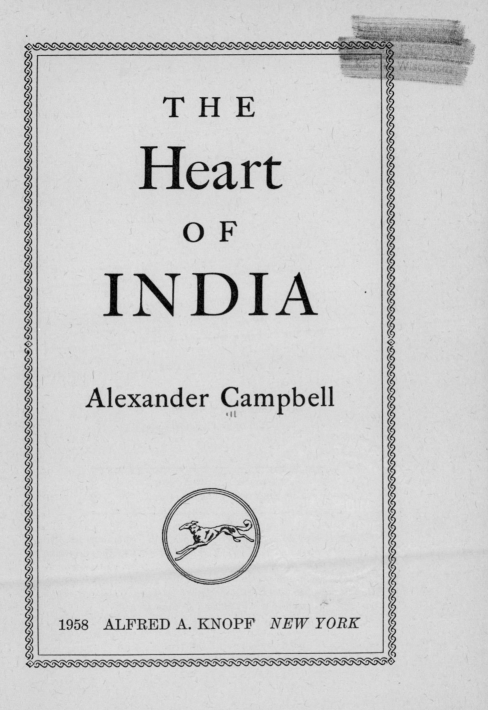

1958 ALFRED A. KNOPF *NEW YORK*

80870

L. C. Catalog card number: 58–6530
© *Alexander Campbell, 1958*

THIS IS A BORZOI BOOK,
PUBLISHED BY ALFRED A. KNOPF, INC.

PUBLISHED APRIL 21, 1958
SECOND PRINTING, OCTOBER 1958

CONTENTS

ILLUSTRATIONS

(FOLLOWING PAGE 150)

THE HEART OF INDIA

I
DELHI:
THE SHADOW UNDER THE LAMP

The dominant fact in India is heat. WILL DURANT

KALI, the wife of Shiva, shook her necklace of human skulls in the dance of death. Under the pounding of the divine feet, the earth shrank to a smoldering ember. It was the end of the world but, with the cunning that comes only in dreams, I had taken refuge inside one of the skulls of Kali's necklace. I could smell the sweat of the goddess's flesh as she grew mad with the joy of the dance. It was a poor refuge, for I was being shaken and jolted over terrifying abysses of space and time. Only Shiva could end the dance, and I wished he would come.

I awoke from nightmare, and the sweat was my own. Kali was the train, rattling the blistered brown boxes of its carriages like castanets. The shaking was real enough, for the train was rocking across a vast glaring plain. It was morning, and I had a taste of cinders in my mouth. Above the compartment's lavatory door, a fan rasped tinnily behind its wire screen. From his corner of the compartment, sitting comfortably cross-legged with his bare feet on the green leather cushions, Mr. Kaviraj Lal was telling Rud about the Godhead.

"On the controversial subject of attaining union with the Godhead," he said, "Krishnamurti has some exceedingly sound common sense."

3

Only in India, I thought, could one awake in a train and hear such a remark start off a new day.

Mr. Lal was a plump man, with a round brown face. He had large, jutting ears, and he wore a white cotton Gandhi cap which he never removed. His brown legs were loosely wrapped in a dhoti, consisting of several yards of thin white cotton, and over this he wore a long white cotton shirt, with several pockets. One of the pockets carried a row of ballpoint pens.

We were bound for Delhi, and Mr. Lal had been with us since we left Bombay. At the Bombay railway station, just before the train started, he had appeared in the doorway of the compartment, smiling his benign smile, carrying a furled black umbrella with a bamboo handle, and followed by a railway porter holding a large wicker basket.

Mr. Lal surveyed us blandly and, it seemed, approvingly. Then he seated himself in the compartment, and with dignity arranged the folds of his ample white dhoti. The large wicker basket was respectfully placed on the luggage rack. The porter slammed shut the compartment door. A bell clanged loudly; the train started. "A warm day, gentlemen," said Mr. Lal benevolently. "Very humid."

Rud responded not just politely, but with positive enthusiasm. He was still in that early stage of the foreigner's acquaintance with India when the fact that many Indians speak English as if it were their mother tongue (which for many Indians it is) comes as a joyful surprise. Rud was a young American, not long out of college. He had broad shoulders, reddish hair and alert, pale blue eyes with sandy lashes, above freckled cheekbones. His name was Rudyard Jack, and he proposed to study at Benares University, learn about Gandhism, and go on a walking tour with Gandhi's land-reforming heir, Vinoba Bhave. And now here he was, at the very outset of his travels, locked up in a railway compartment with an Indian who evidently spoke fluent English and who appeared to be a man of some influence. Rud was plainly delighted.

4

There was no question about the fluency of Mr. Lal's English, but it had one fascinating peculiarity. He spoke it with a strong Welsh accent. At some time or other the schools of India appear to have been staffed almost entirely by Welsh teachers. Little Hindus and Moslems had the message of the British Raj drummed into them in the accents of Cardiff and Liverpool. Mr. Lal might have hailed from Llandudno.

He was agreeably ready to tell us all about himself. He had been imprisoned several times for making speeches demanding Indian independence. Each time he was set free he made more speeches and was invariably arrested again. But British jails and British bayonets had proved powerless against the Gandhian technique of soul-force. "Gandhi taught us that violence can do the country no good," said Mr. Lal. "On the contrary, it further aggravates the economic situation." When soul-force finally triumphed and India was set free, Mr. Lal was elected to the new House of the People as a member of the Congress Party, by a large majority.

"You did well to come to India to sit at the feet of our great teachers," Mr. Lal assured Rud, with a kindly if superior smile. "Americans are rich, but they are also very naïve. India is not interested in material things, but humbly seeks spiritual truths. She has saved herself by her own exertions, and will save the world by her example. I quote Burke. It is not for us to give advice to others, of course, but we are, after all, a very ancient nation. Our past has been glorious and destiny has marked us for great things. You Americans care nothing for us poor Asiatics, we know; but we bear you no grudge. We have forgiven even the British for enslaving us. For us, the means are more important than the end. To adopt bad means leads to all sorts of unpleasant consequences."

When the train halted at stations, Mr. Lal left the compartment to stroll up and down the crowded platform. Magnificent in the billowing white dhoti that flapped to his ankles, he smiled complacently on porters and carefully sidestepped beggars. His nod was sufficient to send a low-caste sweeper scurrying to the compartment, to remove the scum of gritty dust that had accumulated on the cushions, and to stand guard to see that the compartment was not invaded by unfortunates who had bought tickets but could find no place on the train. He was a very well-read man, and could quote Aristotle, Humboldt, and Renan in support of his opinions. Once, when Rud exclaimed at the sight of an emaciated man stumbling past, bent double under an enormous load, Mr. Lal followed Rud's gaze and nodded.

"Ah, yes; a coolie. What is it, Mr. Jack, that Eddington has to say about the universe? I will tell you. Eddington said: 'The world is all mind-stuff.' Nothing material is real, Mr. Jack: let America please remember!" Laughing merrily, Mr. Lal led the way back to the freshly swept compartment.

In Bombay the monsoon rains had just begun, but the countryside through which we were passing was as dry as an abandoned bone. Baked and rolled flat, it looked like a scorched *chapatti* straight out of a gigantic oven: the dread handiwork of some diabolical cook. The train clanked past the crumbling mud huts of a village. A woman with a red skirt was molding flat round cakes of cow-dung and adding them to an immense mound of the fuel. In a field a man wearing only a loincloth and a large white turban was leading two bullocks down a long earth ramp, in order to raise buckets from a well. The man was as thin as a stick insect. Man and beasts moved in a daze, as if they were dragging the sun on their backs.

Rud and I ordered breakfast at a station, and it was brought to the compartment at the next halt, the dishes wrapped in cotton napkins. Unwrapped, they were found to contain thick hot soup, an omelet filled with hot spices, and spiced chicken. Lunch, when it came, consisted of hot thick soup, a highly spiced omelet, and spiced chicken. From his large wicker basket, Mr. Lal produced a number of small brass dishes. One of them contained a fresh green banana leaf, kept rolled and moist. He laid it out flat, and spread on it curds and rice from

6

the other dishes. Then, like a painter mixing oils on a palette, he put in red pepper and yellow mustard. Finally he added a sprinkling of white chopped coconut, and began scooping up the dribbling mixture in skillful fingers, making cheerful sucking sounds. When he had finished, he wiped his fingers carefully on the leaf before throwing it out the window, and rose to visit the toilet.

Seated once more, with his bare feet tucked under him on the green cushions and his black leather sandals discarded on the floor, Mr. Lal turned from religion to history.

"Napoleon said: 'History is pack of lies agreed on.'" He smiled challengingly at Rud. "Isn't it, Mr. Jack?"

From time to time Rud attempted valiantly to argue back at Mr. Lal. He had little success. It was like watching a boy with a catapult trying to halt the massive onsurge of a steamroller.

The day wore on. Behind its wire screen, the ineffectual fan buzzed and whined. Mr. Lal visited the toilet again.

"When I was a child," said Mr. Lal, returning, "the astrologer who cast my horoscope told my father I would spend seven years in prison. My father was a lawyer, and this news made him very peevish. But the astrologer also assured him I would then become a pillar of public life. It has all come true." He beamed. "I also manufacture medicinal drugs. In the arts of medicine, Mr. Jack, the ancient Hindus were supreme. Did you know that the ancient Hindus performed every sort of surgery except ligation of the arteries? It is so, I assure you. Ancient Hindus were fully conversant with all so-called modern Western inventions. Did you know it is established fact that they frequently flew over the Himalayas in airplanes? Also, they had atomic power."

Mr. Lal smiled happily. "They keep those things from you, of course. It is natural. Did you know that latest research proves IIndus were the first people to discover America? Aztec worship of Vishnu demonstrates this conclusively."

I looked out the window. "We're almost in Delhi," I said.

Mr. Lal put on his sandals, and warmly shook our hands.

7

When Rud tried to thank him for making the journey so interesting, Mr. Lal said with his kindly smile: "It was nothing; it was my humble duty."

Old Delhi railway station exploded around us, in an uproar of clanking coaches, hissing steam, and shouting porters. I saw Jane on the platform, and waved to her. She waved back. "My car is here," I told Mr. Lal. "Can I perhaps give you a lift?"

"No, no," said Mr. Lal, beaming. "I observe that some friends of mine have come to the station to greet me."

I stepped down onto the platform. It was like stepping close to the open door of a furnace. I introduced Rud to Jane, and said: "Come along with us, why don't you? We might find something interesting for you on your first evening in Delhi."

"If I won't be a nuisance—"

"Not a bit; that's settled, then."

Singh, tall and bearded and looking more than ever like a maharaja, was twisting his mustache and speaking loftily to the porters who were quarreling over our bags. "Tell them to take the lot to the car," I said.

Rud was looking back along the platform to where some sort of ceremony seemed to be in progress. Mr. Lal was surrounded by men, all wearing white Gandhi caps like his own. One man was smearing vermilion rice powder on Mr. Lal's forehead. The others were busily hanging garlands round his neck. Mr. Lal submitted with smiling grace, placing the palms of his hands lightly together in the Indian traditional greeting.

Outside the station the Studebaker was parked in a dusty glare of ancient taxis, pedal-rickshaws, tethered camels, and laden pack-mules. Though Old Delhi is a city of the plains, it actually lies north of Everest, and it looks toward the hills and the passes whence came the Moslem invaders who built most of it. The hill-folk still trade down along their route. Rud was looking about him, as we drove, at the scarlet battlements of Shah Jehan's Red Fort and the minarets and turnip-shaped dome of Shah Jehan's Great Mosque. Luckily, perhaps, we

8

were too far from the mosque to see the beggars crowding its huge stone steps, or the wooden shacks of the thieves' market, crowded at their foot. But we passed a man who had squatted and drawn aside his dhoti to urinate in the gutter outside a second-hand clothes shop displaying faded regimental tunics; and a cow wandered across the busy street, tangling traffic.

I asked Jane: "What's your news?"

"Kenny shot a cobra," she announced with pride. "It came out of one of the old tombs and tried to eat his pigeons."

"My son," I explained to Rud. "He's twelve." Rud looked suitably impressed.

To impress Rud still more, Singh drove with one hand, steering us skillfully between wildly swerving taxis and furiously pedaled rickshaws. With the other hand he twisted his mustache and caressed his beard.

We passed under a railway bridge, and the refugees who lived there peered out at us from the cool darkness of the vaulted stone arches. Then we were in a narrow sweating street where the air tasted of burning copper and was heavy with the smell of frying food. The buildings had balconies from which washing hung, and the balconies swarmed with people. A cinema hoarding showed a woman, ten feet high, with a red mark on her forehead; she was weeping tears the size of golf balls and praying to a man in a blue turban who floated godlike in the air above her, seated cross-legged on nothing. We approached one of the old city gates, its red sandstone badly crumbling. Singh maneuvered past a water buffalo, and with no break in the continuity we passed from Old into New Delhi.

But beyond Queensway and the open-air stores, gaudy with bales of bright cloth, the scenery changed. On our left was the magnificent stone bulk of the palace of the Nizam of Hyderabad, and on our right the Rashtrapati Bhavan and the Secretariat buildings, with their pink phallic domes. King George V sat inscrutably inside his memorial with an inquisitive myna bird perched on his marble crown and peering down at his

9

marble scepter. We were driving through the Princes' Park, with its artificial stone lotuses in artificial lakes; the park smelled of scorched grass. Beyond the park, on the road to Agra, were the old Moslem tombs. In one of them shirts were hung to dry. The shirts belonged to the policemen in a near-by police post. Two policemen sat in the shade of the tomb smoking cigarettes. They wore khaki tunics and red-and-brown turbans. On their sleeves were white armbands. One armband said in English "May I Help You?" and the other armband repeated this in Hindi. The policemen grinned at Singh, who grinned back. We drove on, past the police post, the tomb, the policemen, and their washing.

Singh's smile vanished abruptly when we came to the railway crossing and found the gate closed as usual. The steel tracks shone like silver and looked as if they were about to melt. They stretched forlornly away on either side, quite empty, with no train in sight. Singh got out of the car and shouted angrily in Hindi at the gatekeeper, who paid no attention. He was a large man, as big as Singh, and with a fiercer mustache. Singh came back, shrugging, and got in the car. The sky was a tent of aching blue and the air was a suffocating blanket. On either side of the tracks the earth was beaten flat and strewn with cinders. On the left side of the road a black water buffalo wallowed in a pit of mud that had once been a pool. Singh pressed the hooter. A youth, quite naked, and smeared from head to foot with ash, suddenly appeared, attracted by the noise. He pranced up and down beside the gate, laughing idiotically. The gatekeeper roughly ordered him away. He left, weeping.

Cars and trucks piled up behind us, all of them hooting. The sugar-cane man had taken his usual stand beside the closed gate, and he now began to squeeze sticks of sugar cane through his hand press. The thick juice ran into a brass pot, and the sugar-cane man filled glasses, adding slices of lemon and handfuls of ice chips. He wore a dirty white cloth wrapped round his head, and he occasionally unwound it to wipe the glasses. People began to tumble out of the vehicles, prepared to risk cholera at four annas a glass.

I told Rud: "During the Partition of India trains passed through here crowded with Hindu refugees from Pakistan. The trains were so crowded that they had people on the roofs of the carriages. The Moslems of Delhi came out with rifles and sniped at them all through the day. Elsewhere other Hindus, and Sikhs, were slaughtering Moslems."

Beyond the railroad tracks we passed a man walking slowly in the thick dust of the roadside. He was leading a shaggy dancing bear on a chain. We drove through a village of refugees, where men in pajamas slept stretched out on charpoys, the Indian rope-beds, outside the huts. A black-haired sow galloped away pursued by eight pink piglets. A string of camels minced toward us, followed by a long slow line of bullock carts. We turned off into the side road that led to our white bungalow. "Home!" said Jane.

The big living-room was comparatively cool, with the shades drawn against the glare and the ceiling-fan whirling. As we entered, the summertime lizards scampered across the walls, twitching their long tails and racing for shelter behind the African shield and the Picasso print of Gertrude Stein, their favorite lurking places. Later, encouraged by our apparent non-violence, they would come out to flick their tongues at the insects that clustered round the wall lamps.

"First you want a shower," I told Rud. "Then a drink. After that we'll see what Delhi has to offer us."

The usual gilt-edged invitations were on the mantel, below the African shield where the lizards hid. While Rud was showering, we examined them. The Vice-President of India had invited us to meet a delegation from a World Religion Society. The Minister of Education offered us Mrs. Nye Bevan, and the Minister of Health was giving a party for a visiting Swedish gynecologist who claimed to have evolved an oral contraceptive

11

from the common pea. We were also invited to a wedding in Chandni Chowk, and to a reception for a world-peace delegation. All these functions were being held that evening.

We decided to look in at the world-peace reception, and afterwards to attend the wedding. I consulted Rud, who was agreeable. "You'll have to wear black tie and cummerbund," I warned him. "But those I can lend you."

The reception was in a house near the tomb of a sixteenth-century sheik. The tomb made an imposing landmark, for it was lit with crimson lamps. In a narrow lane beyond the tomb we passed a string of sewage carts, smelling very strongly and hauled by disdainful camels. Policemen were flashing torches in the lane to guide guests' cars to the reception. In Delhi receptions and official cocktail parties absorbed much of the time of the police. When not thus engaged, they were usually to be found lining the route from the airport to salute visiting or departing delegations. It was an arrangement that well suited the gangs who, in the frequent absence of the police from their normal duties, went about stripping houses of their plumbing and stealing manhole covers, items for which there was always a ready sale on the thieves' market at the foot of the steps of the Great Mosque.

A policeman in a red-and-brown turban saluted us and gave Singh a numbered slip, handing me its duplicate. Another policeman pointed the way to a large striped marquee which had been set up on the lawn, whose surrounding trees were strung with colored lights. The marquee was buzzing with people making polite conversation. Barefoot servants went among them offering drinks, snacks, and cigarettes from silver salvers. Three of those bearers converged upon us. One offered us orange juice. The second offered us lemonade. The third offered us cigarettes, and lit them for us. The upholders of world peace evidently smoked, but did not drink.

We pushed our way slowly through the crowd toward our hostess, an elderly Hindu lady with gray hair and gentle eyes.

She was a cousin of the Prime Minister. Greeting us by pressing the palms of her hands lightly together, she said: "Isn't it grand that so many people are ready to work for world peace? It makes one feel that India, now she has thrown off the yoke, can do great things." She spoke B.B.C. English, not Welsh.

An Indian photographer with frayed shirtcuffs came up and asked if she would pose for a picture beside a large man with blond curls and blue eyes. She did so. Someone said the blond man was a Soviet playwright and a member of the peace delegation. Standing within the marquee was similar to being in a Turkish bath. Little pools of sweat lay in the bags under the playwright's eyes. My shirt was wet where it touched my skin. I finished my orange juice, and a bearer immediately put another in my hand. The ice in it had already melted. A woman with a red caste mark on her forehead, wearing a gold sari, and with a diamond in her nose came up and spoke to Jane. The sari disclosed four inches of pale brown midriff. She was the daughter of a millionaire cotton-mill owner, and was also a member of the Indian Communist Party. Her rouge and mascara had begun to run.

Through the entrance of the marquee I could see a strip of well-lit lawn and the high green hedge that separated the lawn from the lane. The string of sewage carts we had passed came slowly up the lane, and the camels peered inquisitively over the hedge. They seemed astonished by what they saw.

Rud found himself face to face with a stout woman with muscular arms who was wearing a green velvet dress that gaped open at one side. A white rosette surmounted by a white dove was pinned on her chest, like a medal. She pointed to it and said slowly in English: "World-peace delegate. From Uzbekistan. I am a railway-construction model worker." She eyed Rud closely. "You are for world peace?"

Rud said: "Well, ma'am—yes and no."

"You are Ameri-can?" The muscles under the green velvet rippled aggressively. "Americans, bandits," she declared. A convulsive movement of people around us abruptly removed her.

Her place was taken by a tall man with a long face, like a grave horse. He wore a white turban tightly wound round his high forehead. "If you believe in the Absolute," he told Rud, "there can be no problem." Rud said doubtfully that he supposed not. The tall man said: "Separateness is an illusion; there is no otherness. Do you believe in reincarnation?" Rud said he feared not. "But it all becomes so clear once you do," the tall man protested. He waved thin eloquent hands. "Recurrent but illusory deaths—the soul develops continuously . . ."

He vanished in the crowd.

"World Religion Society, probably," I told Rud. "He must have come to the wrong party. It often happens."

We glimpsed the man in the white turban talking vehemently to the woman in the green velvet dress. She was protesting that she was a railway-construction model worker and asking him about the atom bomb.

Jane suggested: "Let's go on to the wedding."

I gave one of the helpful policemen my duplicate number slip and he called for the Studebaker over the public-address system that had been set up on the lawn. We drove through the Princes' Park, now softly lamplit; fountains were spraying colored water on the stone lotuses. Old Delhi's tumult engulfed us. In Chandni Chowk cloth merchants and silversmiths sat cross-legged, and the sidewalks were crowded. The press became so great that we left the car and proceeded on foot. We could hear a street band, and presently a funeral procession crept down the street. It came slowly because of the crowds, but the band blew lustily on trumpets, and the mourners were dancing with ecstatic expressions before the bamboo bier on which lay the corpse, wrapped from head to foot in cloth of gold.

"They seem pretty happy about it," said Rud, bewildered.

One of the mourners, a thin young man with a narrow straight nose, had paused in his dancing and stood near us, breathing deeply. He turned at Rud's words and said in Eng-

14

lish: "We rejoice because the dead man died at a great age: he was sixty. Because the gods favored him, he will return as a high-caste man—perhaps even a Brahmin."

The funeral procession was moving on. The young man searched quickly in his pocket and handed Rud a card. "My jewelry store is just on the corner. You can't miss it. We have special prices for foreigners. There is no obligation to purchase if you care to come and look round. It will be our humble duty to serve you." He danced off after the procession, waving his arms and singing something in Hindi.

The wedding for which we were bound was being held in a large house off Chandni Chowk. We would see the groom but not the bride, for the bride held her wedding reception separately. But the groom would have no advantage over us, for he would not see his bride until his own wedding festivities concluded, when he would meet her for the first time. The wedding had been arranged by the parents after long consultations with astrologers.

We groped our way along an alley, almost pitch-dark and overhung by balconies that nearly touched. Then suddenly a lit doorway spilled us into a bright inner courtyard, with stone walls and inner balconies high overhead. Musicians sitting cross-legged on the floor blew reed pipes and banged on wooden drums. The wedding guests sat in rows on wooden benches; on a raised wooden platform covered with bright carpets the bridegroom sat alone. He was one of the most disconsolate bridegrooms I ever saw, for he wore a heavy gilt crown too large for him with jewels that hung down half-concealing his face; his mouth was sullen and his hands played nervously with the rich embroidery of his scarlet coat. His fingers were covered with rings, and he wore tight white trousers and crimson slippers with curling toes.

The guests were sipping coffee and drinking lime juice. A small boy in a pink turban politely offered us some. Bhada Prakash saw us and came over to join us. He was a small man

15

with black oiled hair and piercing black eyes. He wore a white silk shirt and a silver cummerbund, and there were large sweat patches under his arms. Bhada was the groom's elder brother. The family had lived in Chandni Chowk for several generations. They had once been enormously rich, and were still wealthy, but the family fortunes had been depleted in the troubles that followed Partition. Bhada had been compelled to become a businessman, and had proved to be a very good one. But his younger brother had shown no such aptitude, and so was now being married off to a girl whose family had no history and were of no consequence, except that they were richer than the Prakashes.

Bhada told us all this while we drank our coffee. He was very gloomy. "It will probably turn out badly," he concluded. "They say the girl can't speak a word of English, and that she eats with her fingers and takes her shoes off in public." He sounded bitter. He himself had been educated in England and spent as much as possible of his time in Europe. When he was compelled to pass a vacation in India, he went tiger-shooting.

The bridegroom came down from his platform and started shaking hands with everyone. Then he made his way slowly and reluctantly to the doorway, where his three sisters suddenly appeared and dramatically cast themselves at his feet, clutching his tight-trousered legs and imploring him not to leave them. These sisterly appeals were merely a traditional part of the wedding festivities, as was the bridegroom's next act: someone handed him a large canvas bag, and from this he drew out handfuls of silver rupees and presented them to the sorrowing sisters, as a token that he was still their protector. The small boy with the pink turban came along the alley, leading a richly caparisoned horse. While the guests crowded round, the groom buckled on a large sword and with difficulty mounted the horse. The small boy promptly got up behind him, and the pair rode off. The groom was still looking gloomy and nervous.

We said good-by to Bhada, and left the hall. As we went out,

16

I looked up in time to glimpse a woman, dressed in white and with her head shaved, ducking out of sight on one of the balconies. She was the groom's widowed aunt, and I hoped that nobody else had seen her, for in India widows are rated only a degree above the untouchables and are seldom allowed to watch weddings, even from a balcony.

We walked back to the car, passing shops that displayed mounds of pink, green and yellow sweetmeats. The night was black and greasy. It was hotter than it had been at noon. My cummerbund was a soaked rag and my black tie a wire noose. "Let's go to the Birla Temple," Jane suggested.

Round the temple's outer walls, flare-lit booths were doing a brisk business, selling *pakauras* and *papars*, the former a pastry stuffed with hot vegetables and the latter a thin pastry similar to a potato chip. The smoke rising from the booths overhung the entire area like a thick veil. The air stank of food being cooked in bad oil. The temple's three phallic towers were garish with electric lights. We walked up to the cement elephants at the temple entrance. Inside the temple priests were reciting *bhajans* and *kirtas*, which are Hindu religious verses that are chanted, and verses from the *Bhagavad-Gita*, the song that the Lord Krishna sang to Arjuna on the day of the battle.

The temple bells tolled, and in the temple courtyard conch shells were blown to mark the conclusion of the evening prayers. The crowds began to disperse.

We drove through the dark, baking streets to an air-conditioned restaurant that served Chinese food. The imported Hungarian orchestra was a man short, because the previous night one member, overcome by heat and homesickness, had cut his throat while lying in bed. A Sikh with lascivious eyes was dancing with a French girl with dyed blond hair. At one of the tables three Kashmiris were talking together in whispers. At another table an Indian Government spy was watching them and surreptitiously making notes.

We drove Rud to his hotel, and then drove home. The railway-crossing gate was closed, and we waited in the stifling darkness until a train clanked slowly past. The refugee village was fast asleep. Our bungalow gate was opened for us by the *chowkidar*, the watchman who, armed with a long bamboo stave, patroled all night on guard against plumbing burglars.

Lying in bed in the air-conditioned bedroom we could hear the jackals howling, close at hand, near the old tomb where Kenny had shot the cobra.

If there be a paradise on earth, it is here, it is here, it is here.
                                                                SHAH JEHAN

SINGH, his beard unwaxed and his long unbarbered hair hanging down his back, was wearing pajamas and walking up and down the vegetable garden, crooning to his two-year-old son. Overhead a flock of bright green parrots wheeled against the bright blue sky. In the distance, their outlines ghostlike in a raiment of gently billowing dust, the crumbling Moslem tombs shimmered in an early morning heat-haze. I got out the Studebaker and drove into New Delhi.

Rud was putting up at a small hotel off Connaught Circus. I walked leisurely round the Circle, careful to stay in the shade of the arcaded sidewalks. In the railway booking-office the sign was still up which read: "Please ask for a regret slip if a reservation is refused." I wondered, as I always did when I saw the sign, what one was supposed to do with the regret slip after getting it.

A beggar woman who had been squatting on the sidewalk beside a man who was rolling *bidi* cigarettes rose when she saw me approaching. She grabbed up a feebly stirring, cloth-covered bundle, and ran toward me, uncovering the bundle to show me a week-old infant with hideous-looking sores on its arms. She followed after me, holding up the baby and asking for money in a sing-song voice. She was a professional beggar, and she had hired the baby from an indigent mother. The baby's sores were artificially produced by means of a chemical, did not harm the baby, and were guaranteed removable in a few hours. When she saw I was not going to give her any money, she returned philosophically to her husband, who was still rolling cigarettes.

An unattended leper with no nose and stumps for legs was sitting upright in a wooden box on wheels. When he saw me coming toward him, he beat on the side of the box with his hand, and a ten-year-old boy ran out of an alley and began pushing the leper along the sidewalk. I gave the boy eight annas and the leper thanked me.

In the cool cavern of an enormous bookstore, serious-looking young Indians with rows of ballpoint pens clipped in the pockets of their cotton shirts were industriously reading. There were fat books everywhere, crowding the shelves to the ceiling and heaped on wooden tables. The young Indians were university students, and puffs of dry dust went up from the books when they opened them. The books were mainly studies in history, treatises on economics, works of philosophy, and essays on English literature. They had been there a long time, slowly crumbling in the dry heat and becoming pulpy during the monsoon, only to dry out again in the next dry season. The students visited the bookstore to read them but I never saw anyone buy one.

A fat man with a black beard shaped like a spade caught up with me just beyond the bookstore. He fell in step with me, flourishing a business card and chanting at me in a Welsh accent. "Today you will have very good fortune. It is in the cards. For only twenty rupees I will tell you about the beautiful fair-skinned girl you are going to meet tonight!" The price dropped from twenty to ten and from ten to five. Finally he stopped, out of breath, and panted after me: "Oh, mister, I tell you, your luck is going to be very bad—very bad, indeed!"

Walking in the road and impeding traffic, a procession marched round the Circle. It was a long procession, and it walked three abreast, carrying red flags and banners on bamboo poles. The procession was being taken out by the Delhi Hotel Workers' Union in protest against the workers' horrible conditions, the banner declared. There were no women in it. The men were waiters, bearers, sweepers, and cooks. Several policemen carrying steel-tipped bamboo staves kept in watchful step with the marchers.

Rud had acquired a pleasantly unpretentious room with a balcony looking toward the Circle. It had no air-conditioning but there was a big ceiling-fan. Rud, in an open-neck shirt worn outside the trousers, was sitting on his bed talking to a young Indian with large, bright eyes in a very thin face, who wore a badly patched coat, grimy slacks, and brown laced shoes without socks. His name was Raval Kalpa, and he was a magazine editor; Rud had got a letter of introduction to him from Kalpa's brother, who was studying engineering in Massachusetts. I shook hands. Raval Kalpa's hand was as thin and cold as an emaciated fish, but his smile was warm and friendly. He was smoking a cigarette, and occasionally he put a thin hand to his tattered coat, over his chest, as if he had a pain there.

Raval Kalpa was eager for Rud to meet a Socialist friend of his called Jai Khungar at Kalpa's home that evening, and he asked me if I would care to come, also. I said I would. Raval looked at his watch and said he must return to his office. We arranged to meet him there, for it was on the Circle, and he could take us to his home; "you would have difficulty in finding it by yourselves," he said, with a wry smile.

"I have to go over to the Secretariat," I told Rud. "Then I thought we might have a look at Parliament."

New Delhi was planned by Sir Edwin Lutyens. The planning began in 1911 and Lutyens's city was finished in the thirties. Imbedded in it, as it were, are such older structures as Jai Singh's eighteenth-century observatory, and the thirteenth-century Qutb Minar, a stone tower so exquisitely carved that it looks as if it were made of lace. By the time New Delhi was completed, the number of British officials in India had been reduced to 3,000. Soon afterwards India got her independence and became a republic. But the imposing buildings put up by the British remained, including the two massive red sandstone wings of the Secretariat, which housed the various Indian Ministries.

Rud and I entered one of the wings, and plunged from eye-aching glare into a maze of cool stone corridors. They smelled of *bidi* cigarettes. I gave my card to a *chaprassi*, an old man with a gray beard who wore a faded uniform, a tarnished silver-handled dagger in a faded red scabbard, and ragged slippers. He shuffled ahead of us along the corridor, and ushered us into a darkened room, protected from the outside glare by thick curtains over the windows. A man with a clipped black mustache and hot eyes glinting behind thick spectacles rose from behind a desk littered with flapping papers. There was a big ceiling-fan, and the papers were prevented from blowing away only by being held down under large brass paperweights. Trapped under the weights, the official files fluttered like imprisoned doves.

I introduced Rud to Mr. Vaidya Sharma of the Ministry of Planning. We sat down, and the *chaprassi* was sent for cups of tea. Sharma began telling Rud about India's Five Year Plan. He had a responsible position in the Ministry, but not at the highest level, so he spoke Welsh English. He took his job seriously, and he tended to address foreigners as if they were a hostile public audience. He told Rud severely: "India is carrying out a bloodless revolution. Austerity is our watchword, and we need every man, woman, and child for honest constructive work. As the Pandit has said: 'This generation of Indians is condemned to hard labor.' Unlike the capitalist countries, we cannot afford flunkies, Mr. Jack."

21

The *chaprassi* brought in the tea. Sharma spoke enthusiastically about new housing projects. "Here in Delhi," he said, "we have an immense refugee problem. After the Partition Delhi received 377,000 refugees. The density of population rose from 932 to 2,632 per square mile. The population of Old and New Delhi has increased fourfold in ten years and is now close to 2,000,000. We are very busy with housing developments." He produced plans of a brand-new housing estate—he called it a "colony"—and showed them to Rud. They looked impressive. Rud examined them, then asked: "Who will occupy these homes?"

"Government employees," said Sharma. "Clerks of various grades. New Delhi is like Washington, Mr. Jack. There are thousands of people here working for the government."

While Rud looked at the plans, Mr. Sharma snatched up a cup of tea and drank it off in one gulp. He took off his spectacles and impatiently polished them. His eyes glistened more hotly than ever. The papers fluttered madly under their brass weights. Inexorably the big fan whirled round and round in the ceiling, flailing the hot air. Mr. Sharma's right foot beat a nervous tattoo on the worn carpet, and he clutched his right knee in a thin hand as if to restrain the motion. "We are building homes for the people," he said, "and giving land to the peasants. India has cast off the chains of imperialism and can breathe again." Momentarily we had ceased to exist. Tapping his foot and clutching a shaking knee, Mr. Sharma addressed some large imaginary audience, in sing-song English with a Welsh accent. "The imperialists still seek to divide and rule, and have offered arms to Pakistan to be used against us. Pakistan is like the young man who murdered his father and mother and then pleaded for alms on the ground that he was a poor orphan!" Mr. Sharma laughed sarcastically. "Then there is Goa, where the Portuguese Fascists still lord it over poor downtrodden Indians. They will not do so much longer. Let the Portuguese be warned! Let the Atlantic Powers take heed! We are creating a Socialist society of free men, where there will be no more castes and no more classes, no more wealthy landowners and exploited masses. Free India is on the march!"

Rud pointed to the plan. "Here are the homes, but what are those buildings near them? They look like garages, but—"

Sharma laughed. "They are not garages. India is a poor nation, and very few people can afford automobiles, least of all government employees. No, no; these, of course, are the servants' quarters—the bearers, sweepers, and so on."

He put away the housing-development papers, and talked again about the Five Year Plan. "We have now entered the period of the second Plan. The first Plan built up our food resources; the second Plan will lay the foundations for rapid creation of heavy industry. Delhi, as the capital of India, will play a big part, and we are getting ready to shoulder the burden. We are going to build a big central stationery depot, with a special railway-siding of its own. There will be no fewer than 12 halls, each covering 2,000 square feet. They will be storage halls, and," said Sharma triumphantly, "we calculate that the depot will be capable of an annual turnover of 1,400 tons of official forms, forms required for carrying out the commitments of the second Five Year Plan!"

When we had shaken hands and were once more outside in the corridor, Rud asked: "He did say 1,400 *tons*, didn't he?" I nodded. "Of official forms?" I nodded again. "Uh-huh," said Rud; "that's what I thought he said."

We walked along several corridors, then went up a stone staircase, for I wanted Rud to meet Sett Rao. He occupied a larger room than Sharma, and he sat behind a larger desk. There were no papers on the desk, and he was leaning back and smoking a cigar.

Sett Rao was a handsome man who looked like Hollywood's notion of an Indian prince. He had been educated in England, and he spoke Oxford, not Welsh, English. He also played cricket.

23

We shook hands and I introduced Rud. "You'd better talk fast," I told Sett Rao. "We've just been to see one of your colleagues in the Ministry of Planning. Rud Jack is shocked, for he has been told that India's bloodless revolution means building homes for government clerks first and refugees afterwards, and that the clerks' homes are to have servants' quarters attached."

Sett Rao smiled at Rud. It was a smile that nicely blended cynicism with humor. He said quietly: "I'm afraid you will find Indians are very irritating people, Mr. Jack. In fact, we are probably the most exasperating people on earth. What was it Nehru said? 'There is hardly a country that has such high ideals as India, and there is hardly a country where the gap between ideals and performance is so great.' Nehru also said: 'In India, we live continually on the verge of disaster.' If you remember that, you may begin to understand some of our absurdities."

He looked thoughtfully at his cigar, burning evenly between his slim brown fingers.

"In the beginning we planned a very different India from the one that is represented by the architecture of New Delhi. It was to be—we hope one day it will be—a decent country where decent people can live in decency and some dignity. In fact, what we got, at first, were bloodshed, massacres, and anarchy. Gandhi, a saint, was assassinated; and we gave him the crowning mockery of a military funeral. Only a few months before his death, the Mahatma said: 'I do not want to live in darkness and madness; I cannot go on.' Nehru inherited huge problems. We had columns of refugees 45 miles long pouring in on us from the Punjab. In the Punjab alone, there were 10,000,000 homeless and panic-stricken people. However, we survived, Mr. Jack. Each year things get a little better. The problems are still huge, and the absurdities remain. They will probably remain for a long time. But we are a very old nation, Mr. Jack."

"You yourself don't despair?" Rud asked him directly.

"No," said Sett Rao thoughtfully. "I don't despair." He

24

smiled. "I shrug; I laugh; I work. What else is there to do?"

Outside the Secretariat the sun glared down on the Great Place, and on the huge empty roadway, broad as a parade ground, that ended at the gates of the President's Palace. Across the roadway shuffled the solitary figure of an aged *chaprassi* in his tarnished uniform, clutching a tattered official file and bound for the West Wing. The burnished red sandstone of the vast buildings looked too hot to touch, which it probably was. Behind the sandstone walls in honeycombs of darkened offices, several thousand Vaidya Sharmas sat behind desks heaped with fluttering papers under wheeling fans, busily planning the new India.

We eased ourselves into the Studebaker, trying not to come in contact with the burning leather, and drove round the corner to Parliament.

Parked neatly opposite the large circular Parliament building were a dozen or so of Delhi's small black-and-yellow taxicabs. They had just disgorged a number of men wearing saffron-colored robes and carrying banners. More little taxicabs, similarly freighted, were arriving every minute. One of the robed men took his place under one of the largest banners and began to speak loudly in Hindi. The banner was inscribed: "People of India! Defend the Cow!"

As we parked beside the taxis, I explained to Rud: "It's a meeting of holy men. They're protesting against cow slaughter. Good Hindus don't eat beef, and they worship cows, but the government allows cows to be slaughtered. The holy men are trying to stop it."

"I never thought of holy men riding in taxis," Rud confessed.

"The police have been rounding them up and dumping them outside the city. But the holy men have the support of a Hindu millionaire who calls himself the Friend of the Cow. He hires fleets of taxis to bring them back."

Sheltered from the sun by a black umbrella held by an attendant, the chief holy man thundered his message of compassion for the cow in a voice like a bull. He was a burly man, with arms like a blacksmith, and while he bellowed he shook a fist at Parliament in a menacing manner. The other holy men shouted their approval.

We walked along a circular stone corridor and then climbed a stone staircase to a green baize door which admitted us to the parliamentary gallery. Beyond the green baize door it was suddenly, delightfully cool. Down below us, on the floor of the vast air-conditioned hall, members of the House of the People, wearing white cotton shirts and dhotis and white cotton Gandhi caps, sat on green leather benches. The galleries were filled with spectators. Most of them were men, dressed, like the legislators below, in white cotton. But the pattern of white, matching the writhing plaster lines of the curving ceiling, was slashed and made vivid by the brilliant green and pink and orange saris of several women spectators. The women sat composed and still; but almost every man, his eyes glued on the doings beneath him, was beating a nervous tattoo with his foot and clutching his jerking knee in a thin nervous hand.

It was question-time, and from the floor there came a medley of quick eager voices, echoing tinnily from the small wooden loudspeakers that were placed at intervals along our part of the gallery.

The voices all spoke in English, but the words were run quickly together, in the odd familiar accent, like a Welsh sewing-machine stitching at high speed.

"Mr-Speaker-sir-may-I-know . . . ?"

"May-I-know-sir . . . ?"

"Arising-from-the-last-answer-will-the-Minister-tell-the-House-what-steps-are-being-taken-in-the-matter . . . ?"

Into the microphones, out of the loudspeakers, poured quick question and answer, facts and figures in a torrential stream. White-clad politicians jerked up and down like marionettes. *Chaprassis* scurried in the green aisles with papers. Up in the galleries listening heads nodded in sympathy or comprehension; all around us white-clad knees bobbed steadily, rhythmically, to the sewing-machine's beat.

Presently, when Rud had had enough, we rose and stole out. The green baize door closed noiselessly behind us, the quick querying voices were abruptly cut off, and the heat enfolded us. We went down the stone staircase and along the circular stone corridor, back the way we had come.

The holy men had just made a valiant attempt to take the building by storm, and policemen, swinging their bamboo *lathis* briskly, were forcing them back. A holy man fell, clutching a policeman; three other policemen lifted him bodily by his tangled robes and bore him struggling from the field. Seeing that the battle was lost, his comrades gathered up their banners and retreated sullenly toward the waiting taxis. A few escaped, but the remainder were encircled and herded into a large police van that suddenly appeared on the scene. They entered it without much resistance, and the taxis immediately started up their motors and prepared to follow it. At the outskirts of the city the holy men would, the drivers knew from experience, be released; the taxis would pick them up; and the holy men would return to hold another meeting. The cause of the cow was in stubborn hands.

Jaya Durg's house was not far from the Parliament, and near the Jai Singh observatory. We opened a creaking gate and passed into a garden blazing with flowers. Through a window we could see a small man with a brown bald head fringed with very white hair. He was writing industriously while squatting in pajamas on a mattress laid on the floor. He scrambled agilely to his feet, and I introduced Rud. He inspected Rud gravely, then bowed very low. "I am honored to be visited by the friend of my very good friend."

The room contained, in addition to the mattress, a rope-bed, a chair, a desk, a telephone, and several hundred old newspapers scattered on the floor. It was a narrow room, not more than five feet in width and eight or nine feet in length. Jaya

Durg called it his study. It had no fan and the sun-glare flooded it with heat, for the whole of one side was glass. You could have grown grapes in it.

Jaya Durg led us through a curtained doorway—there was no door—into his library. The curtain swished into place, and we were in cool semidarkness. Jaya Durg seated himself beneath the painted plaster figure of a naked dancing girl, and we groped our way to chairs. The library gradually revealed itself to our returning eyesight as a large room with a lofty ceiling and immense draperies. It contained a signed portrait of the Nizam of Hyderabad, a signed portrait of King George V, two signed portraits of Lord Mountbatten, a small framed snapshot, unsigned, of Jaya Durg talking to Gandhi and Nehru, and several thousand books in English, German, French, Swedish, Hindustani, and Russian.

Jaya Durg usually made a profound impression on all those who met him for the first time. As they got to know him better, this impression deepened. He was a tiny man, not more than four feet ten or eleven, with a broad, ugly face, a small paunch, and small soft hands as immaculately kept as those of a French countess. In his home he always wore pajamas and he almost never shaved. When he left his house he invariably wore London-tailored suits, and his chin was as smooth as brown silk. But he ventured forth only in order to dine with ambassadors and attend receptions for prime ministers and crowned heads. His manners were more courtly than a raja's. He was a brilliant writer and a born actor, had access to the most intimate political secrets, and possessed one of the sharpest wits in India. There was hardly a book he had not read, or a language he could not speak. He knew many famous people by their first names, and there was scarcely one about whom he could not tell at least two scandalous stories.

Looking like a small Buddha in the twilight of his library, with his bare feet drawn up under him and his tiny hands crossed on his little paunch, Jaya Durg told Rud: "You will find that India is a looted dustbin." He had a soft, deep voice and a habit of fixing his eyes hypnotically on whomever he was addressing. " 'Loot' was one of the earliest Hindu words to be adopted into the English language. The riches of India financed Marlborough's wars. Thomas Pitt bought the world's largest diamond at Golconda for £16,000 and sold it to the Regent of France for £125,000. The profit on this single transaction enabled him to buy the burgh of Old Sarum. India made England wealthy enough to be able to afford the luxury of democracy, to beat Napoleon, and to rule the world.

"But that was not the beginning. In the beginning there was Akbar. He was the most powerful and the richest monarch there has ever been. Rajas brought him elephant-trains of gold, and he wore a new outfit of jewels every day. The English wooed Akbar and his successors with burgundy wines, bull-baiting mastiffs, and the cornet. Jehangir was so delighted with this instrument that he persuaded the English cornet-player to take up permanent residence at his court and turn Moslem. The palace of the Moguls here in Delhi was larger than the Kremlin. But by the time of the Indian Mutiny, a century ago, it gave shelter only to armies of beggars. Nothing was ever cleaned or mended, and the Mogul throne was coated with four centuries' accumulation of the filth of birds and bats. Delhi is as you see it today, and the rest of India is no better."

Though plainly overwhelmed by the hypnotic eye and the bland flow of words, Rud made a gallant attempt to argue. "All the same," he said, "it couldn't have been *all* bad." His eye brightened as it fell on one of the signed photographs of Lord Mountbatten with its cheery inscription: "Sincerely yours, Dickie." Rud said: "I mean, the British did give India her freedom."

Jaya Durg unclasped his hands to hug his bare feet. He was enjoying himself.

"The English are a nation of shopkeepers," he declared. "The branch was failing to pay its way, so they closed it down.

As for giving India her freedom: what the English did, my good friend, was simply to give the Indians a tremendous inferiority complex—first by ruling and despising them, then by giving them their freedom without their having to fight for it."

"Didn't they do any good at all, then?"

"Oh, certainly!" Jaya Durg said cheerfully. "Remember what Lady Asquith told our Mrs. Pandit when she asked the same question. Mrs. Pandit is the sister of Mr. Nehru, and she is a widow. She demanded to be told just one good thing the British had done for India. After considering the question Lady Asquith replied: 'If it hadn't been for the British, you would have been burned to death on your husband's funeral pyre.'

"The British when they came to India found thugs who committed horrible murders not for gain but for religious reasons; widows who were burned alive; Bengal children who were thrown into the sea as human sacrifices; and Rajput female children who were customarily strangled at birth. When the British left India, they had abolished most of those practices and had succeeded in irrigating seventy million acres of land—the largest irrigated area in the world and, I believe, three times larger than the irrigated area of the United States. Unfortunately, by putting an end to internal tumult and periodic civil war, they also succeeded in increasing the Indian population from a hundred, to nearly four hundred, million. Consequently the average yield per acre remains just what it was in Akbar's day, and the Indians are wretchedly poor. That is what I mean when I say that India today is a looted dustbin."

Rud coughed deprecatingly. He was very conscious of the hypnotic eye. Even I had to confess to myself that Jaya Durg was in exceptionally fine form.

"All the same," Rud said stubbornly, "India does have her freedom now. And I believe she did fight for it, and with a very noble weapon, soul-force, or nonviolence, or whatever you care to call it. The Congress Party can lead India to a better future—"

"My very good friend," said Jaya Durg, "If you believe that, you will believe anything. Nonviolence had absolutely no existence, outside of my poor friend Gandhi's mind—I knew him rather well; we often discussed those matters in this very room," he added in careless parentheses. "No: when Gandhi told the mobs to be nonviolent, what they did was to go out and murder policemen and then burn the bodies in the policemen's own police stations. The British, being a superstitious people who hold religious zealots in great awe, made polite noises at Gandhi; but they would not have let Gandhi beat them. The mobs did that. The truth is nobody really listened to Gandhi, least of all the mobs themselves. When Gandhi was on his last fast here in Delhi, because of the terrible things that were happening following the Partition, the mobs marched round the house where he lay, shouting: 'Let Gandhi die!' An Indian mob is rather a dreadful phenomenon."

"But a lot of people went to prison rather than use violence to win freedom for India," Rud protested. "The Congress Party—"

"And what did they do in jail, my good friend? They wrote books, and prepared further speeches. This was the extent of the terrible British tyranny, that it permitted its opponents to write books and prepare speeches while they were in prison. And now those jail wallahs sit in Parliament, wearing Gandhi caps, and make more speeches; or they sit in offices, with fountain pens in their hands and, because they have pens and have been taught to read and write, imagine they are very wise. But, my dear good friend, having been in prison is not necessarily a good qualification for becoming a politician. 'The art of government,' said Bernard Shaw, 'is full of surprises for simpletons.' So our politicians are learning."

"Well," said Rud, "there's Nehru."

"I know Nehru very well indeed; he and I have often chatted together in this room. He occasionally allows me to proffer him advice on some matter requiring specialized knowledge, though nowadays he very seldom acts on it. Nehru is a man—I hold him in the highest regard, but without blinding myself to his limitations—who has drunk thirstily but not deeply at the Pierian spring. He wanted in his youth to be a great scientist, then decided to be a lawyer, and has become a politician in constant danger of turning into a mere windbag. Nehru today is being hailed as the Hindu Trinity, but what does his political philosophy consist of? It is one third Socialism, one third Communism, and one third capitalism. That is what he offers India. To the rest of the world he offers the *panch shila,* the Five Principles which he and Chou En-lai concocted together; but the *panch shila* on inspection turns out to be very like the Hindu *panch gavya,* that is to say, the five products of the sacred cow—milk, butter, curds, urine, and dung."

"Jaya Durg," I said, while Rud silently struggled to absorb those Shavian remarks, "will you lunch with us?"

"Alas, my dear good friend, I cannot: I have to lunch with the Ambassador of Iraq."

I had a hotel luncheon engagement with a soft-drink manufacturer called Alpen. New Delhi's lunch-hour stretched from noon until four. Connaught Circle was deserted, the shops were all shuttered, and the beggars and lepers slept in the shadow of the arcades, stretched full-length on the sidewalks. The sun glared down on baking silence. But outside the hotel, where the pseudo-Tibetans normally sat in their dyed robes, selling imposing looking brassware made in Birmingham to credulous tourists, there was considerable movement. The hotel workers' procession had arrived and wound itself tightly round the building, clutching its banners and waving its flags. Large hired limousines had just disgorged a number of foreigners who were trying agitatedly to break through the ranks of the hotel workers and reach the cool sanctuary of the hotel. One of the foreigners was a large, muscular woman in a green velvet dress that gaped at one side. I recognized her. She was the railway-construction model worker from Uzbekistan who was attending the world-peace conference. The world-peace delegates had just returned from a tour of Old Delhi's historic mosques. The conference was being held in this hotel, where the delegates were staying, and they were all looking forward to a sumptuous capitalist lunch. Perspiring freely and looking harassed and not a little frightened, they found themselves suddenly confronted by hostile proletarian faces. The handful of policemen who had marched with the procession to keep it in order were standing a little way off, watching. One of the world-peace delegates went up to them. He pointed to the other delegates, pointed to himself, and pointed toward the hotel, tantalizingly close but apparently inaccessible. The policemen shrugged. It was very hot, and they, too, longed for their lunch; besides, it was a free country and there was no law against the hotel workers picketing a hotel if they wanted to do so. Most of the Delhi police, being themselves underpaid, were in sympathy with the hotel employees.

The world-peace delegate, meeting with no response, threw up his arms in despair toward the burning sky, and said something in Korean. He clearly found himself at a loss in a country where the police stood idly by and allowed the masses to come between important Communists and their lunch.

Finally one of the organizers of the procession addressed the workers, who grudgingly cleared a narrow passage through which the peace delegates hurried apprehensively. Rud and I seized the chance to follow them into the hotel. As we did so, one of the hotel workers thrust a pamphlet into my hand.

Alpen was waiting for us in the bar, sitting on the edge of an overstuffed red plush couch and gazing morosely at a kidney-shaped table with a black glass top. The walls were decorated with improbable-looking murals drawing their inspiration from Hindu mythology and topped by a scroll which proclaimed in Latin that "In Drinking Lay Pleasure." At a near-by table the owner of the hotel, a young Indian with oiled locks, sat swarthily drinking champagne between two blondes, one French and the other Scandinavian. Alpen was a stout man with a blue-shadow chin and stomach ulcers. He greeted us gloomily. "I've had a hell of a morning," he said.

I was acquainted with some of Alpen's troubles. He had arrived in Delhi from Cairo some months before to put up a soft-drinks factory. His company sold prodigious quantities of soft drinks throughout the Middle, Near, and Far East. Alpen proposed to turn out two million bottles a year for Indian consumption. But in this endeavor he had encountered numerous obstacles. Devout Hindus descended on him and demanded to know if his crown corks contained animal glue. He was permitted, at his own cost, to clear a jungle and make a road leading to the factory site; but he sought in vain for months for official permission to build a small shed to protect his workers' bicycles during the monsoon. He had not been allowed to import trucks, but had been compelled to have them manufactured in Bombay and Calcutta; when the trucks were ready, Alpen was not permitted to have them driven to Delhi, but had to rail them, by the state-owned railways, at considerable expense and with much consequent delay. In order to obtain water, he had had to dig two wells, for the Delhi authorities refused him permission to run a pipe to the city mains, even though he offered to pay for its construction. When the wells were dug, the water that they yielded proved to be unfit for human consumption, so Alpen had had to purchase two enormous water trucks to make the eight-mile daily haul to and from the city. Unfortunately the trucks, also, were obtainable only in Bombay, and they, too, the authorities ruled, must be railed.

"And now it's ball-bearings," said Alpen bitterly. "I had to import ball-bearings, and they've arrived, but they tell me they've got to have the country of origin stamped into them. When I point out that this would irretrievably ruin them as ball-bearings, they just nod their heads at me, meaning 'No.' "

The bar swam in a dark green twilight. The overstuffed red-plush couches looked curiously obscene. They had evidently not been dusted for some considerable period, and from time to time things stirred behind them. There were small soft scamperings. While Alpen expounded his woes, Rud's attention wandered elsewhere. He was plainly unable to make up his mind which was more fascinating, the young Indian hotel-owner with the two blondes, or the pink-tailed mouse that had suddenly appeared behind Alpen's head and was scampering along the top of the couch.

We went into lunch. At tables all around us the peace delegates were hungrily consuming large steaks. The Russian playwright was sitting with the railway-construction model worker from Uzbekistan and two black-bearded priests of the Russian Orthodox Church. At another table sat two Buddhists from North Vietnam with two nuns from Red China. The nuns, I noticed, ate their steaks with as much concentration as the others. I was reminded of the pamphlet that had been thrust into my hand, and I took it out to read. It said: "We protest against the anti-people and anti-national policy pursued by the hotel managers, who indulge in barbarous repressions and anti-working class practices, subjecting employees to unprecedented plunder, ruination and exploitation, and employing close relatives and dancers at salaries many times more than our President and Prime Minister while paying workers less than what a donkey-man charges for the cost of his donkey's labor-power." The pamphlet also—rather unfairly I thought, and was sure the peace delegates would have agreed with me, if asked—accused the police of "torturing and beating the workers," and concluded: "Long live working-class solidarity! Workers of the world unite! Long live the Delhi Hotel Workers' Union!"

Alpen, lunching frugally off steamed white rice and a fragment of boiled chicken, resumed the recital of his wrongs.

"This morning I found them installing the factory's roller gates upside down, and the walls have begun to crack. And we're having trouble with a fellow who claims the Hindus invented cokes—he's selling a soft drink called 'Pepsu-cola' and wants us to buy him out. . . ."

After lunch I suggested to Rud we should take a closer look

35

at the world-peace meeting. The meeting was in progress upstairs in the hotel ballroom. At the head of the stairs stood
youthful Indians wearing blue running-shorts: guards of honor
for the peace delegates supplied by the Indian Congress Party.
The platform, flanked by the flags of eighteen participating nations, had for its background a large blue cloth embroidered
with two silver doves pecking at a yellow lotus. On the platform
sat the chief delegates, smiling and wearing garlands of jas-
mines and roses. Red China had sent, in addition to the nuns,
a pretty film actress and the chairman of the National Committee of Churches in China for Self-realization. Russia had contributed a consumptive-looking composer as well as the bulky
playwright; there was an expert on radioactive diseases from
Japan.

An Albanian was denouncing the American bandits and
Anglo-American imperialists; the railway-construction model
worker applauded vigorously. The delegates' Indian hosts were
looking glum and seemed somewhat dazed.

On the way out I handed the Delhi Hotel Workers' Union
pamphlet to a spectacled Chinese. He took it eagerly, rose,
bowed, and thanked me effusively. At the head of the stairs the
guards of honor in their blue running-shorts saluted us. I drove
Rud to his hotel, advised him to take a siesta, and arranged to
meet him at Raval Kalpa's office.

The office when I reached it that evening turned out to be
two small bare rooms up three steep flights of stone stairs, in a
decrepit building off Connaught Circle. The building had a
narrow passageway for entrance, and outside on the sidewalk
a man was selling contraband cigarettes and pornographic magazines, while near by sat a snake-charmer in a loincloth amid
several baskets containing reptiles. I stepped over a python that
was slithering sluggishly from one of the baskets, and climbed
the stone stairs. They were liberally splashed with the red juice
of betel nut, like large bloodstains. On the stone landing outside Kalpa's office a woman sat watching an infant which she

had laid flat on its back, naked, on a heap of rags. Feebly stirring its limbs, the infant made no sound: the state of the landing suggested it was suffering from acute diarrhea, or possibly from cholera. The door of the office was ajar: it bore a sign which said: "*The Intelligence:* A Weekly Review. Editor, Raval Kalpa." The two rooms were divided by a thin partition. Their common ceiling seemed at one time to have collapsed, probably during the monsoon, and was patched with straw and propped up with timbers. In one of the rooms there were two armchairs covered in faded green cloth and a low table with a stack of well-thumbed issues of *The Intelligence*. In the other room a wall fan roared rustily, blowing dust like a vacuum-cleaner in reverse across two battered desks, on one of which stood a black metal typewriter. Three tabs were missing from its keyboard.

Raval Kalpa wore the same patched coat, slacks, and brown shoes he had worn that morning. His face looked even thinner, and when he drew on his cigarette he coughed more violently. But when he gave me an emaciated hand his eyes lit up with the same friendly warmth I had noticed before. Rud had already arrived, and Raval Kalpa said he was ready to go, if we were. He padlocked the door of the office, and we went past the woman with the sick infant and down the stone stairs splashed with red betel-nut juice. Outside the snake-charmer was blowing a sad tune on his bamboo flute, but the python had retired to its basket.

The Intelligence was a very highbrow weekly review. Raval Kalpa wrote most of it. He wrote articles about Indian philosophy, politics, and economics, all with equal ease. They were liberally sprinkled with quotations from the classics, and had such titles as "Democracy or Communism: The Choice Before India" and "The Second Five-Year Plan: A Critique." He also did a literary column, which reviewed English and American books about six months after they were published and compared Indian writers, unfavorably, with Jean-Paul Sartre and

André Gide. The magazine was written in English throughout. It was aimed solely at the intelligentsia, eschewed news, explored large cultural horizons, and sold only a few hundred copies. Raval Kalpa was always in financial troubles with his printer, and spent most of his spare time soliciting advertisements.

In the dark streets the heat was a tangible thing. We drove to Old Delhi through the crumbling city gateway and past the cinema with the tearful female giant praying to the godlike man in the blue turban who floated in the air above her head. Chandni Chowk swarmed stickily with white-clad figures and wandering white cows. "We turn here," said Kalpa. "Drive toward the Golden Mosque; I'll tell you where to stop." I drove along a narrow street looking for the mosque where, two centuries ago, Nadir Shah had sat and enjoyed the massacre of Delhi citizens by his soldiers. "We must stop now," Kalpa said apologetically. "The rest of the way is too narrow for a car. But it is not very far."

He led us into a strongly smelling alley and through it into another, which stank. The ground was soft, as if mud, but our nostrils told us it was not mud. We turned a corner, and surprised a small boy defecating in a gutter under a lighted window. Walls rose sheerly around us and seemed to touch overhead. Here for centuries, I reflected, the nobility of India, both Hindu and Moslem, had lived, fought, murdered, intrigued, and finally squandered away an empire. I thought of Akbar, the richest ruler in the world, and of what had happened to his palace, besieged by beggars and befouled by birds and bats. Now, only a few yards from bustling Chandni Chowk and within a stone's throw of the Golden Mosque, this quarter had become a jumble: thieves live cheek by jowl with still wealthy moneylenders, and the respectable poor, and Brahmins brush shoulders with untouchables. But in scattered darkened rooms throughout the warren, there probably survive a handful of very old men with fading memories of past splendors. There had still in 1857 been a Mogul emperor, even though he dwelt in squalor and was half-blind.

And Raval Kalpa, who quoted Sartre and Gide, also lived here. He guided us eventually up a pitch-dark stair and into a room small enough to be mistaken for a cupboard. It was furnished with two wooden chairs and a bed, and was crammed with books. Sitting in one of the chairs and reading a book was a man with a pear-shaped head and a smooth, pale brown face. "This is my friend Jai Khungar," said Raval Kalpa.

Jai Khungar was a man of about thirty-five, wiry and muscular, wearing a blue-check shirt, open at the neck and with short sleeves, dark brown corduroy trousers, and leather strap-sandals without socks. He stood up, holding the book—it was John Stuart Mill's *On Liberty*—and looked at us with dark, heavy-lidded, passionless eyes.

Raval Kalpa produced coffee; Jai Khungar accepted one of Rud's cigarettes. "What do you think of India?" he asked Rud, smiling.

Rud said it seemed to be a very complex country.

"We are larger than Europe but speak fewer languages. What makes us different is that we are dead. There is nothing very complex about a corpse."

Rud said diffidently that perhaps India had been asleep for a long time, but now she was awakening, like all of Asia and Africa.

"You've been listening to Congress Party propaganda. India doesn't change; it only pretends to change."

He turned suddenly to Kalpa. "I hear you're being married soon. Congratulations!" Kalpa smiled shyly. "But I haven't met your girl yet, you know. Is she really lovely?"

Kalpa seemed disconcerted. "Why," he stammered, "she's—why, you know, she's all right—"

Jai Khungar laughed. He seemed to fill the little room. I found myself disliking him.

"Raval Kalpa hasn't even seen the girl," he said mockingly,

turning back to us. "The whole thing has been arranged by his family and the girl's. His family are very pleased, for the girl's people have money; her family are keen for her to marry an 'educated' man, even though he's as poor as a mouse. They may hit it off; they may not. The point is Raval Kalpa will dutifully accept the bride chosen by his family. Won't you, Kalpa?" It was painfully evident from Kalpa's face that this was so. "Yet Kalpa is an Indian 'intellectual,'" said Jai Khungar, still mockingly. "He writes bold articles; he quotes all the most daring thinkers of the West; he even calls himself a Socialist. Now, Kalpa, I'll ask you something else. How about the caste system? You've written plenty about it, you know. 'The caste system must be destroyed'; 'In a Socialist society, there can be neither classes nor castes.' Well, now, Kalpa, tell me; would you be seen talking to an untouchable? Truthfully, now!"

Raval Kalpa said angrily: "Oh, I didn't ask you here to talk nonsense, Jai Khungar! You know very well I've talked to lots of untouchables. I refuse to acknowledge the existence of caste!"

"So! Some of his best friends are untouchables!" laughed Jai Khungar. "But have you ever, knowingly, shared a meal with an untouchable?"

"I've never said I wouldn't," said Raval Kalpa sullenly. He was throwing us appealing glances, apologizing in eloquent silence for Khungar's behavior.

"And how about the other castes—the castes lower than your own?" inquired Khungar. "You're a twice-born, aren't you? Suppose you were to fall in love with a girl of a lower caste: would you marry her, even though your family cursed you?"

"Of course, I would: that is, if I felt sure I really loved her. But—"

"'But,'" said Jai Khungar. "Ah, always that 'but'! Well, tell me: were you ever invited to the home of a person of a lower caste?"

"No: the lower castes are the most conservative of all. They simply wouldn't suggest such a thing."

"There you are," declared Khungar, shrugging. "Higher castes won't meet, mingle, visit, eat, or marry with lower castes; and lower castes won't either with higher castes! I could quote you scores of examples right here in Delhi. Old Pandit Pant says, rightly: 'Delhi is the shadow under the lamp.' But not just Delhi. The whole of India is in the same state. That's why I say India is dead. A stinking corpse. A nasty scribble on the wall. There's no depth of superstition to which Indians won't sink. We worship cows and cobras. We have 8,000,000 'holy men,' most of them naked and all of them mad. Everything of any value was taken long ago by the conquerors, who have been coming here for a thousand years. They took the strength from the soil, the virtue from the women, and the will power from the men. They left nothing behind but vices and weaknesses: the cunning pliancy of slaves, the intrigues of degenerates, the superstitions of peasants. India is like an empty tomb: the gold gone, the jewels gone, nothing left but bones and a bad smell."

He helped himself to another of Rud's cigarettes. The room was stifling, and great sweat patches had grown under his armpits, staining the blue-check shirt, while his curiously shaped head dripped like a pear that had been dipped in water. But his voice remained coldly sarcastic and his heavy-lidded eyes showed no emotion. I liked him less and less.

"The Congress Party are the heirs of the British," he said. "They sit in the seats the British vacated, wearing Gandhi caps and oozing piety. But they still employ *chaprassis* with silver daggers in silk sashes, just as the British did. India under Congress rule is the mixture as before: four parts filth to one part hypocrisy."

Raval Kalpa said valiantly: "Nehru is a Socialist."

"Nehru's Socialism is a fraud, for he still has the backing of the big landlords and the industrialists."

"You talk like a Communist," said Kalpa accusingly.

Khungar merely laughed. "The Communists!" he said contemptuously. "The Communists are simply the new imperialists. The Russians 'liquidated' God knows how many millions,

41

to what end? In order to create a bourgeois state with bourgeois morals, ruled by bureaucrats who surround themselves with flunkies and attend dull parties where they drink too much, talk too much, and play at being Napoleons. In Russia and China the 'revolution' has become an affair of clinking champagne glasses, solemn toasts, and stupid intrigues. India does not have to go Communist to achieve that, for the Congress Party has achieved it already. Congress Party officials behave like butchers put in charge of goshalas—the societies for the protection of cows. At the first opportunity they cut the cows' throats. A government clerk won't look at a poor man's application unless it has a 50-rupee bribe attached to it. The Gandhi cap now signifies that its wearer is open to the highest bid. Congress Party politicians pose as sniveling saints while they plunder the peasants. In Central India 10,000,000 people exist by eating the barks of trees. The cotton workers still sweat in fetid mills, children in coalmines do the work of pit ponies, and women are put to mending roads. Our 'intellectuals' worship the Soviet Union, but still wear their caste marks. Most of them have never set foot in a village, though four fifths of Indians live in villages. What they have in common with the Bolsheviks they admire is a contempt for the common people."

He got to his feet, yawning. "I must go. I hope I haven't bored or offended you. Raval Kalpa said you wanted to learn the truth about India. Go and see the 50,000,000 untouchables who are still shut out of temples and compelled to drink from ditches, and you'll realize I'm not far wrong."

When Khungar had gone, Raval Kalpa said defensively: "You must not take him too seriously. He is very fond of talking."

"I can see that," I said. "But tell us more about him."

"He is a member of the Indian Socialist Party—which opposes both the Congress Party and the Communists—but he has no job. His brother is in the government, and offered him a post."

"He refused, I suppose."

"Oh, no. He eagerly accepted. But he was no good at it, and moreover he was caught taking bribes. Even his brother could not protect him, and he had to go. That is why when he talks about the Congress Party he sounds so peevish."

Presently we said good-night to Raval Kalpa, stumbled down the dark stairway, and groped our way cautiously along the alleys, fearful of what we would tread on.

"What do you make of it all?" I asked Rud.

"I still think it's a very complex country," Rud said.

Who does not get intoxicated by drinking of the vanity of office? THE *Nitisara* OF SHUKRACHARYA

ALL ALONG the ten-mile route between New Delhi and the airport, flags had been planted and ceremonial arches erected. The archways were made of bamboo poles, thickly twined with marigolds. Straddling the highway at half-mile intervals, they bore such inscriptions as "Long Live the God of Peace," and "Welcome Home, Jewel of Asia." The crowds had been on the move since dawn, converging on the airport on foot, on bicycles, and in bullock carts. They squatted in thousands on both sides of the road, which was being kept clear for official cars. Delhi's hard-worked police were out in force. There was a policeman every few yards, wearing a freshly pressed khaki uniform and a new red-and-brown turban, and armed with a businesslike bamboo *lathi*. But the crowds were good-humored despite the stifling heat and the long hours of waiting, and the policemen were disposed to relax while they had the chance. They sat in the shade of the trees, removed their shoes in order to wiggle their bare toes pleasurably in the dust, and exchanged broad witticisms with bullock-cart drivers while they broke their fast on cold *chapattis*. Only when an automobile showing the Congress Party colors appeared in a cloud of dust did the policemen spring to their feet, snatch up their *lathis*, and stand rigidly at attention. When it had passed they went back to the shade and to their *chapattis*.

At the airport itself, steel fences had been put up to prevent the vast crowds from swarming on to the field. Beyond the fences, near where Nehru's plane would land, a large tent or *shamiana* sheltered dignitaries from the blazing sun. Inside the *shamiana* the President of India chatted with foreign diplomats, all looking excessively uncomfortable in glossy top hats and black frock coats; behind the tent a pipe-band practiced martial airs.

Rud and I occupied a semiprivileged position, on the airfield side of the steel fences but not too close to the *shamiana*. We could keep an eye on the dignitaries, and at the same time listen to the crowd. There was a good deal of jostling. Remarks in English floated toward us from time to time.

"Please move, you are obstructing our view."

"But I mean, kindly inform me to where I shall move in this crowd?"

"That is not my outlook."

The plane bringing Nehru from Russia first appeared as a white speck in the blue sky. A great roar went up from thousands of Hindus. The plane came in view again, traveling much more slowly but appearing very much larger. Momentarily the noise of its engines drowned all other sounds. Then, its wings dwarfing the crowd, it wheeled massively into place, and came to a stop. The engines ceased to throb. In the aftermath of their silence a gangway was pushed forward. The door of the plane opened, and a broad-shouldered man with a handsome, lean brown face appeared at the top of the gangway. He wore a dazzlingly white coat, with a single red rose in one buttonhole, and a white Gandhi cap.

In India things seldom go off according to plan. Nehru was to have descended with dignity from the plane and walked across to the long line of diplomats now drawn up ready to receive him, amid the huzzas of the enthusiastic but immobile thousands restrained behind the steel fences. What happened instead was that, with one accord, the people surged forward with wild shouts; the steel fences toppled and were trampled underfoot; and in an instant the crowds were surrounding the plane in a tumultuous, screaming mob. The pipe-band blew valiantly, but no one could hear them; when they got in the way, they were thrust impatiently aside. Officials ran forward, waving their arms and opening and shutting their mouths; presumably they were shouting, but whatever they shouted was lost, and they were quickly swallowed up by the crowds. Women screamed; children tried to run away and were trapped amid grown-up legs; intense pandemonium prevailed. The line of diplomats, already wavering, was abruptly blotted from sight and overwhelmed. A handful of hatless ambassadors fought their way manfully back to the shelter of the *shamiana*, only to find that the mob had overrun that, also, and were breaking chairs by trying to stand on them. Several score of policemen, belatedly summoned from the rear, came on the scene waving their *lathis*. Less fortunate than their comrades back on the roadway peacefully eating *chapattis*, they suddenly found themselves called on to quell a riot in which they were grossly outnumbered. The best they could do was to form a thin khaki cordon and try to hold back fresh thousands from rushing on to the airfield to join the thousands already there.

I stooped to pick up a sandal that had fallen from some panicking foot. Then Rud and I continued to follow cautiously in the wake of the crowd as it surged ever closer to the stationary plane. The first human tidal wave had passed over us, leaving us as it were in slack water. As it was impossible to retreat, we advanced. Looking over my shoulder, I could see the policemen's long, steel-tipped *lathis* forming a sort of background frieze to the tumult. They rose and fell with almost monotonous regularity, contacting heads with a dull thwacking sound.

Someone with good sense had dispatched a jeep to the Pan-

dit's rescue. In order to reach the plane, it had been compelled
to make a complete circuit of the airfield. It now appeared,
coming slowly toward us and forcing the mob to clear a lane
for it. The people cheered loudly. Nehru stood up in the jeep.
He was perspiring heavily and holding a short swagger cane
in both hands. The crowd began to pelt him with roses. Dropping his cane, the Pandit began to throw the roses back. He
was laughing, and showing a flash of white teeth. The white
hair curling out from under his Gandhi cap contrasted oddly
with his still youthful face.

The jeep went slowly past, moving toward the *shamiana*. We
fell in immediately behind it. Suddenly we were leading a procession instead of being at the tail of a mob. At the *shamiana*
Nehru jumped down from the jeep. He had picked up his cane
again, and his expression abruptly altered from good humor
to moroseness as he looked at the tangle of broken chairs and
ripped-down cloth. People were still milling amid the wreckage
and loudly protesting as policemen tried to hustle them out.
The first person to greet Nehru was an immensely tall man
wearing a high turban. He overtopped the mob, and in the now
subsiding tumult the long blue streamers attached to his white
turban fluttered like a victor's banner. His composure was unruffled, and he greeted the Pandit with a bland smile. He was
the Pakistan Ambassador and, judging from Nehru's tightened
lips, the Pandit regarded this as an unfortunate omen.

Catching sight of Nehru, the portion of the crowd that the
policemen in the background had so far managed to restrain
came surging forward with renewed shouts. This further demonstration of unruliness sparked an exhibition of the Pandit's well-
known temper. He thrust aside his swagger cane, snatched a
lathi from the astonished hands of a passing policeman, and
leaped up on one of the few unbroken chairs that stood in the
entrance of the *shamiana*. Wires trailed in confusion on the
trampled ground, and Nehru's eye fell on one of the microphones to which they were attached. He made an imperious

46

gesture, and a disheveled official handed it to him. Brandishing the *lathi* in his other hand, Nehru shouted: "Stop this uproar at once!" Unfortunately the microphone was not working. But even the deafest and most obtuse person present could hardly have failed to grasp the Pandit's meaning. The sweat was rolling down his face. His lower lip was outthrust belligerently, and his eyes glared. From the benign God of Peace laughingly tossing roses to the worshipping crowd, he had transformed himself in a twinkling into a very picture of malignancy. An awed silence fell. Nehru said, more quietly: "Thank you for your reception. It was a little overwhelming. I have many things to tell you, and I had meant to tell some of them to you here. But now they will have to wait until a better time."

Someone cheered, but faintly; perhaps the crowd felt that cheering would have been only an added impertinence. They had been thoroughly cowed, and looked as sheepish as scolded schoolboys. Nehru leaped down from the chair. A large black limousine nosed its way towards the *shamiana*. Driven by a liveried chauffeur, it contained the President of India, returning, perhaps belatedly, to the stricken field. He embraced the Pandit; the Pandit embraced him. They entered the car together, and drove away.

I found I was still holding the sandal in my hand. An official, the official who had given the microphone to Nehru, came up to me. He looked as if he had been having a very bad time. His face was streaked with sweat and dust and his coat had been half torn from his back. "I think I know whose that is," he said. I surrendered it to him. Presently, as we were leaving, I saw him giving it to a limping man, who accepted it gratefully and immediately put it on. He was the Minister of Defense.

The President was giving a garden party to celebrate Nehru's return. Jane and I were invited, and I also secured an invitation for Rud. The invitation said: "Dress—Official or Formal." This meant wearing neckties—but was not strictly observed. We drove past saluting sentries and parked in the Palace courtyard.

Crowds were streaming through a stone gateway and toiling up an inner stone staircase, leading to the gardens of the Rashtrapati Bhavan. At intervals along the pathways, rigid, motionless, looking straight ahead and with their index fingers laid along the creases of their regimental trousers, men of the Household Guard in white and scarlet were stationed. The 3,000 guests poured along the paths, ignoring these living statues. The gardens glowed with flowers. Fountains splashed musically and goldfish darted in artificial ponds. The many-windowed bulk of the Palace, which had been the Viceroy's, looked silently down on the throng. Formerly only Indian princes and the very highest Indian officials had been invited here to mingle with their British masters. Nowadays the Palace gardens were opened to a wider public. There were still a bejeweled raja or two, but most of the guests looked seedy. A few wore long, high-collared, tightly buttoned coats and tight white trousers; the majority wore dhotis, flapping white cotton shirts without collars, or ill-fitting Western clothes. I ceased being conscious of my rather crumpled tropical suit, and Rud, who had been apprehensive about his suit, was reassured.

But if the guests looked nondescript, their reception remained impressive. The rigorous traditions of the British Raj had been fully preserved. A band, gorgeously uniformed, dispensed appropriate music. On either side of the huge lawn long tables had been laid with snowy cloths, and behind them hovered Palace waiters, wearing slashed velvet hats, ready to serve tea. Trumpets suddenly shrilled. The band began to play the Indian national anthem. Everyone stood at attention. Down one of the pathways from the Palace, heralded by trumpeters and preceded by military aides in white uniforms hung with yellow cords and tassels and stiff with epaulets, advanced the President and the Pandit. They came amid the guests with slow and ritual steps, and the guests respectfully fell back to make way for them. The President, a cheerful-looking elderly man with a grizzled mustache, pressed the palms of his hands together in the *namasthe* greeting. Nehru did likewise. The guests responded. The garden party had officially begun, and would last for exactly an hour and a half.

Indians love appearances, but seldom keep them up for very long. On this occasion they did so for the two minutes that it took the President and Nehru to step from the pathway onto the verge of the lawn and to commence to chat with the people who happened to be nearest. The others made a beeline for the tables where free tea and cakes were to be had. Those who got there first and grabbed quickest had to fight their way back out of the line, precariously balancing cups and plates. The wisest did not even attempt this, but remained where they were, drinking quickly and gobbling down cakes, and then demanded more. Latecomers in the stampede freely used elbows and knees to secure places, and many loud arguments ensued. The waiters in the slashed velvet hats had a busy time.

Jane had said she was dying of thirst. But when I extricated myself from the squash—bringing her a cup of tea—she and Rud had wandered off. Seeking them in the crowd, I came face to face with Nehru. He was slowly pacing the garden, head bent and his hands behind his back. There was a fresh rose in his buttonhole; but, amid the hubbub, he seemed a strangely neglected man. People fell back respectfully at his approach, but offered no conversation; he passed on, and I suspected he was as shy as they.

Being a great man had many disadvantages. Nehru's sister Krishna Hutheesingh, had just accused him, in a highly publicized article, of becoming harsh and cynical, overbearing and peremptory with too much power: a dictator. "Nowadays," she had written, "he brooks no criticism and will not even suffer advice gladly. He is highly conscious of his place in history." Nehru on this occasion did not look overbearing to me: I could see only a man, still almost boyishly handsome despite his white hair, with a very sensitive face, who looked very tired.

He might be very conscious of his place in history, and probably was; but he himself had said, with a deprecatory sarcasm not usual in dictators, that "listening to others I sometimes feel

I must be very wise and brilliant and important, then I look at myself and begin to doubt this." I had been long enough in India to cease to be astonished by the adulation Nehru received. He was described daily as "the greatest man of our time"; "the world's most talked of man"; "the idol of millions not only in India but everywhere"; and much more in the same vein. Nehru's own view of himself was considerably more modest. He had written: "I have been a dabbler in many things; I began with science at college, and then took to the law, and, after developing various other interests in life, finally adopted the popular and widely practised profession of gaol-going." He had also written: "I have become a queer mixture of East and West, out of place everywhere, at home nowhere; a lover of words and phrases and an ineffective politician; being somewhat imaginatively inclined, my mind runs off in various directions; as I grow old, I tend to philosophise and to dole out advice to others."

It was easy for his critics to attack him, for he himself supplied them with all their best phrases. As early as 1937 he had published an article about himself, written anonymously and in the third person, in which he declared: "He has all the makings of a dictator—vast popularity, a strong will, ability, hardness, intolerance of others, and a certain contempt for the weak and the inefficient." This warning about Nehru, by Nehru, had been taken to heart by many and, apparently, never forgotten by some.

In India Nehru-worship had replaced Gandhi-worship, but Nehru was far from returning the compliment. He had great ambitions for India—"India cannot play a secondary role in the world," I had heard him cry; "she will either count for a great deal or not at all." But he often seemed to doubt his people's ability to play the part he wished to assign to them, for I had seen him get up and passionately declare before huge abashed audiences, who had come to cheer him and who went away bewildered: "You are slaves, and have the minds of slaves: why do you bicker and quarrel over trivial nothings?"

50

Pacing slowly over the lawn, apparently sunk in melancholy reflections, his face suddenly quickened into a smile. He had just caught sight of his daughter, Indira.

The first time I saw Mrs. Indira Gandhi she had just returned from a visit to Peking and was full of enthusiasm for the new China. "China today is a disciplined nation, marching resolutely towards the future," she declared ardently. "Even infants are taught the benefits of collective life." It struck me as a singularly humorless remark, and many Indians agreed, but Indira remained unshaken. "Progress calls for a certain amount of regimentation," she said simply. At this time she had begun to go everywhere with her father. The Congress Party had made her the first woman member of the election committee that selected all Congress Party candidates; she addressed numerous meetings on the need for India to emulate Chinese discipline. Indian newspapers are no respecters of persons, and with their tongues in their cheeks they began reporting that "Mrs. Indira Gandhi is greeted wherever she goes by enthusiastic but disciplined masses." The second time I saw her was at a party given for bearers and sweepers at the Prime Minister's house; she was seated on the floor, chatting familiarly with squatting servants and feeding a saucerful of milk to a tiger cub called Bimi. It was an impressive sight, but not an unusual function for Indira. She recalled: "My public life started at the age of three. I have no recollection of playing games, or playing with other children. My favorite occupation as a small child was to deliver thunderous speeches to the servants, standing on a high table." When she was four, she was already accompanying her mother to political meetings. When she was twelve, she organized a troop of politically conscious children called "the Monkey Brigade," who carried urgent Congress Party messages under the noses of British soldiers and policemen.

Nehru's favorite name for her was Priyadarshini, which means "Dear to the sight." When she was thirteen he was in prison at Naini, and from there he wrote to her on her birthday: "Do you remember how fascinated you were when you first read

51

the story of Jeanne d'Arc, and how your ambition was to be something like her? The year you were born in, 1917, was one of the memorable years of history, when a great leader, his heart full of love and sympathy for the poor and suffering, made his people write a noble and never to be forgotten chapter of history. In the very month in which you were born, Lenin started the great revolution that changed the face of Russia." The following year, still in prison, Nehru in another letter reminded her again: "You are a lucky girl. Born in the month and year of the great revolution that ushered in a new era in Russia, you are now a witness to a revolution in your own country, and soon you may be active in it. It is the twilight of capitalism, which has lorded it so long over the world. When it goes, as go it must, it will take many an evil thing with it."

With such fatherly advice being constantly showered upon her, it was scarcely surprising if Indira displayed revolutionary ardor. At twenty-four, after an expensive education abroad, in Switzerland and at Oxford, she was in a British Indian prison. She was Nehru's only child, and her marriage to a young Indian lawyer called Feroze Gandhi—despite his name, he was not a relative of the Mahatma—evidently had done nothing to alter her devotion either to the cause of Indian freedom or to her father. When India gained independence, Indira moved with her two young children into her widowed father's home to act as the new prime minister's housekeeper and hostess.

I watched Nehru greet his daughter. The tiredness had gone from his face, and he spoke animatedly. Indira was wearing a silk sari, and she had white flowers in her glossy black hair. They made a handsome couple as they moved slowly toward the Palace. The heat-flushed evening sky was barred with pink and lemon, and flocks of green parrots flew across it, screeching hideously. The gardens were emptying. Jane had found a raja, more helpful than I, to bring her tea. "He talked about polo, skiing in Switzerland, and tiger-shooting," said Jane. The great revolution seemed very far away. The waiters, whose slashed velvet hats fascinated Rud, were busily clearing away the debris. Accompanied by the military aides in their yellow-corded white uniforms, the President retreated slowly indoors, past the stiff figures of the Palace Guard. The band began packing up their instruments. The garden party was over.

Sensitive people cannot put up with the vast gap between human beings: it seems so vulgar. NEHRU

UEHHARANGRAI NAVAISHANKAR DHEBAR carefully placed a large, loudly ticking watch on the plain deal table in front of him. The watch was to remind us both that he was a busy man. He had already told me he had to catch a plane to Saurashtra in an hour's time. "The Congress Party," he told me in a soft voice, with a deprecating smile, "is a tear dropped from the heart of suffering humanity."

He was a man in his fifties: small, dark-skinned, wiry, wearing a white cotton Gandhi cap and clothes of the coarsest hand-spun cotton, for he was a staunch believer in the revival of simple village crafts as the salvation of India. He had a small black mustache that made him look like Charlie Chaplin playing the part of the humble tailor who exchanged identities with the Great Dictator. He was the president of the Congress Party and one of the most powerful men in India.

I had gone to see him because the Congress Party was undergoing a severe bout of self-criticism, and he was popularly supposed to be chiefly responsible for it. The Congress Party's All-India Working Committee had set up a subsidiary body called a Constructive Working Committee, which had just issued a severely worded report. Cataloguing the Party's sins, it found that it was suffering from too much pomp; loss of its sense of function; and growing cleavage between the Party heads and the rank and file. The report roundly condemned Ministers, Members of Parliament, and high officials for living in luxury homes, riding in large limousines, surrounding themselves with "elaborate security arrangements," and indulging in other "glaring disparities between the life of Congress Party leaders and the life of the masses."

There was nothing luxurious about Mr. Dhebar's present surroundings. I made the appointment through a secretary, who instructed me to go to the Parliament building, the *Lok Sabha*, and ask to be taken to the Congress Party president: he warned me to be on time. I was guided along a gloomy stone corridor to a small, basementlike room. Its walls were painted a very dark green; it had no windows; and it contained a single, naked electric lightbulb, a plain deal table, two wooden chairs, and Mr. Dhebar.

Or, as the secretary said devoutly: "Dhebarbhai," meaning Brother Dhebar. For Mr. Dhebar was a Gandhian. He was one of the last persons the Mahatma spoke to before his assassination; and Gandhi's blood had actually flowed over his foot on that tragic day. Like Gandhi, he was a Gujerat, having been born in the village of Gangajala in Kathiawar: a village with only fifty inhabitants, of whom the Dhebars constituted a fair fraction, for Mr. Dhebar had been the fifth child in a family of eight. He did not drink or smoke; he lived on only one vegetarian meal a day; he hand spun sufficient yarn to make all his own clothes; he had never been abroad; and among Gandhians he enjoyed enormous prestige. So much I had learned from the devout secretary, a thin, spectacled, and talkative young man. I recognized the loud-ticking watch as an old Gandhi trick: on one occasion, the Mahatma had placed his watch prominently on a table before him at a Congress Party meeting and announced that, as the meeting was starting half an hour late, India's freedom would also be postponed by an avoidable half-hour.

Mr. Dhebar said gently: "Rivers of sorrow have flowed, and we have committed some Himalayan blunders. We must purify the Congress Party and come in closer contact with the people."

Mr. Dhebar was a lawyer. He had twice been jailed by the British. On the second occasion they offered to release him because his wife was dying, but he refused their clemency and insisted on being taken to the hospital each day under jail escort; after the visits he duly returned to his cell, where he diligently read the works of Tolstoy.

I asked him how he thought the Congress Party could best be purified.

"Neither bullets nor bribery can corrupt us. Our richest inheritance from the Father of the Nation is his gospel of pure means to attain pure ends. We must strengthen our internal organization and convey Gandhi's message of love to every hamlet. We must be goodhearted and keep our minds open to all suggestions for improvement."

When the Nawab of Junagadh, a Moslem ruler, tried to take his state into Pakistan, Mr. Dhebar urged the Nawab's Hindu subjects to seize power. Indian troops were sent to help them do so; the Nawab fled to Pakistan. Hundreds of tiny principalities —222, to be exact—were merged in the new state of Saurashtra, with a total population of 4,000,000. Mr. Dhebar became Chief Minister of the new state. In its capital, Rajkot, he lived austerely in four bare rooms. His entire worldly possessions consisted of a cot, a chair, a table, a lamp, and his clothes. Saurashtra was infested with dacoits: traveling about with jeeploads of armed police, Dhebar fought the bandits so strenuously—and caused so many people to be imprisoned under the Preventive Detention Act, which the new Indian government inherited from the British and which allowed no habeas corpus—that he became known, to his distress, as "Jenghiz Khan and Timerlane rolled into one." Nehru, however, called him "one of the humblest and quietest men in India."

The watch ticked loudly. Mr. Dhebar looked at it pointedly.

55

We did not seem to be getting very far. I had heard that his only hobby was chess; I suspected he was probably very good at it.

I asked if he could perhaps be a little more specific about how the Congress Party was to be purified.

"There is still too much speechmaking, and too little action. We must all work harder. But the Congress Party must not lose faith in itself. If it does then it will fail, and if it fails there is no other party that can save the country."

"The Congress Party's goal is said to be Socialism," I said.

"A socialistic pattern of society," he corrected with a deprecating smile.

"How is that to be achieved?"

"We have the responsibility of viewing the whole problem of needs and resources in their totality. We must work on the basis of comprehensive planning, but the planning must bear in mind India's own social values. Only if that is done can there be proper social utilization."

I puzzled over this reply, and the more I puzzled, the more confused I became. I decided to try another tack.

"Do you think Socialism is the only way to cure Indian poverty?"

"A human being is not simply a mass of matter. We are interested in more than merely material considerations."

"Is India in any danger of ever going Communist?"

"India is the largest democracy in the world."

"What in your opinion is the future of Communism?"

Mr. Dhebar smiled. At the same time he rose, and pocketed his watch. "For a clue to the present and future of Communist power," he said pleasantly, "I refer you to Gibbon's *Decline and Fall of the Roman Empire*."

He paused in the doorway and pressed the palms of his hands together in the Indian gesture that serves as both greeting and farewell. Then he was gone, to catch the plane.

Rud was leaving shortly for Benares, and I myself was going on a trip that would keep me away from Delhi for some time.

But before we left we followed Mr. Nehru on a tour of the city's worst slums. It was highly educative.

On both sides of a foul-smelling *nala* running from the Mori Gate to Tis Hazari, an area about half a mile in length and only thirty yards wide, five hundred families lived in shacks constructed out of empty kerosene cans, straw, rags, and mud. I had seen the ghastly shantytowns of Moroka and Tobruk near Johannesburg, but this was worse. No shack was roomier than eight feet by ten feet; the families were large; and the interior of each shack was fetid, stifling, and almost pitch-dark even at high noon. Countless children, either wearing filthy rags or stark naked, played in the muddy ditches: none of them, we were told, had ever attended a school. "These," said Raval Kalpa bitterly, "are the next generation of poverty-stricken illiterates." And, despite the fearful overcrowding, the five hundred families had sorted themselves out into a rigid caste pattern. The highest caste were the hereditary sweepers. They were in regular municipal employment, they earned as much as sixteen dollars a month, and they felt very superior to the porters, odd-job men, and beggars. They kept themselves to themselves and, amid the filth, had their own "colonies."

This Sunday, Raval Kalpa said, the place was comparatively clean, and smelled comparatively sweet. In anticipation of the Pandit's visit, the municipal sweepers had been busy, patching up the most dilapidated shacks and, above all, dumping large quantities of bleaching powder in and around the *nala*. "It drives away the flies, and helps to lessen the stench," Kalpa explained.

We had got there early. An hour before Nehru's arrival large squads of policemen suddenly appeared. Swinging their *lathis*, they went systematically through the shacks, asking few questions but making a rigorous search. "They went to make sure that there are no assassins lurking, waiting to throw a bomb," Kalpa added. "He's always complaining about having too much police protection. But you can't blame the police: if anything did happen, they would be blamed. They might even be accused of having arranged it."

When they had finished searching, the police took up positions along the route that Nehru would follow. It became obvious that no one was going to be allowed very close to the Prime Minister. Perhaps, in the minds of the authorities, if not in Nehru's, the incidents at the airport still rankled.

Time passed; the heat steadily grew; so did the smells, and more bleaching powder was hastily dumped in the *nala*. Nehru arrived, in a large black limousine. It halted abruptly, and Nehru got out, wearing his summertime white coat, with a red rose in a buttonhole, and his white Gandhi cap. He was hastily joined by two municipal officials, who approached him at a stumbling run, apparently somewhat agitated. The police exchanged significant glances. Things were not going according to plan. Nehru, as was his way, had suddenly disapproved the original arrangement, which was for him merely to drive slowly past the shacks. He insisted on going on foot, and seeing things at closer quarters. Impatiently clutching his short cane, and talking vigorously to the two officials who trotted alongside with bowed heads, he walked smartly to the nearest shack. He vanished inside, ducking his head, and came out a moment later looking like a thundercloud. He inspected several more, and his expression grew steadily more forbidding. A trembling small boy, coming unexpectedly face to face with the great man, backed hurriedly away. Nehru pounced on him, and put a gentle hand on the boy's head. He addressed him in Hindi.

"Do you live here? Do you go to school? Why do you live here? Do you have a father and mother? What does your father do for a living? How much do they pay him? Do you have any brothers or sisters? How many? Seven!"

He released the boy, who immediately ran away. "Shocking!" said Nehru in English. "A scandal!" He repeated it in Hindi. The officials bowed very low.

Their curiosity overcoming their timidity, the people of the *nala* began to gather in groups. They followed the Pandit, though at a respectful distance. A policeman with more zeal than discretion darted forward to shoo them off. Nehru gave him a dark look that stopped him in his tracks. "Why do the police always try to come between me and the people?" he demanded loudly. "Ridiculous! Intolerable!" The officials, and the police, looked abashed. I looked at the people, rather hoping that one of them would raise a cheer at those words, but their expressions were disappointingly vacuous.

At the conclusion of his tour Nehru insisted on making a short speech. It was plainly addressed not so much to the people as to the officials. "It is a disgrace, it is intolerable, that people should have to live in conditions like these. We talk of building a new India, of having Socialism and all that; how can we look the rest of the world in the face, when some people still live in places like this? And here, almost in the heart of Delhi, the capital of India! We talk of our ancient culture: it is folly to talk about culture, or even to talk about God, while human beings starve and rot and die. I hope something will be done about this place, and immediately; it must be cleaned up." He stopped as suddenly as he had begun, gave the *namasthe* greeting, and got into his limousine, which drove quickly away.

"Well!" said Rud admiringly. "Did you see those officials' faces? That's telling them!"

"Ah," said Raval Kalpa cynically, "but that's just what he said back in 1952, when he visited this place for the first time. He travels about India constantly, and he sees many places like this, but he cannot remember them all: India is a very large country."

Out of curiosity, we went back to see the *nala* a couple of days later. Nothing had changed, except that the bleaching powder had lost its effect and the shacks that had been hurriedly patched up for Nehru's visit were once more falling down. The flies and the stench were back, and the children who never went to school still played in the deep muddy ditches, wearing filthy rags or no clothes at all.

59

II

MEERUT: CLUBS AND CANNIBALS

*People with a cow-dung mentality, living in a cow-dung coun-
try.* NEHRU

A FAIR proportion of India's 10,000,000 bullock carts seemed
to be on the road to Meerut that morning. The patient, slow-
moving beasts plodded along in vast clouds of dust, the clumsy
cart wheels screaming like souls in anguish. As Singh cautiously
edged the Studebaker past those interminable processions, we
were faced with a difficult choice. When we opened the car
windows, the dust choked us; when we closed them to keep out
the dust, we were in danger of frying to death. Dozing on top
of their carts, the farmers protected themselves by wrapping the
white cloths of their turbans across their faces; bullocks require
little steering. Once a bullock defecated; its owner got down
and solicitously wiped its behind with his headcloth before re-
suming his journey.

Crumbling stone tombs. Crumbling mud huts. An occasional
rounded stone, worshipped for its phallic shape and lovingly
smeared with bright red clay. The scenery of the Indian plain
is singularly monotonous. I tried to forget the heat, and the 42
miles of bullock carts which presumably lay ahead of us, by
meditating on the strange tale I had heard, which was taking
me to Meerut.

At a *mela,* or religious bathing ceremony, at Garhmuktesar,
across the river from Meerut, the police had arrested 17 young
men whom they found hiding in a sugar-cane field. Seven

hundred thousand people had attended the *mela;* and several agitated parents among the 700,000 reported to the police that their children had disappeared. Indian *melas* and tragedy frequently go hand in hand; at a recent *mela* near Benares almost 500 people had been crushed to death. Numbers of children are always reported missing on those occasions. Some are kidnapped by a wandering gypsy-like tribe that specializes in the capture and sale of children—which is a recognized caste; some get drowned; many simply wander off and later turn up again, safe and sound. So the Meerut police were understandably a little blasé—until they found the young men hiding in the sugar-cane field, and discovered that one of them, a youth of nineteen, was going about with a child's skull, which he was using as a candy bowl. The police promptly took the young men to Meerut, for questioning. I was now on my way to Meerut from Delhi to try to discover what the outcome of the police investigation had been. There were ugly rumors that the missing children had not only been murdered, but had been eaten.

Meerut was no better and no worse than most Indian towns. It looked as if it had just been through a severe bombardment. Many of the buildings appeared to have recently fallen down. In fact, the rubble had lain for years, perhaps for centuries. But it was overlaid with a more modern accretion of rusting mounds of scrap iron. In India clay pots are smashed and discarded if a casteless person or an untouchable has used them, and human corpses are ceremonially burned; but anything more durable is never thrown away. In Meerut, amid the rubble of houses that had simply collapsed with old age, there was the rubble of machinery that had been worked to death but was still being hoarded. Both served the same purpose. When people wanted to build new houses, they carted away as much as they needed of the ruins of the old, to serve as their building materials. When a machine broke down, they rummaged in the piles of old worn-out machines for spare parts. We drove past a factory

61

that called itself "The Northern Indian Steel and Iron Corporation." It was no more than a large open shed in which workers naked to the waist banged energetically at large sheets of metal. The yard in front of the shed was heaped with gigantic rusting springs, broken iron rods, gaunt wheel spokes, and the remains of ancient engines. On the shed's flat roof, levitated there by who knows what mysterious means, there crouched the wheelless, engineless shell of an entire omnibus.

Next door to the factory was a small brick building with dirty windowpanes and a flaking wooden door. A sign above the door read, in English: "Dr. B. C. Raji's University and Commercial Business College."

The road became a narrow street running through the bazaar. Cows foraged contentedly off the garbage outside vegetable stores. A man sat, cross-legged, stirring an immense iron pot. The low-roofed open shops were gaudy with brassware, green celluloid combs, dusty bottles of violently colored soft drinks, cotton saris. A man in pajama trousers furiously pedaled a sewing-machine. A grain store sold red peppers. A shoe store sold crimson slippers with curling toes. There was a profusion of wicker baskets, stools, and charpoys. The buildings were scrawled with inscriptions in Hindi and English. The street overflowed with merchandise and swarmed with people, cows, dogs, bicycles, and bullock carts. There were thin-cheeked young Hindus, white-bearded Hindus, girls with long black pigtails, aged crones, ragged children with infant sisters and baby brothers strapped on their backs, beggars, Brahmins, snake-charmers, fortunetellers, and a youth beating a big drum outside the inevitable cinema, which was showing an Indian version of *Hamlet* in which the gloomy Dane became a dusky raja who joined Ophelia in nine specially written song-hits. Loudspeakers blared outside tea shops, the snake-charmers' flutes reedily pierced the air, bicycle bells rang, dogs barked, street-vendors hoarsely called their wares, beggars whined, and children cried.

Beyond the bazaar area, the road climbed and widened and was lined with bungalows behind high walls and thick hedges. We had come out of what the British, an alien handful in a swarming land, used to call the "native town" into the "cantonment." A heavy hot silence brooded over it. Here one blistering Sunday evening a century ago, the 3rd Bengal Cavalry regiment revolted after 85 of their comrades had been imprisoned for refusing cartridges that the Hindus said were greased with cow-fat and the Moslems said were greased with pig-fat. The British were all at evening service: the rebels marched off toward Delhi and began the great Indian Mutiny. We drove along the deserted Mall, past the church and the cemetery, and after some difficulty located the white-pillared Meerut Club.

It seemed to be deserted, too, for our voices echoed vainly in its vast entrance hall. My footsteps clattered loudly as I wandered through a dusty library whose shelves were filled with decaying books and into an enormous smoking-room solemnly lined with huge leather couches and bulky leather armchairs. Beyond the smoking-room was an empty inner courtyard. I tried a door at random, and found myself in a gargantuan washroom with high white walls, great white porcelain washbowls, and rusting taps dripping discolored water. The slow dripping made a melancholy sound. In a huge billiard room, the windows were shuttered, and the green-clothed tables swam in a semi-dusk: they looked larger and longer than normal billiard tables, as if only giants had ever played on them, standing nine feet high and using poles to strike cannon balls. And while they played they had smoked giant's cigars, and drunk down enormous whiskies and sodas, for I could still smell cigar smoke and the fumes of alcohol. But the smell of decay was stronger. The green cloth on the tables had begun to rot.

A door other than the one through which I had entered took me back into the smoking-room. Tables were scattered about among the great black leather couches and armchairs, and some of the tables still held old magazines: *Tatler* and *Punch* and

63

The Illustrated London News. There were a few shelves of books, mostly about sport, and many volumes of an encyclopedia, partly eaten by mice. Round the walls ranged the mounted heads of big game: mostly tigers, but also some boars and buck. Their glassy eyes stared vacantly. Below the heads and above the shelves of moldering books the walls were lined with old photographs, with waggish handwritten inscriptions. They were regimental photographs. Bald colonels, mustached majors, and toothy captains looked accusingly out of their frames at me. They seemed to be asking if I had been properly introduced. The handwritten inscriptions made a strange contrast, for they had an almost feminine skittishness. "Captain Dash at the Mess Dinner raises his glass to a Certain Miss!" "Where had the Gallant Major been, the Night BEFORE?" But a graver note was sometimes struck. "The Colonel and his Lady—God bless them!" "For He's a Jolly Good Fellow; We'll Miss You, Major Blank!"

While I fingered the dusty books and looked at the faded photographs, Singh had been exploring on his own, and shouting lustily as he went. At length there was the faint shuffle of bare feet, and a very old, bearded Hindu appeared in the doorway. I asked him if we could have anything to eat or drink, and he nodded tremblingly and vanished eagerly, presently to return miraculously with good beef and cheese sandwiches and very good cold beer in bottles. I ate the beef; Singh ate the cheese; we both drank the beer. The old man hovered anxiously, and the animal heads on the walls stared glassily.

"Do many people come here," I asked.

"Oh, no, sahib: very few; hardly ever."

The old man replied in English, but haltingly, as if he had not spoken it for a very long time.

"But the club is still open?" I asked, surprised.

"Oh, yes, sahib!" He was eager again. "Club always open. Sometimes people come."

After that, his English broke down completely. I never did

discover who kept the Meerut Club mysteriously going: vast, empty, desolate, falling steadily into decay, its great billiard tables unused, its enormous washroom echoing only to the faint dripping of rusty taps, its mounted heads slowly moldering, and its magazines and encyclopedia accumulating dust; but with a servitor still on the premises and able at a moment's notice to produce excellent sandwiches and cold beer. When we had finished, the old man collected the empty bottles and glasses and plates, humbly requested a ridiculously small sum—it was about a third of the price that the same meal would have cost anywhere else—panted out broken gratitude for a modest tip, and bowed himself out of the room backwards. We never saw him again. When we drove away from the white-pillared building, nesting in the neglected greenery that gave it protection from the blazing sun, it was utterly silent and seemed utterly deserted. But for the beer and sandwiches, the old man might have been a ghost, at one with the fading photographs in the smoking-room and the gigantic forgotten tables in the billiard room.

It stays in my mind as a monument to a ruling caste that was almost exclusively male: Spartans who were soldiers, horsemen, pig-stickers and, at heart if not in mind, schoolboys. They were schoolboys who kept themselves too busy to have more sex-consciousness than the archly old-fashioned waggish inscriptions on the photographs displayed. This was the society that produced Dr. Watson, the patient foil to A. Conan Doyle's detective hero for schoolboys. ("My old Afghan wound still troubled me.") Richard Hannay could have walked out of *The Thirty-nine Steps* into the Meerut Club, performing his favorite trick of tossing a Kashmiri dagger up in the air and catching it in his teeth, with no questions asked. (There might have been some good-natured applause in the smoking-room.) India, which is also a male society, and which understands caste, accepted them. The British lost India when they began to bring out their women. Nobody loved the *mem-sahibs* and the relations between British and Indians grew sour. The women brought color-consciousness as well as sex-consciousness, and in the great wave of anger and fear which followed in the wake of the Mutiny both got full play. Things were never the same again.

Before we left the club, Singh had asked the old man the way to the police station. The *chowki* was a small brick building, and its single office had instead of a door, very sensibly, a rolled-down bamboo screen, on which a bucket of water was thrown at intervals, to lay the dust and keep the air comparatively cool. Behind a battered desk sat a sergeant, who was diligently scratching on a piece of yellowing paper with an ancient pen that needed frequent dipping in a cracked ink bottle containing an eighth of an inch of muddy ink. He welcomed our interruption enthusiastically, called out in Hindi for another chair and some tea to be brought, and spoke to me in a friendly Welsh accent.

"Oh, yes!" he said, nodding and smiling briskly. "The men have confessed everything."

"To murdering the children?"

"They are Aghoris. The Aghoris are a strange sect, and we don't know much about them. People say they live in graveyards and get their food off funeral pyres. That is to say," the sergeant explained, with happy relish, "they eat what's left of cremated bodies."

"And these men you have arrested—seventeen?—they admit they are Aghoris, and they admit that is what Aghoris do?"

"They say they assembled together in Delhi, and came on here from Delhi when they heard there was to be a *mela*." The sergeant, a middle-aged man with a long humorous face, vigorously shook his head from side to side, which is the Indian way of nodding. "But they came originally from Allahabad. I'll read you a bit of one of the confessions."

Unexpectedly he donned a pair of spectacles, which made him look solemn, and from a drawer of the battered desk he

66

pulled another yellowing sheet. He translated fluently from its Hindi.

" 'In Allahabad our father dwells. I am nineteen years of age and have been an Aghori since childhood. The father called us together in Allahabad and said, if we did such-and-such things, which would revolt all mankind, we would achieve salvation. We were to go to Delhi by diverse ways, and there the path would be made known to us. In Delhi, we were told of the *mela*, and so we separated, and by twos and threes we came here. This is the truth, I swear it. Do not use the leather belt ag—' "

The sergeant coughed loudly, and put the yellowed sheet back in the drawer.

"What sort of things were they supposed to do?" I asked.

"Ah!" said the sergeant, darkly. "We haven't got to the foot of it all yet, no, not by any means. We are still chalking it out. But this one who confessed said: 'such things as killing and eating children.' "

"In Allahabad our father dwells." It sounded vaguely like the opening words of a Christian hymn. And then the dreadful things to revolt all mankind, including the killing and eating of children. Rud had said, cautiously, that India was a very complex country. Happily now on his way to the University of Benares, Rud didn't know the half of it.

I said: "I thought you said they had all confessed?"

"Not all," said the sergeant, suddenly turning cautious himself. "Not yet. But they will."

"Have they been charged with murder? When will they come to trial?"

"The superintendent could tell you that."

"Do you have them in jail here in Meerut? Could I see them?"

The sergeant abruptly became evasive. "You should talk to the superintendent."

But the superintendent was not immediately available.

Meerut, the sergeant explained, was holding a show of local crafts in the community center. A Congress Party M.P. was opening it. The superintendent would almost certainly be there.

We drove to the community center, but on the way a prominently displayed poster caught my eye. I hastily called on Singh to stop, and got out of the car to inspect it. Printed in English, it read:

"A new star has risen on the horizon! Kaviraj Lal, M.P., is a man of the masses. Simple and unostentatious, he lives his life as they do. He speaks in accents which they understand. His heart is large enough to find a place for all, without distinction of race or creed. Honest to the core, his moral authority strikes terror into the corrupt and the greedy. Speaking truth and only truth, he seeks neither power nor pelf for himself, but everything for the poor. His heart bleeds for the oppressed and downtrodden throughout the world, and he is a determined fighter in their cause. As long as India brings forth sons like Kaviraj Lal, her place in the vanguard of human progress is assured. A prince among patriots, Kaviraj Lal takes pride in everything indigenous. Much practiced in ancient Hindu arts of medicine etc., Kaviraj Lal has himself invented a rare sovereign specific for all human ills. A revival of *Ayurveda* in all its pristine glory! Only it can guard the people's health! Cures nervous debility and brings happiness into woebegone lives! Buy Kaviraj Lal's famous remedy! (Patented)."

Singh had joined me, and we read this effusion together. "Gentleman at the railway station?" Singh inquired. "Very rich man, Mr. Kaviraj Lal." He was twirling his mustache, and his tone was not without irony.

There was a crowd outside the community center. There were also plenty of posters advertising Kaviraj Lal's famous remedy. I asked for the police superintendent, and was told he was expected but had not yet arrived. I was asked to wait. A chair was brought, and was placed with much ceremony in the shade of a tree. The crowd read the posters, chattered among themselves, and came to gape at me. I sat under the tree, feeling foolish. The man who had brought the chair dashed into the community center. Presently he came out again. He was a stoutish man who had not shaved for two days, but in spite of the intolerable heat he was wearing a black jacket and a blue-striped shirt with a collar, and a brown woolen tie. He perspired rather freely. "Please come," he said. I was wearing a bush shirt without a tie and khaki shorts. I followed him nervously.

Inside the community center the local crafts were laid out on long tables. They seemed to consist mainly of garden shears. "Best in India," said the man in the blue-striped shirt. There were also some odd-looking rubber tubes. "Medical supplies," my guide explained. In vivid pantomime, he pretended to swallow one of the long tubes. "For examination of patients' interiors."

At the far end of the room, a group of people were listening to a blandly delivered lecture. There was no mistaking that urbane voice, those jutting ears. His magnificent white dhoti ballooning round his ankles, wearing his long white cotton shirt like a Roman toga, Mr. Kaviraj Lal advanced upon me and greeted me with enthusiasm. "My dear fellow, what a pleasant surprise to find you at our little function! You should have informed me you wished to attend, I would have sent special invitation!"

"As a matter of fact," I said, "I'm looking for the superintendent of police."

Mr. Kaviraj Lal looked surprised but not a bit disconcerted.

"Nevertheless you are interested in our local crafts? Permit me to conduct you round the exhibit personally. These are garden shears—pure fine steel—best in India. All manufactured here in Meerut. Perhaps on your way in you saw the Northern India Iron and Steel Corporation factory? I have a small interest. We poor politicians must also live!" He laughed heartily. The people who were following us round laughed po-

litely, all save the stoutish man in the black jacket and brown
woolen tie, who laughed uproariously. "My secretary," Mr.
Kaviraj Lal explained in an aside. "Very efficient." He picked
up one of the long rubber tubes. "These are medical supplies,
also manufactured here in Meerut. For examining patients' interiors. The tube is introduced orally. I myself am a manufacturer of medical supplies: pharmaceutical."

"I saw the posters," I said.

He nodded, well satisfied that I had done so. "Ninety per
cent of the people of our country are poor. It is beyond their
means to resort to foreign medicines. I decided *Ayurvedic* drugs
were the answer. I studied the ancient arts, and produced my
remedy after much toil. Results have surpassed all expectations,
I am happy to say. Millions are getting their desired relief." He
beamed with pride.

The secretary tugged his sleeve and whispered something in
his ear.

"Ah, yes! I am called upon to say a few words. Please remain."

I said: "If I could find the superintendent—"

"Yes, it is very annoying. He should be here, but he must
have been delayed. I hope he does not miss my few remarks.
He is a highly intelligent man, very interested in the current
political situation." Mr. Lal's brown eyes unexpectedly
twinkled. "Some years ago it was his painful duty under the
British to have me put in jail, but he is now a loyal supporter of
the Congress Party."

The secretary then called the gathering to order, including
two small boys who were trying to cut one of the rubber tubes
in half with a pair of garden shears, and Mr. Lal made his
speech. He talked about the need for industrialization, and referred glowingly to the outstanding achievements of the Northern India Iron and Steel Corporation. Then he turned to politics, and declared that public office was a sacred duty, which
should not be lightly abused. He had begun to talk about democracy, and was quoting Burke, when a lean brown-skinned

man in a dark blue uniform came up to me and said, in a whisper, that he believed I wanted to see him.

The superintendent and I tiptoed out of the hall. In the open he pulled out a pipe and looked at me with alert eyes. "What can I do for you?"

I told him what I had heard about the imprisoned Aghoris, and asked when they would come to trial. The police superintendent bit thoughtfully on the stem of his pipe, and crinkled his eyes. He looked rueful.

"I don't know if they ever will come to trial. I doubt it. The boy's confession wasn't made before a magistrate, and now he's withdrawn it. They deny everything, except being Aghoris. We could charge them with loitering in cemeteries"—he wrinkled his nose—"but that wouldn't mean very much."

"But why did they confess to killing and eating the children in the first place?"

"Ah," said the superintendent cheerfully, "I suppose some of my men might have banged them about a bit."

"And the child's skull that one of them was using as a candy bowl?"

"He could have picked it up after a cremation. The skulls seldom get burned, you know. Anyway the skull has been examined by the experts—we sent it to Calcutta—and they think the child probably died a natural death. Very hard to tell, without the rest of the body, of course. As for the children reported missing from the *mela*"—he shrugged—"that happens all the time. None of them has been found; but they could have been drowned, or kidnapped. I don't suppose we'll ever know."

And, the superintendent's tone implied, there wasn't much use bothering about it in a country where a baby was born every four seconds or so, and the already enormous population increased by 5,000,000 each year. He was being neither cynical nor fatalistic, only realistic.

There was a burst of hand-clapping, and Mr. Kaviraj Lal came out of the community center, holding his dhoti, like a

71

Victorian lady holding her skirts, and beaming. He greeted us jovially.

"Ah, there you are! I hope you liked my little speech." His eyes fell on one of his own posters, and he paused to admire it. "I think our local crafts must have astonished you, eh? We Indians are not so far behind the West as you had thought!" He looked about him: at the brand-new concrete community center, at the sparse little garden in front of it where I had waited under the tree, at the slowly dispersing crowd. "A beautiful day —perhaps a little warm. How is Mr. Jack? I hope he is very much enjoying India."

I could have asked again to be allowed to see the Aghoris, but it would only have embarrassed the superintendent, whom I rather liked. He said he had to get back to his duties; we shook hands. Inexorably, Mr. Lal took me by the arm. "And now you must come and have a cup of tea with me. I always have time to spare to talk to a friend. Our meeting like this is very propitious. No doubt it was written in our horoscopes! Have you ever seriously studied astrology? You should certainly do so. While we are having our tea, I shall tell you what the ancient Hindus had to say about astrology."

III

JODHPUR: DEATH OF A LADY

And lay me down by my master's side to rule in Heaven his only bride. KIPLING

"I SUPPOSE you want to visit the cemetery first," Mr. Bhatkal bawled briskly. He stood before me, his head cocked to one side and a hand cupped over a hairy ear with the alert expectancy of the very deaf, wearing a pair of spectacles askew on his broad nose, a brown-check sport jacket with five ballpoint pens clipped in the breast pocket, and a green tie fastened with an imitation gold pin. Mr. Bhatkal, it was plain, was ready and eager to go.

The Circuit House at Jodhpur stands on the side of a hill, and is enclosed by a stone courtyard and sweet-smelling flowering trees. I had been ushered into a spacious bedroom with a splendid view of the fort that peers down on the town from a precipitous crag. Adjoining the bedroom was an enormous bathroom. The huge bed, unlike the beds in most Indian hotels, looked soft and inviting. I was tired and, after Meerut, I fancied I had had my fill of cemeteries. But I weakly muttered that I supposed I ought to see it, and Mr. Bhatkal led the way downstairs at a brisk trot.

We drove into town with Mr. Bhatkal sitting in the front seat beside the driver and shouting directions. When the car had inserted its way into a narrow corkscrew lane, he bawled at the driver to stop. He rushed up an outside wooden staircase, and emerged triumphantly with a large woman and a small child. "My wife," explained Mr. Bhatkal loudly. "My son." He bundled them unceremoniously into the back of the car beside me. "Thought they might like to have a look," Mr. Bhatkal shouted. "Gives the child an outing. Hope you don't mind."

Mr. Bhatkal was a lawyer and a newspaper correspondent. He also owned a small stationery store which sold newspapers and paperback novels with lurid titles. He wrote articles, indefatigably, for a large number of Indian papers. His office, which was in a small room at the back of a local cinema, was a hive of activity. The steep stairs leading to it were always crowded with people seeking legal advice. They remained huddled on the stairs, sometimes for hours, while, inside the office, Mr. Bhatkal instructed his clerk to hold them at bay until he finished an article. He wrote his articles very quickly in a large flowing hand, for he disdained the use of a typewriter, and signed them all, with a flourish: "P. D. Bhatkal, Special Correspondent." Then he thrust them into large brown envelopes, stuck the envelopes down with gummed tape, and dispatched them posthaste. The tedium of waiting was relieved for his clients by the fact that the cinema's walls were very thin. While Mr. Bhatkal wrote furiously, the entire building vibrated to snatches of magnified dialogue and the thunder of film music. It was this daily assault of sound that had made Mr. Bhatkal go deaf.

The car successfully corkscrewed itself out of the narrow twisting lane. But then it came to a halt again, for the main street of Jodhpur was packed with expectant crowds. "Just in time for the procession!" bawled Mr. Bhatkal, and instructed his wife to stand the child up on the seat so that it would have a good view. Presently, over the heads of the crowd, we saw a large, flower-smothered chariot pass slowly down the street. Propped up in it, amid the flowers, was the effigy of a woman, wearing a red-and-gold sari. The chariot rolled ponderously on: the crowds as it passed knelt down and said loud prayers. I

74

looked at Mrs. Bhatkal: she was praying, too, her eyes closed
and her lips moving. The child leaped excitedly up and down
on the leather seat. Mr. Bhatkal was not praying: he had
whipped out one of his ballpoint pens and was making rapid
notes. "Fifteen papers have asked me for a descriptive," he
shouted cheerfully at me. With every flourish of the pen, Mr.
Bhatkal was briskly earning rupees.

After the chariot had passed, we drove at a crawl toward the
cemetery, for the crowds were still thick. The cemetery had
wrought-iron gates and was full of people. Outside the gates
stood a barrow full of coconuts. It had the name "B. Ravi"
painted on its side in white letters, and B. Ravi was doing very
good business. The people streaming into the cemetery, mostly
women, all paused to buy a coconut. We got out of the car and
followed them in, along a winding path, to where the crowd
was densest. Undaunted, Mr. Bhatkal shouldered his way
through. I followed closely. Mrs. Bhatkal, who had purchased
a coconut, came last, pulling her child by the hand.

We struggled through toward a cleared space, in the midst of
which a fire was burning. Women were pacing slowly round the
fire, their heads bent and their faces covered. As they walked,
they chanted and, when they had circled the fire seven times,
they laid their coconuts reverently in the flames. The ground
was covered with scorched and blackened coconut shells. Mrs.
Bhatkal, still clinging to her child, joined the women who were
walking round the fire, her coconut held ready. A woman knelt
and kissed the ground, then took a handful of ashes, kissed
them, and placed them on her head. She knelt before a pitcher
filled with flowers and began to pray. The other women went
through the same ritual.

Mr. Bhatkal, notebook in hand, surveyed the scene through
his spectacles with a proprietory air. As he jabbed down notes,
he shouted explanations at me.

"This is where the *sati* took place. The fire has been kept going ever since. The coconuts are offerings to the *sati*, who has

passed through the fire to become a goddess. The pitcher beside the fire is the one she used for her last bath, on the day she threw herself into the flames."

The background to the scene was a large marble tomb which dominated the entire cemetery. Carved and fretted, it must normally have been an imposing and dignified piece of work. It was far from normal now, for it was luridly strung with colored electric lightbulbs that robbed it of its dignity and reduced it to the level of a gaudy exhibit at a fair.

Mr. Bhatkal pointed to this monstrosity and shouted: "That is the tomb of the *sati*'s grandfather. It has been decorated in her honor by the Jodhpur Electricians' Union, entirely at their own expense."

Presently, after Mrs. Bhatkal had cast her coconut, smeared her head with ashes, and finished praying, we left the cemetery. At the gate a colored print was thrust into my hand by a street-vendor, who promptly demanded five rupees and tried to sell me, in addition, a garland and a poem specially written for the occasion. The print showed a woman, dressed as the effigy in the chariot had been dressed, seated amid decorative flames and cradling a dead man's head in her lap. Hovering over the flames was a *viman* or mythological Hindu airplane, heavy with gilt and shaped like a balloon's gondola. In the gondola, smiling happily, sat the same woman and the man, both transfigured into deities. Brahma, Krishna, and Sita looked on approvingly, and two Hindu saints sat on two prancing white horses, holding lances. At the top of the picture other Hindu gods and goddesses rode lions, played lutes, held tridents, and showered down flowers.

We drove Mrs. Bhatkal and her child home. "Now you and I will go and meet the *sati*'s family," shouted Mr. Bhatkal.

The house to which he took me was very large and very gloomy. Several opulent looking motorcars stood in the driveway. People were grouped on the veranda, and as we approached, Mr. Bhatkal striding forward purposefully and I lagging apprehensively behind, a thin figure in white slipped away from the group and hurried off, looking nervously over its shoulder.

Mr. Bhatkal waited for me to catch up and yelled in my ear: "That is the family priest. He is skulking, because he fears he may be in trouble with the police for aiding and abetting the *sati.*"

I felt somewhat relieved. For what they were worth, these were the first words I had heard that even hinted at disapprobation of the event that was attracting great crowds to Jodhpur. Suttee—the self-destruction of a Hindu widow on her husband's funeral pyre—still occurs in India, but usually only in villages far off the beaten track and among obscure people. The Jodhpur suttee was unusual, for it had occurred in full view of some five hundred people, and the victim was the widow of a high-ranking and high-born soldier. On the day of the funeral, the inconsolable widow, it was said, had dressed herself in her wedding sari, entered the cemetery heavily veiled, and suddenly cast herself into the flames. Now she was being worshipped as a *sati*, or goddess.

Mr. Bhatkal strode briskly on to the veranda and loudly introduced himself. Then, in equally stentorian tones, he introduced me. I found myself unwillingly shaking the flabby hand of a large unshaven man in a white turban. He looked at me with dull eyes, said something in Hindi to Mr. Bhatkal, and walked into the unlighted house. "He has gone to fetch the dead man's brother, who has come to take charge of the family's affairs," Mr. Bhatkal explained.

A slim man came on to the veranda. His handshake was muscular but perfunctory. He wore a small, neatly trimmed mustache, and had a soldierly bearing.

"Happy to meet you," he said. "Shall we sit down?" He threw himself carelessly into a wicker chair, and swung a neat, well-shod foot. "What can I do for you?"

"Ah, major," shouted Mr. Bhatkal, happily, "you can do a

great deal. I want to write several articles. Whole country is
agog, isn't it?" He began pulling out handfuls of crumpled tele-
grams. "All my newspapers demanding special-correspondent
articles!"

"Not much I can tell you, actually," said the major. He spoke
in the clipped accents of Sandhurst Royal Military College. "Bit
of confusion, naturally. Of course I came dashin' up here as
soon as I heard about my brother's death. Poor old chap!" He
shook his head. "Not old, actually. In his forties. My sister-in-
law was some years younger. I got here too late for *that* part,
though. Missed the funeral altogether." He shook his sleek head
again, and I thought he was going to add: "Bad show," but he
didn't. Instead, he turned to me: "Know Jodhpur well?"

I said: "No."

"Very good huntin' country. Gone off a bit now, of course."

I said we were extremely sorry to intrude upon him at this
time of tragedy.

The major blinked. He was plainly disconcerted. "Sorry, I
don't quite follow."

"The tragedy of your brother's death and then your sister-
in-law's—er—suicide."

"Oh. Oh, yes." But the major was evidently still puzzled. "Of
course. Naturally. Yes, quite a shock." He considered: there was
a point he wanted to put, and he did not quite know how to
put it. Finally, brightening up, he said: "Only I don't know
that *tragedy* is quite the word, you know. We hardly look at it
that way. By dying the way she did, my sister-in-law felt she was
doing the right thing. After all, widows don't have much of a
life in India. And now instead of being a widow, she's become
a *sati*. And that's a very big thing for a family like ours; people
look up to us." He rose. "Well, hope you'll excuse me. Lots of
things to attend to, you know."

As we walked down the drive toward our car, Mr. Bhatkal
shouted enthusiastically: "Very fine chap, the major. Very big
sportsman."

"Polo, I suppose," I said.
"And pig-sticking!" Mr. Bhatkal bawled.

The number of holy men increases every day. FROM THE PRE-
AMBLE OF A BILL FOR THE COMPULSORY REGISTRATION OF *Sadhus*

A LUNCH was being given in honor of the Chief Minister of
Rajasthan, who had come to Jodhpur to inquire into land dis-
turbances. Disgruntled former landlords who had been promised compensation but had not yet received it had launched a
satyagraha. They were taking out processions, holding up trains
by squatting on railroad tracks, and invading government offices armed with cudgels. About two thousand of them were already lodged in the city jail.

Despite those exciting events, the lunch was a leisurely affair. Several speakers, all of them belonging to the Chief Minister's faction within the Congress Party, praised him extrava-
gantly to his face. He responded with a beaming smile, and finally made a speech himself, in which he poured ridicule on
his political opponents, accused them of being in league with
the dacoits, and declared he intended to uphold democracy at
all costs. Meanwhile, in the broiling streets, mobs were fasting
outside the jail, smashing windows, and stoning passing automobiles.

I found myself next to a gray-haired man who turned out to
be the superintendent of police. He might have been the brother
of the police superintendent in Meerut. Heartened by this coincidence, I asked him about the *sati*.

The superintendent took his time in replying. He looked like
a man who weighed his words.

"We've arrested the family guru," he said. "But we may not
be able to prove anything."

I remembered the white figure that had slipped away so furtively from the big gloomy house where we had met the sport-loving major. I also recalled Mr. Bhatkal's words.

"You mean," I said, "you suspect the family priest helped her to reach the cemetery and commit suicide?"

The superintendent looked rather grim. "Not necessarily. This isn't the first case of suttee I've investigated. Some of these women become hysterical when their husbands die, and say they mean to throw themselves on the funeral pyre. The word gets about. There were over 500 people at that cremation, and they had gone there expecting to see something." He paused. "But often these women change their minds. Being burned alive isn't the most pleasant of deaths."

"But this one evidently didn't change her mind."

The superintendent looked at me strangely. "Perhaps we'll never know."

I was appalled. "You mean you suspect foul play?"

"What I suspect and what I can prove may be two different things." He sounded tired and bitter. "All I know is that 500 people were crowded into that cemetery at the time the thing happened, and not a single one is prepared to testify. Not one. They all say they saw nothing, heard nothing. I know some of the people who were there; a number of them are quite prominent citizens. But they aren't talking." He paused again. "This woman announced her intention of committing the act of suttee: a religious act of tremendous and solemn significance in Hindu eyes. I know just what it means, for I'm a Hindu myself. Well! If you say you are going to become a goddess, you may find you have to go through with it, whether you change your mind at the last moment or not."

A policeman came up and leaned over to whisper in the superintendent's ear. The superintendent looked exceedingly annoyed. "All right; I'll come at once." He excused himself to me, and quickly slipped away. The Chief Minister, still on his feet, was announcing that in a democracy public office was a sacred duty. The lunch, already interminable, looked as if it might continue being very dull. Unobtrusively, I followed the superintendent.

He was just getting into a police car, and it began to move away at once. Temporarily separated from the invaluable Singh, I looked helplessly around. A most elegant young man with a cheerfully impudent grin hailed me. He was driving a brand-new Chrysler.

"You are Mr. Bhatkal's friend? Please hop in!"

I hopped in. "They are going to the police station to pick up more men," my unexpected ally explained. "I heard them say so. Let's see the fun."

"Is it the land business?"

He shook his head. He had a handsome face, smooth as a girl's, and very lively dark eyes. "No; they are going out to a place called Lohardi. It's about eleven miles. A *sadhu* has taken *samadhi* and is attempting to engrave himself alive. The police disapprove, and will try to stop him."

We reached the police station in time to see a small cavalcade set off: three police cars, with the superintendent's in the lead. They evidently felt they had no moments to lose. Suitably disguised from inquisitive eyes in a thick cloud of red dust, we followed. My accomplice introduced himself as Suni Aiyyer. "I am a qualified architect," he said proudly, "but have not yet found a job. However, my father owns several cement factories, so I should have no difficulty."

He drove with skill, swerving adroitly past bullock carts that had already been pulled hastily into the side of the road to allow the police cars to pass. He wore a white silk shirt, with his initials embroidered on the pocket, and cream-colored slacks. He chattered happily as we sped along, plainly delighted to have the tedium of a very hot day interrupted by so odd an adventure. "A *sadhu*, I suppose you know, is a holy man. They have a great influence over our superstitious villagers, and do a great deal of harm. There are millions of them, and their num-

81

ber is growing all the time, for it's a good life: a couple of cheap conjuring trucks are all that's needed to pose as a new incarnation of the Lord Krishna, or Vishnu returned to earth, or some such nonsense. A *samadhi* means a trance. Great renown attaches to a *sadhu* who has himself engraved alive while in state of *samadhi*, so that he may emerge after many days, even weeks or months, without having had food to eat, water to drink, or air to breathe. The villagers then perform *puja* before him and he is worshipped."

Shortly—for even over a very bad road the new Chrysler rode swiftly—we came to a hillock at the entrance to a small and wretched-looking mud village. A large, curious crowd had assembled; Aiyyer got out of the car and pushed his way through without ceremony. I followed meekly. The police cars had halted untidily by the roadside, but the police at first glance were not in evidence. We found them, farther round the side of the hillock, busily attacking huge slabs of rock with pickaxes. Aiyyer watched them for a while, then turned to the nearest bystander, a villager with one blinded eye and a rapt look in the other, and spoke to him vigorously in Hindi.

"The *sadhu* is in a pit, under those rocks," he explained to me, dismissing the villager presently with a cavalier nod. "He was engraved yesterday, and these village people have been here all night and all today, saying prayers and waiting to see a miracle. The police have already arrested one of the men who put him in; the others are said to be hiding in the village temple— the people here are Shivaites—and some policemen have gone to arrest them, also." He inspected the laboring policemen critically. "If they find the *sadhu* dead, it will be a bad thing for those who engraved him, even though he was engraved of his own free will."

But the *sadhu* was not dead. Having finally loosened the slabs of rock, the policemen began heaving and levering them aside to reveal a small dark pit cut in the side of the hillock. It was barely four feet square; and curled up inside it was a small, thin naked figure whom the policemen briskly hauled out. Extremely dirty, he lay on the ground with his eyes closed; but his thin chest moved, and an eyelid fluttered. The crowd behind us exclaimed and muttered. Ignoring the police, Aiyyer peered inquisitively into the pit. "There are some coconuts," he reported. "Not for food, of course, as the *sadhu* was in trance, but as a religious offering; and there is also money—quite a lot of money." He straightened up grinning. "This *sadhu* was doing quite well."

The *sadhu* was carried to a police car. The police began to disperse the crowd. I kept cautiously out of the superintendent's way. Presently the policemen who had gone off to search the village temple returned with three thoroughly villainous looking men in tow. They also were stowed in a police car. The villager with one good eye, seeing the police busy elsewhere, scrambled eagerly into the pit. He was disappointed: the police had already removed the *sadhu's* money hoard, as well as the coconuts. The police cars drove off. Aiyyer had vanished into the crowd, and I waited patiently beside the Chrysler. Presently he reappeared and slid into the driver's seat.

"It is all the fault of the recent *sati* affair," he explained, as, more sedately than we had come, we followed the police cars back into Jodhpur. "That has drawn big crowds, you know, and some people have made a lot of money out of it already. The gurus, the garland-makers, and the sellers of coconuts have been making business. The *sadhus* of Lohardi decided to try a 'miracle,' also. They persuaded this man—he is only an apprentice *sadhu*—to allow himself to be engraved. Thus they proposed to exploit the blind faith of the people, sharing the income from the *samadhi*. The *sadhu's* sealed pit would have become quite famous; people would have come many miles to see it and to make offerings before it. You saw how much money the man had himself collected even before he was engraved in the pit."

"But how would he have got out again?" I objected.

"Ah, his comrades of course would have persuaded the peo-

83

ple to go away for a short while, on some pretext. Then they would quickly have released him, and sealed up the pit again before the people returned. After that they might have exploited the situation for years.

"Or," said Aiyyer brightly, a fresh thought striking him, "perhaps they would not have done that. Perhaps they would just have let him die. Then they would not have had to share the money with him. He looked a very dull-witted fellow. His name is Nathu, and he is from Bikaner. Yes, on the whole, I think they would have let him die and told the people that, as he had not come out of the pit, he must have ascended to heaven."

"But now, thanks to the police, he is alive and the people know it was a swindle."

"Yes, that is so." Aiyyer sounded dubious. "But there will be another *sadhu* along next week or next month, and the villagers will believe him when he tells them he can perform miracles, and will make him coconut offerings and give him cash. We Indians are very credulous people." He shrugged his elegant shoulders. "Have you visited the Jodhpur Fort yet? It's well worth seeing. Let's go there."

We drove up the steep winding road to the fort on its spur of precipitious rock 400 feet above the town. There were seven enormous gates, with spike-studded doorways yawning open. Each was large enough to admit two elephants walking side by side. On the wall just inside the last gate were the prints of fifteen tiny palms. "These are the handprints of the widows of the maharajas," Aiyyer explained. "All of them committed suttee. Six were the widows of the Maharajah Man Singh, who signed a treaty with the British." He halted the car. "We shall have to walk from here, I'm afraid: cars are not permitted to go any farther."

It was a long, hot, steep walk over giant cobbles, but we saw no one until we came to the first great courtyard on top of the rock. Above us rose the round and square towers of the fort;

peering over the thick wall, we could see far below us the cramped yellow hieroglyphs of the town houses, lapped by the sunbaked plain. In the courtyard, seated on a stone step and paring his toenails, was a young man with thick black hair and a scowl. When he saw us he got to his feet and exclaimed in English: "Come and see how the exploiters lived! Palaces, jewel-rooms, jade, women! Abolished by the great Congress Party but kept for the proletariat to see monument of feudal past. The guided tour lasts approximately thirty minutes and the fee is only one rupee, unless you wish to pay more. You may walk on the battlements, if you wish, at no extra charge. Come!" He bounded up the stone steps and disappeared inside, though we could hear him still calling impatiently.

Aiyyer grinned and winked: we followed. Through vast rooms, brocaded and many-windowed; up great staircases and along corridors that seemed to stretch endlessly as in a dream; out in the open again, under the hot sun, stone courtyard within courtyard; sheer walls and dizzy balconies; more courtyards, and the windows of the secluded women's quarters, now empty. We paused to admire a vast green jade bowl of infinite coolness, inspected a roomful of miniatures, gaped at very bad full-length oil portraits of black-whiskered fierce-looking rajas clasping curved jeweled swords. The young man with the black hair and the scowl padded swiftly, predatorily ahead, talking angrily through it all, but as a guide he was poor, for he had but little historical information to impart. His subject was Marxist-Leninism.

We paused breathless in a glittering ballroom hung with crystal chandeliers and lined with stately high-backed chairs in blue velvet.

"Congress Party is Marxist but first task was overthrow of feudalism. Thus the revolution in India contains bourgeois elements. This is unavoidable. Lenin said—"

We panted down yet another corridor and were stunned by

85

the magnificence of a throne room, slashed with crimson, heavy
with gilt, with tiger skins spread casually on a polished dark
floor.

"Rich mill-owners and landlords supported Congress Party
not because they loved the masses but because they hoped for
own selfish purposes to oust British finance-capitalism. This
was capitalist contradiction we were entitled to exploit. In this
way even Indian capitalists helped to smash the yoke of imperialism. As Palme Dutt has written—"

Abruptly, unexpectedly, we were ushered into another world.
The rooms were modern, and ordinary. The furnishing was
heavy, unimaginative, outmoded, and rather shabby. There was
a great deal of it, but it might have been picked up in an auc-
tion sale. Here, evidently, in the very last days of their fading
glory the feudal Rajput rulers had tried to come to terms with
the twentieth century. One could imagine the last maharani,
no longer in danger of suttee, sitting on that overstuffed couch,
knitting, while the maharaja tried to get the B.B.C. on that for-
biddingly upright knob-studded radio. I felt they had sought,
not very successfully, to make themselves cosy; and the guide
evidently felt the same.

"Bourgeois," he said, with emphatic disgust.

At last, for a space, he left, allowing us to stroll alone on the
battlements, inspect the ancient gaping-mouthed cannon, and
peer over the topmost walls down on the town, which from
this great height looked smaller than ever.

"A very trying fellow," said Aiyyer, annoyed. "In feudal days
I think he would have been trampled to death by elephants."

"Or engraved," I said.

After a few minutes the guide came bouncing back. He jin-
gled keys, looked impatiently at his wristwatch which was fastened with a shiny metal bracelet, and hustled us back along
the corridors, through the courtyards, past the silent women's
quarters, down the final great staircase, back to where we had
come from. But he had one last thing to show us.

He heaved up a great stone slab with an iron ring attached to it, and led the way down steep, narrow stone steps into a tiny gloomy chamber, in which candles gleamed palely. They lit up a monstrous image, which at first sight looked like a decapitated man, for on the ground there rested a huge head. The head of stone was wearing a painted turban, with heavy painted eyes, a simpering painted smile, and with two great, black painted mustaches. We regarded this object in astonished silence, which the guide at length broke.

"This was prince's chapel," he said. "Prince worshipped dead ancestor." He pointed. "Prince daily offered the ancestor food and drink. If not forthcoming, then the prince's ancestor would go to Hindu hell, which we call *put*. The Sanskrit word for a son is *putra*, meaning one who frees the ancestor from *put*."

His tone was solemn. He regarded the stone head with reverential awe. I suddenly realized that he was speaking in utmost seriousness. The pseudoscientific claptrap about "feudalism" and "capitalism" had dropped from him like a cloak.

Slowly we climbed back into the hot sunlight out of the dark little chamber. The guide pocketed our rupees with alacrity, and vanished with his usual abruptness. Aiyyer was choking with laughter. "I told you we Indians are a credulous people," he said. "Even Marxist-Leninists!"

Husband wanted for beautiful graduate girl, 23, with fine arts and classical music qualifications. Domesticated. ADVERTISEMENT IN JODHPUR NEWSPAPER

NEAR JODHPUR dacoits captured a train. They robbed the passengers and crew and forced them into the jungle. Then they sent the train crashing into a station, killing the stationmaster and three porters. In Jodhpur itself, 10,000 beggars and prostitutes joined the disgruntled ex-landlords in a mass meeting and quoted copiously from the Constitution of India.

But all this was put in the shade by the high priest of the monkey-god temple, who after consulting the stars suddenly proclaimed an *Akha Teej*, or Auspicious Marriage Day. Families frantically busied themselves with matchmaking, and the newspapers were filled with advertisements of marriageable girls. Sisters were married off in batches at joint ceremonies. One bride was twelve and her groom was only eight. A two-week-old girl was joined in matrimony with a four-month-old boy, the two infants being carried seven times round the sacred fire by their respective mothers. A grown man turned up at his wedding with a nine-month-old girl in his arms. He explained she was an orphan whom he had adopted. Now he wished to marry her because this would be cheaper than providing her with a dowry when she grew up and married someone else.

The beggars, the prostitutes, and the dispossessed landlords continued stoning traffic and invading government offices: they developed a particular passion for smashing tabulating-machines, which were supposed to have something to do with the land question and the nonpayment of compensation. Daily, at its appointed hour, the flower-strewn chariot with the effigy of the *sati* was taken through the hot narrow streets. But fewer people came to watch it, or they only turned their heads casually to follow its progress. The marriage epidemic gripped public attention to the exclusion of everything else. Every street had its wedding procession, complete with brassy trumpets and prancing horses. The many houses where weddings were being celebrated blazed nightly with colored lights, outshining the marble tomb of the *sati*'s grandfather.

The rush of weddings produced some unfortunate incidents. A middle-aged bridegroom keeled over and died in the midst of his own wedding feast. The news was carefully kept from the guests who were separately attending the wedding feast of his fourteen-year-old bride, lest the food that had been so elaborately prepared should be wasted.

Aiyyer and I sat in the Jodhpur court all through one long hot day, watching perspiring lawyers leap up and down excitedly arguing the points of a complicated case. The complainant, shrilly voluble, was a trembling old man with a dirty gray beard. The defendants were his new, eighteen-year-old bride and her entire family. The old man, who was rich, had ardently sought a young bride, and finally one was produced. But after the wedding he discovered that she was of a different and lesser caste than his own, and, moreover, that her father was in jail. The indignant groom called the police, charging the bride and her family with fraud. The girl spiritedly claimed that in the new India caste discrimination had been legally abolished, and demanded her wifely rights. The old man's caste promptly disowned him, but that, though fearful enough, was not the end of his troubles. Emerging from jail where he had just finished his sentence, the bride's father brought a counter-charge against his new son-in-law: of kidnapping his daughter and marrying her without getting her father's consent. The affair looked as if it would keep the lawyers busy for a very long time.

The marriage fever was not confined to Jodhpur. Pleased to have a good excuse for driving his father's air-conditioned Chrysler—and for temporarily abandoning the fatiguing business of looking for a job—Aiyyer took me on long exploratory forays into the Rajasthan countryside. In a village near Jaipur we watched a young man who was securely tied to a bamboo pole spinning around 50 feet above the ground, like a human ceiling-fan. He was lowered to earth only after he had completed 21 giddy turns. The young man emerged grinning cheerfully from the ordeal. He was a Bhil, and he had passed successfully through the tribe's *manyata* ceremony in order to propitiate the gods and win a bride. No self-respecting Bhil girl will look twice at a suitor who has not performed *manyata*. The young man's place on the whirling pole was immediately taken by another, and more young Bhils were eagerly queuing up for their turn. A crowd of Bhils, men and women, sat at the foot of the bamboo platform that had been specially built for the occasion, watching the wildly gyrating figure on the rotating pole, clapping their hands, and singing loud cheerful songs. When the ceremony was over for the day, a man decapitated a tethered sheep with one stroke of a curved sword, and feasting began.

Rajasthan covers an area of over 132,000 square miles. A square-shaped state, cater-cornered between Bombay and West Pakistan, it is half as big as Texas. Much of it is desert, and the desert is eating eastward at the rate of a half a mile a year, spreading in a vast convex arc and bringing with it savage hot winds and blasting duststorms. There are also 13,000 square miles of scrub jungle and thorny forest. The old state of Jodhpur, now incorporated in Rajasthan, was called "The Land of Death." Rajasthan is full of thick-walled forts built on top of sheer rock cliffs, the eyries of the Rajputs.

Aiyyer and I explored the fort at Jaipur, then drove south to the even more awe-inspiring fort at Chitor, which crowns a cliff 500 feet high and 3 miles long.

Comfortably insulated from the roasting heat, our eyes protected from the glare by tinted glass, we rode over shocking roads through a strange world. It was as strange to Aiyyer as it was to me, this world of jungle, desert, and mud villages; for until he had talked his father into letting him take the trip, he had never set foot in a village at all. At first he was even more chary than I of eating village food, or drinking the scalding brown tea, thick with coarse sugar and mixed with oily buffalo milk, that the villagers brought us in great brass cups. Aiyyer had lived a sheltered life, for he had never left Jodhpur except to go to college in Bombay. "They are filthy places, those villages," he remarked with disdain. "Gandhi described them as manure heaps, and he was right."

"But, Aiyyer, 84 per cent of the people of India live in villages."

"That is why we are building Socialism, in order to rescue the people from the idiocy of village life."

From Chitor we drove northwest, for Aiyyer wanted to call on a raja's son who had been at college with him. "His name is Udai Jaswant," Aiyyer said, "and he flies his own plane." In all other ways a charming youth, Aiyyer was a bit of a snob.

The raja's palace was a small fort, crowning a hill and overlooking a gorge. The road to it was narrow, winding, and full of loose stones. But we passed a small field, where cattle browsed round an incongruous object colored bright red: a Piper Cub. Aiyyer pointed to it proudly. "There is my friend's plane." We drove through a large open gateway. In the burning stone courtyard a dirty old man was dispiritedly carrying slop pails. He gaped at the Chrysler, as if petrified, then ran indoors. Starting on a low trembling note, a gong began to boom inside the square stone building, which at close quarters looked extremely dilapidated. One expected men-at-arms to spring to attention. Instead, a plump young man wearing spectacles and what looked like a white nightshirt came out and blinked dubiously at us.

"Udai Jaswant!" yelled Aiyyer. They shook hands. I was introduced. Udai Jaswant shook hands with me, also. His handshake was flabby and perfunctory; he also looked somewhat annoyed. But he led us indoors.

Aiyyer chattered excitedly. We were on a short trip, and he had decided to give his friend a little surprise. Wasn't that Udai Jaswant's plane, in the little field: the Piper Cub? He still flew regularly? Aiyyer shot me a triumphant look. He had suspected me of disbelieving the part about the plane. Was Udai Jaswant's father, the raja, at home?

"No, he is away in Delhi, on business." Udai Jaswant spoke in English. His eyes, behind the spectacles, were evasive. "You will want to wash up. Then we shall have tea."

The place was full of echoing corridors and awkwardly built staircases. It was also dark and seemed dingy. Aiyyer's face be-

91

gan to fall. This was not what he had expected. On a corridor wall someone had scribbled with chalk in English: "Merry Xmas To All." The greeting seemed strangely out of place in the middle of August. The notes of the gong had long since died away, and the palace was shrouded in a brooding silence. We had seen no one since encountering the dirty old man with the slop pails. "This way," said our host, and opened the door of an enormous bedroom.

Quick as light, a girl rolled off the bed and flashed out through another door, too startled even to squeal. She was slim, brown-skinned, and wore no clothes whatever.

Udai Jaswant did not say anything. He merely paused momentarily, frowning, then marched into the bedroom. "I think you will find everything you need here. Unfortunately most of the servants are away at the moment, but, if you pull the bell-cord, the old man will come." His *savoir-faire* was remarkable. He regarded us with eyes that were no longer evasive, but were expressionless. I had the uncomfortable feeling all the same that he was in a towering rage. "Excuse me, I think I would like to change my clothes." He nodded coldly and left us.

Aiyyer was carefully not looking at me. I crossed to the window, and peered out. Below the old man was slowly tottering across the courtyard. I could see the gorge, and the Piper Cub in its field was a bright red toy. Beyond the gorge the wooded countryside flattened out into a dusty plain, shimmering in a heat haze. The silence became oppressive. Aiyyer began to whistle nervously. Then he stopped. In the next room people were whispering. They were girls' voices. One of them suddenly giggled.

"I think we'd better go down," I said.

Directed by the old man, who popped up in our path in one of the dark corridors, we found the raja's son in a large room which was clearly a library. From floor to high ceiling, the walls were lined with books, behind glass. They were uniformly bound in bright red leather, and on the spine of each the raja's crest was stamped in gold. It was an odd collection to find in so gloomy and tumbledown a building, but just how very odd it was I had still to discover.

Udai Jaswant had changed into a long buttoned *achkan* and tight white trousers. The buttoned-up coat made him look plumper than ever. He was about Aiyyer's age, or perhaps a couple of years older, but his manner was suave. Whatever had been troubling him he had evidently determined to put at the back of his mind.

"Ah, there you are!" He smiled jovially. "Tea will be along presently. You must tell me all about your interesting journey." He saw me looking at the books. "These are my father's collection. He is a great reader, and dotes on books. These he has been collecting for years, for they represent his special interest. I myself do not read very much, I'm afraid." His eyes gleamed behind his spectacles. "*I* like to have fun! Flying, for example. I like flying very much. And then there are other things. Really, one does not have time to pore over books as well!" He laughed good-naturedly. I thought of the girls upstairs. While his father was safely out of the way, the raja's son had clearly been having fun. He must have found our unexpected arrival exasperating.

One of the sliding glass doors that enclosed the bookshelves was open. I lifted out a book, idly and at random. Bound in red leather, stamped in gold, it was called *Death Strikes at Midnight*. The one next to it, by the same author, was called *Death for Company*. I roamed the shelves, and the raja's special interest became clear. The library contained nothing but mystery stories.

"You will notice that they are all first editions," said Udai Jaswant. "My father goes to a great deal of trouble to obtain only first editions. Then he has them specially bound."

The old man brought in tea. It was served in cups of thin china, but tasted little different from the tea we had been drinking in the villages. There were also sugar cakes, and biscuits imported from Britain. Aiyyer had found his tongue again, and was talking about Bombay. The raja's son let him do all the talking. I sipped my tea. Gradually Aiyyer ran out of reminiscences. The raja's son contributed none. When a pause ensued he raised a plump wrist and slowly, not casually, inspected his gold watch.

"I think we must be getting along," I said.

Aiyyer jumped to his feet. Udai Jaswant got up more leisurely. "I am sorry you could not stay longer," he said pleasantly. "But I suppose you have a long journey still ahead and are anxious to make a start."

Politely he accompanied us into the courtyard. It was still very hot. Above us the fortlike palace towered, square, rather shabby, and utterly silent. The old man was nowhere to be seen. I thought I glimpsed a girl's face peering down from a window.

"Perhaps we will meet in Jodhpur," Aiyyer said.

"Perhaps," the raja's son agreed. "Well, good-by." He turned, and entered the building without glancing back.

We drove down the winding road, past the field with the red Piper Cub and the cattle. Aiyyer drove more fiercely than usual. "I am sorry," he said. "He was not very polite, was he?"

"He was perfectly polite," I said. "In the circumstances. We ought to have let him know, somehow, that we were coming."

Aiyyer said he thought we could make a western detour on the way back to Jodhpur, that would take us a little way into the desert. It was I who insisted it should be only a little detour. Left to himself, Aiyyer would cheerfully have driven all the way to Jaisalmer. I did not want to ruin his father's Chrysler, or have it purloined by bandits. The dacoits were reported to be very strong in the desert fringes; one band was said to operate with an anti-tank gun.

We left the gorge country behind, and entered a vast, flat, desolate land. The road degenerated to a mere track. Great dustclouds were drawn across the sky like a gray curtain, and ahead of us there were wind-tossed sand dunes. We seemed to be the only living things in those wastes.

Then out of the dust there suddenly appeared a jeep, bump-

94

ing over the track toward us. The jeep advanced steadily, coming very fast in its own dustcloud. There were white men in it. They wore goggles and dark shirts, and they passed us without a second glance, sitting upright and looking stolid.

"Russians," said Aiyyer simply. "They are prospecting for oil in the desert, under an agreement with the Indian Government."

"There are Russian prospecting-teams operating between here and the Pakistan border," Aiyyer said. "Also, the Canadians frequently fly over the desert, hoping to locate oil from the air. And just across the border in Pakistan there are American prospectors who are also seeking oil." Rajasthan, it was plain, was being stirred out of its long feudal sleep.

Meanwhile there were still the dacoits. Late on the following afternoon we saw on the horizon, before the dust curtain dropped again to blot them from sight, a long string of camels. The men who rode them wore high striped turbans, and ready to each man's hand was a rifle stock, sticking up out of his saddle. The Indian Camel Corps has a formidable reputation. It fought in China in 1900 under the Maharaja of Bikaner. Three years later it was fighting in Somaliland. In the First World War it fought in Egypt and in the Second World War in Abyssinia.

"Nowadays they patrol the Pakistan-India border, and they also hunt the dacoits," said Aiyyer. "The Pakistanis, of course, welcome the dacoits and give them sanctuary." (I found that every Indian believed this; later, in Pakistan, I was assured that the dacoits raided across the border into Pakistan and were a great nuisance, but were difficult to catch because when pursued they simply crossed back into India, where they were sure of getting protection.) "If it were not for the Pakistanis, the Camel Corps would long since have exterminated dacoits."

We stopped for tea at a desert village called Rama. The week before the dacoits had paid it a visit, and Rama was still buzzing with excitement. For people who had been visited and presumably robbed by an armed dacoit band, the villagers seemed extraordinarily cheerful. A lean old man with a wrinkled leathery face described the incident with gusto.

"They came riding through the village gate on horseback, yelling their heads off and brandishing rifles. A fierce-looking lot of men. The first thing they did, they forced us poor people to point out for them the houses of the moneylender and the goldsmith." His sun-faded eyes twinkled; I had a feeling the villagers had perhaps not been unwilling. "Well, they caught them and trussed them up like chickens, saying they would carry them off into the desert, and hold them until their ransoms were paid. The moneylender wept, and said he had only one son, who lived in Bombay and was a bad lot: he would never pay a rupee's worth of ransom to save his poor old father. The dacoits laughed, and said that would be most unfortunate, they couldn't afford to feed prisoners for more than a couple of weeks." The old man grinned in a leathery way. "But the dacoits didn't ride off at once. They said they wanted to give a party. They had us prepare a feast—it was the goldsmith's food, and his daughter did most of the cooking—and then they sat around, eating and drinking, and playing accordions, and singing songs from Indian films." He smacked his lips reminiscently. "It was a fine feast, I never tasted such food. . . . Oh, yes, we were all invited. And then the dacoits gave what was left of the food to the poor people, and gave sugar cakes to the children, and handed out money to the untouchables. After that they went away, taking the moneylender and the goldsmith with them. The goldsmith's daughter had taken quite a fancy to the dacoit chief—he was a big, handsome man, with tremendous mustaches—and offered to go along with them: to look after her father, she *said*. But the dacoit leader said the desert was no place for a woman, and promised to send her father back, just as soon as the ransom money was delivered. He said to her: 'If you feel like delivering it yourself, of course, that's a different matter.' She collected the money from her father's family, and left yesterday after getting a message from the dacoits, telling her where to bring it. So I expect the goldsmith will soon be back; but I'll be surprised if we ever set eyes on *her* again."

"It's perfectly true," Aiyyer said, as we drove away from Rama village. "Women do sometimes fall in love with dacoits. I suppose it's their Rajput blood. In the old days Rajput princesses were always running off with their lovers. Anyway, many of the dacoits are descendants of Rajput nobles. They are very reckless and very brave—and also very ruthless, just like the old Rajput warriors."

"Don't they ever get caught?" I asked.

"Yes, but not very often. Take Kalwan Singh, for instance. When a police chief's daughter was married at Pali, Kalwan Singh's men came to the wedding disguised as cooks and serving-men. In that way they learned all about the plans the police were making for Kalwan Singh's capture. So Kalwan Singh had no difficulty wriggling out of the net the police had spread for him. Of course, when a dacoit gets caught, he's usually doomed—unless he has political protection. There was Suraj Bham. The police caught and hanged him. But he was so revered by the poor people that the police had to burn his body in secret, otherwise the villages would have built a shrine over Suraj Bham's remains."

"Do some dacoits have political protectors?"

Aiyyer laughed. "If the dacoits happen to be supporters of the Congress Party. There is a well-known dacoit called Bhanwar Singh. In 1952 he surrendered himself to the police. He said he had seen the error of his ways, and wanted to help build the New India. He received a pardon, and helped the Congress Party win an election at Jalore. That was easy, for the village people loved him; he was so generous to the poor. But after that he quarreled with an important Congress Party man, a member of the State Parliament, and unfortunately killed him. So he had to go back to being a dacoit again, at any rate, until the affair blew over."

97

"But I thought the Congress Party wanted to wipe out the dacoits?"

"Ah, yes, of course," said Aiyyer patiently; "if they are really and truly *dacoits*. But, you see, most of the dacoits are actually just Rajputs."

I said I didn't see.

"Well, there is very bad feeling here in Rajasthan between the Rajputs and the Jats."

I thought I saw a gleam of light.

"The Rajputs support the Congress Party, and the Jats perhaps are opposed to the Congress Party?"

"Oh, no: they *both* support the Congress Party. But for many years the Rajputs lorded it over the Jats. The Jats were not allowed to wear jewelry, or even to ride horses: the Rajputs treated them like a lower caste. So, of course, when India got independence and elections were held, the Rajputs and the Jats fought each other *within* the Congress Party. At first the Rajputs controlled the party in Rajasthan. But now the Jats control the party. They are kicking the Rajputs around. When the big estates were broken up, the land set aside for distribution to the poor—half a million acres—was taken from Rajputs, and given to Jats. That is why some Rajputs became dacoits. Naturally those Rajput dacoits, who as you see are not really and truly dacoits, get much sympathy and help from the Rajput members of the Rajasthan Congress Party, who dislike the present Rajasthan Congress Party Government, which is controlled by Jat elements."

"Yes," I said, my head whirling. "I believe I see now." But I didn't. Aiyyer clearly perceived this, though he was too polite to say so. Instead, he tactfully suggested that when we got back to Jodhpur, I should have a talk with his father, who was, of course, a leading member of the Congress Party, and therefore very knowledgeable on the subject of Rajasthan politics.

In Jodhpur the marriage fever had subsided and politics were again in the forefront of public attention. The beggars and prostitutes had all been arrested, and the ex-landlords had formed a *Bhooswami Sangh*, or Landlords' League, and were trying to have the Home Minister impeached for unparalleled brutality, including the murder of the founder of the *Bhooswami Sangh*, who had been killed by a bus.

Aiyyer renewed his invitation to me to meet his father. He warned me, however, that his father was a devout follower of Gandhi, and therefore lived in extremely simple style.

We drove to the house in the Chrysler. The house was a simple, flat-roofed, two-story affair, set down in three acres of lawns and gardens. Several *malis*, men of the gardener caste, were diligently watering the lawns and pruning the rosebushes. A savage-looking goat was tethered at the side of the house, near the double garage: Aiyyer explained that its function was to supply milk for his father's frugal needs. A number of expensive-looking automobiles were parked in the driveway, with liveried chauffeurs slumped asleep in the driver's seats. In the drawing-room Aiyyer's father sat amid his guests on a long red leather couch. The guests were all men, impressively handsome Indians in well-fitting dinner jackets. They were talking loudly in English. Soft-footed servants glided about the large room, offering cigarettes from silver boxes and tall iced drinks on silver trays.

Aiyyer's father, the owner of cement factories, was a very tall man with a patrician nose and dark flashing eyes. He towered over me, shaking my hand in a strong grip.

"But I mean," one of the men said heatedly, "it is very undemocratic to push people under buses."

"There is no proof of that," said another, shaking his head. "It is only a bazaar rumor."

"So now you are taking the side of the police," said the first man, enraged. "I tell you that Kujal, our *Bhooswami* leader, was standing quite aloof. The police commandeered a bus and crushed him under its wheels."

"It is true!" declared a third man. "They are seizing *bhoo-*

swamis and pushing them under buses in batches. They arrest them and beat them, naked, until they bleed. They take them into the jungles and leave them there to starve to death or be eaten by wild animals."

"I think you are being unnecessarily fretful," said the man who was defending the police. "Besides, it is well known that some of the *bhooswamis* are working hand in hand with the dacoits. That is shameful."

"Who said the *bhooswamis* have anything to do with the dacoits?"

"Everyone knows it. The dacoits hand over part of the ransom money to the *Bhooswami Sangh*. Also, they have pledged at the next election to force the villagers to vote only for *Bhooswami Sangh* Congress Party candidates."

"All the dacoits are not evil men," someone declared. "Some of them were very respectable before they had their land taken and were compelled to become outlaws."

"It is all the fault of the Jats," someone else said.

"I do not defend the Jats," said the man who had defended the police. "I am a Rajput."

"But the Congress Party in Rajasthan contains Rajputs as well as Jats. It is time the Jats understood this."

"There is too much intrigue in the Congress Party," one man said gloomily. "Yesterday's enemies are today's bedfellows, and today's bedfellows will fly at one another's throat tomorrow."

A girl in a crimson sari came smiling into the room. The men's eyes sparkled appreciatively. Those who had mustaches twirled them. I did not blame them. She was an extremely pretty girl, with glossy dark hair and sparkling teeth. I was not surprised when Aiyyer introduced her as his sister. They might have been twins.

Smiling prettily, she offered me a green sweetmeat from a silver dish. "Please try it," she begged. "I myself made it." I nibbled a piece, and said it was extremely good. She sighed. "Oh, I am so pleased! It took me a long time to make. It contains sixteen separate ingredients. One of them is goat's brain. That is very hard to get." I declined a second helping. "But it is very good for the virility," one of the men whispered in my ear. He took three pieces.

Aiyyer's father listened indulgently as the political discussion continued. He was the oldest, and also the handsomest, man present. He radiated personal magnetism and intellectual force. His brow was calm and unruffled. He had a quiet, confident smile, and gave the impression that he could, if he chose, supply the complete and definitive answer to any problem, including the problem of landlordism in Rajasthan. But he never opened his mouth. My admiration for him grew. He plainly found the discussion jejune. These absurd accusations and counter-accusations, his manner quietly suggested, were tiresomely immature. These were the sort of wild charges the Indians had hurtled against the British, and were now busily hurtling against one another. The new India could do better than that. I looked forward eagerly to hearing him expound his own views. I was sure he would do so when he judged the time ripe.

When at length the disputants fell silent, he leaned forward and said with simple authority: "You are all wrong. You are approaching the matter in too petty a spirit. You should reflect more, as I have done, on the teachings of the Father of the Nation. What India and the world need is a new philosophy. We must try to give an activist interpretation to the *Vedanta* of Sankura. Man is a being with two directions, the spiritual and the material. We must reaffirm the individuality of man without denying the reality of God."

In India political discussion is apt to take some surprising turns.

Before leaving Jodhpur, I wanted to say good-by to the police superintendent, but he had been summoned to Bali, a district where the Shakta sect flourished. A young Shakta called

Odia Patel had walked into the police station at Bali wearing a loincloth and carrying a blood-stained knife and his wife's nose, which he had just cut off.

Shakta is one of the many names for the wife of Shiva. Those who worship her under that name hold that the five best things in life are sex, liquor, meat, fish, and grain. The highlight of their worship is a communal sex orgy called *kanchalia dharam*, or the ceremony of the blouse. After feasting and drinking, the women take off their *kanchalias*, or blouses, and place them in a large earthen jar. The men then fish them out, and each man is entitled to spend the night with the woman whose blouse he holds—even if, as usually happens, she is someone else's wife.

Bali was a Shakta area, but Odia Patel had recently married a girl called Naji, who was not a Shakta and who knew little about their peculiar customs. On the night of the *kanchalia dharam*, he told her to put on her wedding costume—a black *kanchalia*, with a billowing scarlet skirt, a scarlet headdress, and bangles, toe-rings and nose-ring of heavy silver. She obeyed unquestioningly, and her husband then placed a silver *lingam*, or phallic charm, on her forehead, and led her to where 84 other Shaktas and their wives were gathered, with a guru in attendance.

Naji was ordered to put her blouse in the jar along with the others but when she discovered the significance of the ceremony she fled. Angered by this affront to his religion, Odia Patel followed her home and there cut off her nose. When he turned up at the police station with the nose, the knife, and this tale, the police went with him to his hut; there they found Naji, still wearing her wedding finery, noseless and hanging from a beam, quite dead. Thus she had been faithful after her fashion.

So I left Jodhpur without seeing the superintendent, and drove east to Bharatpur, on the way to Agra. Bharatpur was in a state of tumult. Several pandits and two Brahmin priests from Benares were investigating a miracle.

The local temple contained an idol of the Lord Krishna, and the temple priest was in the habit of walking reverently round it waving a piece of lighted camphor in the presence of worshippers. This was supposed to lull Krishna to rest, so that, when the temple was closed for the night, he would sleep peacefully. One morning the priest opened up the temple, and Krishna instead of being upright was lying down, with his head on a silk pillow.

Five pandits were immediately summoned, and they recommended that the idol be restored to its original position, amid chanting of *mantras*, to be followed by twenty-four hours of prayer. It took four men to raise the idol, which was extremely heavy. Meanwhile thousands of people streamed toward Bharatpur from outlying districts to visit the temple and witness the scene of such miraculous happenings. Unfortunately there were skeptics who claimed the idol had merely fallen down—in spite of the presence of the pillow, which believers accepted as conclusive proof that a miracle had indeed occurred. Unabashed, the skeptics demanded that the idol be removed and that a new and less unstable one take its place. There were lively arguments, and a number of heads were broken. More pandits were called in. They in turn appealed to the Rajasthan State Government, which sent for the two important priests from Benares. Soon three committees of pandits and priests were sitting in acrimonious session at the temple—unable to agree on their verdict.

When I passed through Bharatpur, the temple was still closed, and the pandits and priests were still deliberating. Up to that point the controversy had cost Bharatpur and the Rajasthan Government some 20,000 rupees in fees paid to the three religious committees.

IV

AGRA: WOMEN AND TIGERS

"This is a national monument and under the care of the Government of India. No tipping. SIGN AT THE TAJ MAHAL

ALL ALONG the road the trees were wrapped in an early morning mist, grape-blue, under a flat bright sky. Then the mist evaporated in the furnace breath of a new day. The heat grew steadily, hour after hour, and the road, yellow with ancient dust, passed through villages that looked as if they had not known rain for centuries. Toward evening the sky turned yellow and then molten gold. Finally, when I reached Fatehpur Sikri, the deserted city's huge red temples, mosques, and tombs were ablaze under a fiery setting sun.

At Fatehpur Sikri I met a man called Ferguson. The guides were all asleep, or had gone home. We wandered unattended through echoing acres of red sandstone and across vast empty courtyards, and climbed five massive stone staircases to the top of the Panch Mahal. Ferguson remarked that it was a good place to watch the sun go down and think about India's history.

Ferguson was a large gray-faced man. Despite the manifest absence of rain, he carried a dark blue raincoat over his arm. He was hatless, and wore a rather shabby brown suit and brown shoes. He had European features but an Indian's brown eyes, and I guessed, correctly as it turned out, that he was an Anglo-Indian.

Akbar, the Mogul Emperor, built the city of Fatehpur Sikri to commemorate his conquest of Gujarat in 1572. The Emperor's stables held 12,000 horses and camels. Water for the city's immense baths was raised by giant Persian wheels, turned by elephants. Nevertheless, the water supply unaccountably failed, and, within ten years of its completion, Fatehpur Sikri was abandoned.

From the flat roof of the Panch Mahal, reared on 176 stone pillars, we could see Akbar's Hall of Audience, the Diwan-i-Am, 365 feet long, and the fantastic tapering tower, 70 feet high, its sides bristling with elephant tusks carved in red sandstone, from which the court ladies used to watch the games and tournaments.

"Akbar was a great man," Ferguson said. "In Europe, in his day, the Catholics and Protestants were slaughtering one another. Akbar was a Moslem; but he invited Jesuits to his court, befriended the Jains, and listened attentively to Hindu priests."

"Did all those people listen to Akbar?" I inquired.

Ferguson laughed. "No, when he forbade the killing of cows in order to please the Hindus, the Moslems were enraged. And when he proposed to build a 'temple of all religions,' the Jesuits were furious with him. They wanted him to turn Christian, and then to brand all other faiths as damnable heresies, punishable by beheading, disemboweling, and burning at the stake."

The walls of the deserted palaces were casting long shadows, and nothing stirred below us, in all that wilderness of stone. We were the day's last, belated visitors. The sun was setting very fast, and soon Fatehpur Sikri would be given over to darkness, and the bats. We climbed down hurriedly from the roof of the Panch Mahal, and passed through the Buland Darwaza: 176 feet high, and the tallest gateway in India.

On its archways there are two inscriptions, one of which runs: "The King of Kings, Shadow of God, Jalal-ud-din

Muhammad Akbar, the Emperor, on his return from conquering the kingdoms of the South and of Khandash, came to Fatehpur in the forty-sixth year of his reign, and proceeded from thence to Agra."

Ferguson read it aloud, and added: "Akbar tried to put an end to wars, and to unite India by marrying Hindu and Moslem wives. But when he failed to persuade men to follow the paths of reason and religious toleration, he returned to wars of conquest."

The other inscription on the great gateway reads: "Jesus, on whom be peace, says: 'The world is a bridge: pass over it, but build no house on it.' The world endures but an hour: spend it in devotion."

Ferguson explained: "That was written, to Akbar's order, in 1601. Four years later Akbar was dead. Every man has two sides. Akbar never resolved the contradiction that those two inscriptions pose; and neither has anyone else."

We left the empty city together, and drove the 20 lonely miles to Akbar's tomb outside Agra. Here, despite the thickening twilight, there was more bustle. Outside the main gate, elaborate with mosaic, thin energetic touts were selling peanuts and colored picture-postcards to tourists. The tourists fed the peanuts to large gray monkeys that swarmed in the trees around the Emperor's mausoleum.

Amid marble minarets and cloisters a corridor, 60 feet long, slopes down to an underground chamber, where Akbar was laid to rest. On the marble walls of the underground chamber are inscribed the 99 names of Allah.

"There are four outstanding dates in Indian history," Ferguson said. "Akbar ascended the Mogul throne in 1556, when he was only fourteen. The sun set on the Mogul Empire in 1757, the year of the British victory at Plassey. The British Empire in India received its death-stroke in 1857, the year of the Mutiny, though the British didn't realize it at the time. The fourth date is 1947, when India became a Republic, 391 years after Akbar was acclaimed Emperor." He smiled, somewhat bitterly, I thought. "It'll be interesting to see if Nehru succeeds where the Moguls and the British failed."

Presently we left the ornate tomb to the hucksters and the tourists, and drove, through narrow streets and past crumbling yellow walls covered with Hindi scrawls, to a hotel for dinner.

In the ceiling a fan whirred listlessly, fighting a sad, hopeless battle with the heat, which the coming of night had not diminished. A waiter brought us thick, greasy soup, followed by fish fried in dubious butter, followed by highly spiced roast chicken. "A ghastly meal," said Ferguson gloomily as we stirred our cups of muddy brown coffee. "Let's have some brandy."

After dinner we went into the hotel's large bare lounge. Ferguson ordered another brandy. An Indian conjuror was amusing the hotel guests. He was a small, smiling, deft man who made coins vanish and reappear, separated steel hoops that appeared to be indissolubly interlinked, and turned knotted black shoelaces into a string of brightly colored flags. The brandies had cheered Ferguson up. "Clever devils, some of those Indians," he remarked, and lit a seedy-looking cigar.

I suggested we drive to the Taj Mahal to see it by moonlight. Ferguson agreed, but insisted on struggling into his dark blue raincoat, though he still wore no hat. On the way we passed a furiously driven horse-drawn tonga. The driver lashed his horse; the little carriage bounced perilously up and down. Under the canopy the solitary passenger clung on with one hand and with the other clutched at his khaki-colored sun helmet. He was a frightened-looking man who despite the sweltering heat wore a thin topcoat and a gray muffler as well. Ferguson, whose good humor the brandies had not only restored but had broadened into exuberance, chuckled loudly. "He's a Eurasian," he said. "Funny chaps. They always wear those sun helmets, and wrap themselves up well. God knows why."

The moon had risen in a dark and starless sky. Suddenly,

just before the moon vanished again behind trees, we glimpsed a second moon. White and softly round, seeming to float in the breathless air, it was the marble dome of the Taj Mahal.

We passed on foot through the massive red sandstone gateway, topped by 12 cupolas, into the garden of the Taj. Directly before us at the end of an avenue of cypresses the marble tomb, silvered by moonlight, was reflected in still water.

Mumtaz Mahal, the second wife of Shah Jehan, died in 1631. They had been married 18 years, and she died giving birth to their 14th child, a daughter. The Taj is her monument. Twenty thousand men took 22 years to build it. It is probably the most beautiful building on earth.

The Hindus' attitude to women was harsh. Manu, the great Hindu lawgiver, taught: "The source of dishonor is woman: the source of strife is woman." He adds: "A faithful wife must serve her lord as if he were a god, even though he be devoid of every virtue." Manu declared that disobedient wives would be reborn as jackals. Not surprisingly, perhaps, the wives seem to have been frequently unfaithful. A Hindu poet writes bitterly: "Women are as constant as the waves of the ocean; their affection is as fugitive as a streak of sunset glow upon a cloud." And another Hindu poet says women have the curves of creepers, the bloom of flowers, the sweetness of honey, the gaiety of sunbeams, the glances of deer—but also the fickleness of the wind, the vanity of the peacock, the cruelty of the tiger, and the coldness of snow. The Moslems seem to have shared those opinions, for they kept their women closely veiled and confined and were obsessively jealous. To those harsh attitudes, the mutual devotion of Shah Jehan and Mumtaz Mahal constitutes a refreshing and touching exception.

In the garden of the Taj, meanwhile, on this moonlit night, people strolled quietly up and down, or sat on marble benches. I had never seen an Indian crowd behave so quietly. Hardly anyone spoke, and those who did so seemed to whisper. The heat that had endured all day was no less oppressive now; we might have been standing in a Turkish bath. You could smell the grass, and the people, and the clothes they wore, for in this sultriness everything and everyone gave off an odor, as in a hothouse. But no one minded the heat here. The vision of almost unearthly loveliness which had drawn us all to this spot created its own climate, like an oasis of white coolness in an arid desert. To look at it was to feel the touch of snowflakes; in the presence of this marble coolness all fevers subsided. We stood where we were, a little inside the gateway, just looking, for what seemed a long time. Ferguson had fallen silent, and in silence he took off his dark raincoat and hung it slowly over his arm. In the moonlight his face looked grayer, like a sick man's.

Then suddenly a soft-footed man appearing seemingly from nowhere was tugging impatiently at my sleeve and whispering too fast in my ear.

"Very best time to see the Taj, by moonlight. You are very lucky! My name is Bharaj. I can show you everything, explain everything. You are lucky, for I was just going off duty, but for you I will wait. One hour, two hours, as you please."

"We don't want a guide," I said. "We only want to look."

"Official guide appointed by Government," said our tormentor relentlessly. He was painfully thin, with a pocked face and mean eyes. "I can show you everything. Other guides are not as good. Ask anyone. This year I act as guide to American millionaires, the Sultan of Zanzibar, the Austrian Ambassador, the French Ambassador, the American Ambassador, the Crown Prince of Cambodia, and Marshal Tito. All very pleased, very impressed. The name is Bharaj. I am the official guide appointed by the Government of India. The other guides will rob you, cheat you. I charge only fifteen rupees—no: for you, only ten." His voice became anxious, changed gear, and went into a practiced whine. "I am very poor. I have a wife and seven children. My wife is sick. The children have no shoes. They are hungry. Times are very hard. I am a college graduate.

I took high place in history at Calcutta. I know all the dates: when the Taj was built, dates of Shah Jehan, dates of the mosque, date of—"

Ferguson was swearing under his breath. "Indians!" he said bitterly. "Bloody Indians!"

"I'll give you five rupees just for going away," I told the official guide appointed by the Government of India. "We don't want a guide and we don't want to be told about dates. We just want to be left alone."

I was dumfounded when, without an instant's hesitation, he nodded and shot out his palm. "All right: five rupees and I go away."

I gave him five rupees. He salaamed deeply. "A thousand thanks, sahib. My wife will bless you. My children will bless you. I am not offended. I see you do not want a guide, not even the best. You only want to look at the Taj, by yourselves. There are other guides here, but they will not trouble you. I will see to it. The name is Bharaj. I am the official guide appointed by government. They do what I tell them. You will see. Good night, sahib."

He vanished swiftly into the warm darkness, but as he turned away, it seemed to me he was smiling spitefully.

"You shouldn't have done that," said Ferguson severely. His name was not as inappropriate as I had at first thought: somewhere in Ferguson, there really was some Scottish blood. "Waste of money."

"I'd have paid double to get rid of him," I said.

Ferguson muttered something about a boot up the backside being a better way. "Anyway," he added, "I'll bet he'll be up to some trick."

Ferguson would have won his bet.

We strolled toward the beckoning miracle of the Taj and had got halfway, as far as the marble pool where the fountains plashed, when a second soft-footed man darted from behind a cypress and started to tug insistently at my sleeve.

I raised my voice. "We don't want a guide: understand?
No guide! Please go away!"

"Sahib, you need someone who knows the Taj to show you
all its wonders. I know every stone. Only this year I acted as
guide to the American Ambassador and to Tito of Yugoslavia.
They were full of praise of my work: I can show you their
fine testimonials. Let me conduct you and your friend to the
mausoleum, the minarets, the sepulchers—"

I shouted. "Go away, d'you hear?"

He stood his ground: a thin man, even thinner than the first,
with a sly face and a relentless voice.

"I am the brother of Bharaj," he said simply. "You gave him
five rupees, to go away. When you give me five rupees, I will
go away also."

We passed into the interior of the Taj. Eight marble walls
surrounded us. The floor and ceiling were also of purest marble.
We stood in the heart of loveliness, bathed in purity. Across
the marble floor quickly shuffled an old man with a dirty
beard, clutching a lantern. His voice was rusty but his English
well rehearsed.

"I am the guardian of the tomb. The walls you see before
you were inlaid with the following precious stones: emeralds,
sapphires, onyx, and jasper. Some have now gone from the
settings, especially the emeralds. This way to the twin sepulchers."

Flourishing his lantern, he led the way to a tall marble
screen, lacy with the most delicate floral designs. "The screen
you now see is eight-sided. It is six feet two inches high. It
guards the sepulchers of Mumtaz Mahal and Shah Jehan."

He led us behind the screen. "Here you see the two graves,
executed throughout in marble. This is Shah Jehan's, that is
the grave of Mumtaz Mahal. The inscription on the tomb of
Shah Jehan reads as follows: 'The illustrious sepulcher of
His Most Exalted Majesty dignified as the guardian of Paradise
having his abode in Paradise and his dwelling in the starry

heaven inhabitant of the region of bliss the second lord of the
Kiran Shah Jehan the King Valiant he traveled from this
transitory world to the world of eternity on the night of the
28th of the month of Rajab 1076 A.H.' " He paused, breathing
hard. "We now have a little ceremony."

As if by magic, another old man, identical with the first, appeared before us. Quickly, before we could prevent him, he
smeared a vermilion paste mixed with yellow rice first on my
forehead, then on Ferguson's, muttering something in Hindi
as he did so. The two graybeards stepped back and regarded us
vulturously. "That will be five rupees," said the first graybeard.
I handed over five rupees: too eagerly. "And another five for
the other guardian of the tomb," he said quickly. I parted with
five more rupees, and we fled from the Taj Mahal.

Behind us, as we passed out through the great sandstone
gateway, the gardens were bathed in moonlight. The water
had a pearly gleam. The crowds moved slowly and solemnly,
unmolested, protected from rapacity by their darker skins: no
Indian regards another Indian as a tourist, even when he all
too obviously is one. In the midst of the gardens the Taj
gleamed whitely, softly, a giant flawless pearl floating in the
warm darkness of the night.

As we got into the car to drive back to the hotel, Ferguson
said morosely: "These fellows would never have dared do that,
under the Raj. But India is no place for a white man any
more."

The velvet tigers in the jungle.   W. J. TURNER

THE HOTEL bedrooms were built round an inner courtyard.
Attached to each bedroom was a small, austere chamber, with
a sloping stone floor, containing a tin basin on an iron stand,

and a wooden commode with a hinged lid. I splashed tepid water into the crumpled tin basin, and shaved without a mirror. When I had finished, I unlatched the door to the courtyard, leaving it meaningfully ajar. In the courtyard the hotel's untouchables patiently squatted, waiting to empty the slop pails and remove the chamber pots from the commodes.

A party of American tourists had arrived from Delhi in tourist limousines to visit the Taj Mahal. They wore gaily patterned shirts, smoked cigars, and were festooned with 35-millimeter cameras. They chattered happily, for they had not yet investigated the plumbing. That would come after a few more cups of the muddy brown coffee they were so lightheartedly drinking. Later, purged by terror and self-pity, they would fall an easy prey to Bharaj and his fellow pirates.

Ferguson and I breakfasted lightly off omelets stuffed with peppers and weak tea. Ferguson wanted to go to Gwalior; I was bound for Bhind. But it would be simple enough for me to make a slight detour, and besides I had no objection to visiting Gwalior. I offered to drive him there, and he readily accepted.

Our bags were put in the car. Waiters, room-boys, sweepers, *chowkidars*, and untouchables lined up expectantly. We tipped them annas, and drove off. Some of the American tourists were already wandering about the inner courtyard, looking puzzled and harassed.

Ferguson, fortified by a couple of after-breakfast brandies, was in a good humor. He lit a cigar, and talked exuberantly about the cotton trade, of which he appeared to know a good deal. "I managed a textile mill at Kanpur, once," he explained. "It was owned by a Hindu who gave money to Gandhi and who used to make speeches about Robert Owen. The mill made 300 per cent profit every year and the workers were treated worse than pigs."

Seen in the full light of day, Ferguson appeared to be in his late forties or early fifties, large and gray and beginning to get fat; in his faded dark blue raincoat—which he persisted in wearing in spite of the torrid heat—he looked like a seedy bagman.

"My father was I.C.S., but before him our background is purely Indian Army. My grandfather fought in the Mutiny— he was a British colonel—and I believe there was a Ferguson at Plassey. As an Indian Civil Service wallah, my father was pretty close to the Viceroy, but they couldn't see eye to eye over the Indian National Congress. My father helped to start it, along with Alan Hume, another I.C.S. man and a Scotsman. The Viceroy—it was the Marquess of Dufferin—didn't approve. Personally I think the Viceroy was right and my father was wrong. He didn't get any thanks for it from the Indians. They're an ungrateful lot of beggars." Ferguson shook his head. "There's no future now in this country for anyone who isn't a Hindu."

We had left the dusty and arid countryside around Agra behind us. The road ran through green country, bright with peacocks.

The term "Anglo-Indian" originally meant an Englishman who lived in India. Later it came to mean a person of mixed English and Indian descent, and in 1911 the Government of India officially designated Eurasians as "Anglo-Indians." I had no doubt at all, and shortly was to have complete confirmation, of which kind of Anglo-Indian Ferguson was. But I held my tongue and, though neither of us was deceived, Ferguson's self-esteem was precariously preserved. He freely admitted having had his ups and downs. "Being born and brought up in India is no joke, if you're not an Indian. They'd like us all to go, you know. But there isn't anywhere else for a chap like me to go *to*." He gave me a sidelong glance. "After all, India is my country. I'd be lost back Home. The trouble is the Hindus have always got dozens of brothers and cousins and nephews wanting jobs. If you're not an Indian you find you've been squeezed out.

"As a matter of fact," Ferguson went on, in a sudden burst

of confidence, "that's why I'm going to Gwalior, to try to find
something to do. There's a chap I used to know in Kanpur
who has a business here. I wrote him and he didn't answer,
but probably he was away, or the letter went astray. He's an
Indian, of course, but rather decent."

Presently Gwalior appeared, a huddle of wretched-looking
houses, dominated by a huge and ancient fort on a rocky hill.
Ferguson pointed out a monstrously large white building,
shaped like a wedding-cake, behind high walls. "That's the
palace of the Maharaja. He's a great shooter of tigers, and he
likes to give banquets. He has a toy electric train made of solid
silver which runs round the banquet table."

Ferguson asked me to drop him off at a local hotel, which
almost rivaled the Maharaja's palace in size, but looked considerably more dingy. Above us, on its sandstone hill, towered
the fort. In front of the hotel was a small park, its rusty gates
securely padlocked. Around us lay the wretched tumble-down
houses, their yards crammed with all manner of junk and their
narrow lanes jungle trails of filth. Ferguson shrugged when I
remarked on it. "It's just the usual filth and spit of India," he
said. "What else d'you expect?" He was right, of course; all the
same, I could not help thinking of the Maharaja's banquets,
and his solid-silver toy train.

I left Ferguson to his business, promised to call on him later in the day to see how he had got on, and drove in the
direction of Jhansi, to have a look at the countryside. I had not
driven very far when I came on a group of women down on
their hands and knees in the middle of the road. They were
sweeping its dusty surface with small brooms, and clearing it of
loose stones. The stones were being collected in wicker baskets,
and when the baskets were full they were taken up and their
contents dumped in the roadside ditches. The women made
way for me, and bowed low as I passed. I drove on, puzzled,
for the roads of India do not usually get this careful treatment,
and presently came on another group of women doing exactly

the same. In a distance of two miles I passed several road-sweeping gangs—all were women—and my bewilderment grew. Then from behind me, from the direction of the Maharaja's white palace, came a melodious hooting, and presently a cavalcade of automobiles swept grandly past me. At the head was an open car, done in powder-blue, containing men in green shooting-jackets and green hunting-hats. The second car was similarly filled with hunters. The third car contained policemen. There were four more cars, which were crammed with retainers of some kind.

The cavalcade hooted past me; but it did not get very far. Round the next bend in the road I found it stationary and in a state of disarray. The leading car, the open powder-blue one, had skidded abruptly to a halt, and the others had jammed on their brakes behind it. Some faced across the road, and some had skidded round to face the way they had come. The occupants of the cars, including the men in green coats, were standing in the roadway, looking dismayed. In spite of the roadwork of the women sweepers, the leading car had picked up a sharp stone and got a flat. Along the road, coming from the opposite direction, lumbered a number of high-piled haycarts. They were summarily halted, and soon peasants had been inspanned to change the car's wheel, while other peasants from the carts stood around, gaping. It was very hot, and dust swirled thickly about the stranded cavalcade. Bits of straw floated about. The policemen, fierce-looking, dark little men, shouted orders; the peasants worked on the stranded car, or stood shuffling their bare feet; the green-coated hunters sneezed. I maneuvered my way past the scene, and drove on.

After about a half an hour there was a melodious but impatient tooting from the rear, and the cavalcade once again swept past me.

I drove for some more miles, through a countryside that grew progressively less inhabited and more jungly, and was thinking of turning back to Gwalior, for tea, when I came on the cars,

this time neatly parked in a side road. The hunters had left
their automobiles and, armed with rifles, had clambered on to
the backs of two enormous elephants with long white tusks.
The elephants were moving slowly and grandly into the jungle.

The opportunity seemed too good to miss. I swung my car
into the side road, parked it alongside the others, and got out.
Two men, who had not mounted the elephants but were
carrying rifles, were going along behind on foot. Luckily I had
my binoculars and camera in the car, and I hurriedly slung
them on.

The policemen stood in a semicircle round the parked cars.
When one of them moved inquiringly toward me, I smiled,
pointed to my binoculars and camera in a businesslike way,
pointed toward the retreating elephants and the two riflemen
following on foot, and started briskly after them. The policeman nodded and fell back, saluting. A little self-assuredness
and, above all, a white face are still the best passports in India.

The elephants vanished into a ravine, and the two men
carrying rifles followed. The road dwindled to a mere track
through long grass, and presently, after a perspiring half-hour
walk, I came suddenly on a large white noticeboard, which
said: "On this spot, on November 10, 1932, Lady Butterfield
shot a tiger which measured seven feet three inches." I con-
templated it with some misgiving. If there had been seven-foot
tigers about in 1932, it was reasonably certain that there were
still some about now. Lady Butterfield had presumably been
armed—though for some reason I vaguely imagined her as
carrying nothing more lethal than a parasol—and I was not.
Then, as I hesitated, I was much comforted by the appearance
of a small ragged boy carrying a wooden box on his head and
marching along stoutly about two hundred yards ahead. I resumed my forward progress.

The small boy, it soon turned out, was only the first of a
long file. All of them were ragged, and all of them carried
wooden boxes on their heads. The boxes appeared to be heavy.

There were fully a hundred boys. Their average age was about twelve, and they were walking barefooted round the lip of the same ravine into which the elephants and the hunters had plunged and which now took the shape of an ellipse. I peered down into the ravine. The elephants were just visible, standing up to their bellies in long grass. Near by, on a concrete ramp higher than the elephants, stood the hunters. Their rifles were held loosely under their arms, but they had an expectant air.

From the wooden boxes the small boys took objects that looked like hand grenades. These they cast into the ravine, in the area of the thick jungle between the platform and the ravine's steep western slope—where the tigers had been spotted —and they went off with loud and terrifying explosions. They were made of clay and were filled with gunpowder. Still throwing the missiles, the boys marched round and round the edge of the ravine, yelling fiendishly, balancing the boxes on their heads, and beating wooden sticks against large pieces of tin. The shrill ululations of a hundred pairs of young lungs combined with the noise of sticks banging on tin and the continuous sharp explosions to produce a hellish cacophony that must have been heard back in Gwalior.

Presently, in the long grass of the ravine, there appeared two frightened-looking tigers. The boys saw them, and increased their shouting: clay grenades were showered on the tigers' hindquarters from all sides. In order to escape the grenades, the cowed beasts were compelled to advance. In this fashion they were driven toward the concrete ramp and, when they had approached close enough to constitute targets that it would have been very difficult for even a bad marksman to miss, the rifles banged briskly, the tigers leaped convulsively, another fusillade followed, and all was over. On the concrete ramp the hunters began to shake hands with one another, and the elephants, prodded by mahouts, lumbered forward to collect the carcases. I put away my binoculars and took some photographs of the small boys.

By the time I got back to my car, walking slowly, the motorcade had departed. It was dark before I reached Gwalior, and I called at Ferguson's hotel. He had taken a room for the night, and I walked along a dingy passage and knocked on his door. There was no reply, but when I pushed the door it opened.

Ferguson was lying on the bed with all his clothes on. On the bedside table was a brandy bottle, two thirds empty. His one shabby bag, only half-unpacked, spilled clothes on to the threadbare carpet. At first I thought he was asleep, but he opened his eyes, grunted, and struggled upright. His skin looked even grayer, and the whites of his eyes had turned yellow.

He squinted at me, then swung his legs over the side of the bed. Morosely, he eyed the brandy bottle. "I'm drunk," Ferguson said.

"You will be, if you drink any more brandy."

"I'm drunk now." He fumbled in his pockets. "Do you have a cigarette?" I gave him one.

"I'm a Eurasian," Ferguson said suddenly. "So was my father. My grandfather wasn't a colonel; he was a British Tommy who married a Hindu woman. My father was a government clerk. He was a Christian, and every night he prayed to the Viceroy as well as to Jesus Christ.

"He called himself an Anglo-Indian—it didn't mean what it means now. 'We are Anglo-Indians,' he used to say, 'just as Mr. Kipling is an Anglo-Indian.' He called Britain 'Home,' or 'the Old Country'; and he was always talking about 'our Empire.'

"He did join the Indian National Congress, but only because my mother made him. She was a Eurasian, too, and a Christian, but she had more spirit than he had. My father supported the Congress as long as it gave three cheers for the Queen and was respectful to the Viceroy. He quit it when it began talking about independence. He said it had got into the hands of extremists.

"He was sure there would always be a Raj, and he regarded

119

Gandhi as a Hindu agitator. 'The Viceroy must stand firm,' he would say; or, 'the people of this country are fundamentally Loyal at heart.'

"When Gandhi and the Congress won the first constitutional reforms, my father said: 'I don't know what they're thinking of, back Home: they must have taken leave of their senses.' "

Ferguson mashed out his cigarette, and defiantly poured himself a stiff brandy.

"My father despised Indians, but he called every white man 'sir.' Indians hated him, and the Europeans laughed at him behind his back. In his heart, he despised himself. But he couldn't help putting on airs, and talking about his father as 'the colonel.'

"After my mother died, he became quite ridiculous; I think he went a little mad. He made up stories about my grandfather's share in putting down the Indian Mutiny. 'We need men like that now,' he would say, 'to deal with the trouble-makers and the disloyal elements.'

"It got him into a lot of trouble," Ferguson said, drinking his brandy. "I'm glad he died before independence came."

Hearing a man unbare his soul is always embarrassing; and Ferguson was drunk.

"The old man's crazy blood is in me," Ferguson said. "You heard me, bullspitting about my grandfather, the colonel, and about my father having been in the Indian Civil Service, and being pretty thick with the Viceroy. God, what crap! And, what's more, you knew it was crap, and I knew that you knew. But it didn't stop me from telling it.

"A couple of brandies, and I start spouting about the dear old Raj. Then a Hindu looks me up and down, and talks to me in an Oxford accent, and I start to bawl with self-pity."

"Did you see your friend?" I asked.

"Yes, I saw him." He shrugged. "I told you he was a decent fellow. We did a lot of back-slapping. All very hearty. So I get the job. But inside of me I was saying: 'You damned grinning little oily Hindu, for two pins I'd knock your teeth down your throat.' And, at this moment, he's explaining to his friends: 'I hired a man called Ferguson today. Oh, no, not a European, naturally; he's a Eurasian, but a good chap. Rather tragic, in a way: please try not to laugh when he starts talking about his Indian Army forebears. Now that we've got our independence, I feel sorry for those Anglo-Indians, especially ones like this Ferguson, who find it so damned difficult to adjust. One feels one has to do something for them.' "

"I don't see why you shouldn't be able to adjust," I said. "Lots of Anglo-Indians have already done so. After all, India is your country; you were born here."

"Ah, but the trouble is, I don't really want to adjust," Ferguson explained. "I don't *want* to be assimilated into Hindu society. That's always been the trouble in India, and not just with the Anglo-Indians. Look at the Moslems, and the Parsees; look at the castes."

Somehow he had drunk himself back into a state of almost sober cheerfulness.

"Already, Anglo-Indians are marrying only other Anglo-Indians; and the children stay Anglo-Indian. Probably, we'll end up as yet another caste. That's India for you; that's the way things go here."

On that note, presently, I left him. I had a feeling that, had I stayed longer, he would have lit a cigar, called for another bottle of brandy, and begun reminiscing again about his grandfather, the colonel, who was on close terms with the Viceroy. We parted quite amicably, and I never saw him again; for all I know to the contrary, he is still there in Gwalior selling cotton, or whatever it was his Indian friend sold, near the old fort and the Maharaja's white wedding-cake palace, where the solid-silver toy train runs around the banqueting table after tiger shoots. He was in many ways a remarkable man, well educated, with a wry philosophy and an unusual personal problem. But he was quite unlike most of the Anglo-Indians I met, who were solid citizens with keen senses of humor and great ability to adjust themselves cheerfully to vastly changed circumstances.

The people call Putli Daku Rana, *the bandit queen.* INDIAN POLICE REPORT

THE COUNTRY between Gwalior and Bhind is a maze of deepcut ravines. The ravines have long been infested with dacoits, who have found them an excellent ready-made Maginot Line against the tiresome interference of the police. The most popular of the bandits was a Thakore clansman of considerable dignity and charm called Man Singh. A white-whiskered, Indian Robin Hood in a white turban, he murdered and pillaged the rich, but gave generously to the poor. Over a period of 27 years Man Singh's gang committed 185 murders and over 1,000 robberies. Harassed officials collected a whole ton of documents against the day of Man Singh's capture and conviction. The day never came, for the old warrior died in battle. Not long before his death, Man Singh caught two policemen and proposed to sacrifice them in a Shivaite temple. When the policemen cried out that they were Moslems, Man Singh ordered their release. "The Lord Shiva would not accept the blood of Moslems," he said contemptuously. The Home Minister of Madhya Bharat State, Mr. Narasinghrao Dixit, was also a worshipper of Shiva. He announced that, all other methods having failed, he would visit a Shiva shrine and there pray for Shiva's help in bringing Man Singh and his gang to book. At the same time, however, he prudently dispatched a company of Gurkhas into the ravines. The combination of prayers and

Gurkhas proved efficacious. The Gurkhas trapped the dacoits in the village of Kakekapura, and there, under a banyan tree, Man Singh at last met his end. The bullet-riddled bodies of Man Singh and his son Subedar, who had been his chief lieutenant, were taken in triumph into Bhind, and 40,000 people from the surrounding villages came to look at them. But, to the chagrin of the authorities, the villagers came weeping and bearing garlands. They had long hailed the bandit chief as their champion against rapacious merchants and moneylenders.

It was a lonely drive to Bhind over very bad roads. Bathed in full moonlight, the ravines stretched ghostlily on either side, an endless vista of steep treeless ridges and deep dark chasms. The bright moonlight only made the chasms blacker. Houses were few and far between, and were only wretched huts, showing no lights; nothing stirred on the road, not even a bullock cart. I might have been traveling on the moon. I had little fear of being challenged by dacoits, who prefer raiding villages and seldom bother to pounce on solitary travelers. Even if I had encountered any, I should probably have been allowed to pass unmolested, for the dacoits have their own peculiar code: a policeman, a moneylender, or an Indian merchant is fair game, and police informers are executed without ceremony; but foreigners are a different matter altogether. In the days of the Raj, Englishmen not in uniform were seldom killed by dacoits, and when it occasionally happened, both sides realized it must have been an accident, and the dacoits were always quick to apologize. The dacoits in the new India have so far continued to observe this admirable custom. All the same, it was a lonely journey through eerie country.

Abruptly, the road descended into a dried-up riverbed. I rattled over an interminable wooden causeway of loose planks. At the end of it men stood waving lanterns and calling on me to halt. Out of the sultry night appeared a villainous bearded face wrapped in a dirty white headcloth. Its owner carried a lantern in one hand and clutched a formidable looking brass-tipped *lathi* in the other. The other men, equally villainous, clustered behind him.

"Where are you going?"

"To Bhind."

The man shook his head. "You won't get through, sahib. All the roads through the ravines are closed tonight. They are being patroled for dacoits."

"Well, I've come from Gwalior. I don't propose to go all the way back."

He scratched perplexedly in his beard. He was plainly anxious not to offend me, but didn't seem to know what to do with me. An Indian traveler, I guessed, would have been peremptorily ordered back—unless he were a Congress Party dignitary; but Congress Party dignitaries were highly unlikely to be wandering about the dacoit-infested ravines of Bhind at night, and especially not alone. The patrolers had not bargained for a foreigner.

"You'd better go on to the government bungalow," he said at last. "It's only a couple of miles along the road. One of my men will go with you and show you the way."

They might be police patrols hunting dacoits; on the other hand, they might equally well be dacoits, pretending to be a police patrol. But in any event I was given no choice. A particularly villainous-looking man, wearing cotton pajamas, got in the car beside me. The door slammed. I drove off with my unexpected passenger.

He lit an evil-smelling brown *bidi* cigarette, and proceeded to make cheerful conversation in bad English.

"Plenty dacoits in ravines," he remarked. "Killing lots."

"But I thought Man Singh was dead."

"Man Singh shot. Subedar shot. But now Putli."

"Putli? I never heard of him."

"She is worst of dacoit. Kill many men already." His tone was full of undisguised admiration.

"She? You mean Putli is a woman?"

"Wife of sultan," he explained. "Very brave; very bad."

I could make nothing of this. A female bandit who was also a sultana was inconceivable. I wished that either I knew more Hindi, or my companion knew more English.

"Turn here," he said, pointing. Obediently, I turned into a sidetrack, which after many upward twists and turns led to a high shelf of ground on which stood a solitary bungalow. My guide got out, and presently reappeared with a bearer, who took my bags and stood waiting for me to follow him. My passenger raised the heavy bamboo *lathi*, of which he had not once let go, in a cheerful salutation, and padded off barefoot back down the winding track.

The bearer led the way up stone steps into the bungalow, explaining in English as he went that unfortunately there were no lanterns, and not even a candle. He brought me to a large, bare room; in the filtered moonlight I could dimly discern a large wooden table, and a rope-bed in a corner. There were no other furnishings. I had left Gwalior without dining and was extremely hungry; but in response to my inquiry, the bearer explained apologetically that there was no food of any kind in the bungalow. "Perhaps manage breakfast tomorrow," he said optimistically. Government bungalows can usually provide the traveler with some sort of a meal; and they are usually tended by more than one bearer. I had plainly come to a very solitary place. Then I reflected that it was surprising to find a government bungalow here at all. My suspicions revived. "Are you sure this is a government resthouse?" I asked sharply.

The bearer grinned, showing a bearded mouthful of blackened teeth.

"This is a *new* government bungalow, sahib," he replied. "Only, nobody ever comes. Dacoits keep everyone away." The thought seemed to amuse him; he went off chuckling.

I was too hungry to feel sleepy. I was also very thirsty, and cursed myself for not having asked the bearer for some water: water there must be, even in the newest and least visited of government resthouses. I decided to explore, and groped my way out of the room. The bungalow, built of stone, stood high off the ground, and a stone veranda ran all the way round it. I walked cautiously along the veranda, turned a corner, and halted abruptly. I was not as alone as I had imagined. Reclining almost full-length on a long wooden restchair, his long legs asprawl, was a figure in white. He sat with his back to the bungalow, gazing out over the moonlit ravines, and he was smoking a cigar. For a wild moment the cigar made me think of poor Ferguson; then the figure spoke in excellent English.

"How the devil did you get here, my friend, and who are you?"

"Sett Rao!" I exclaimed. "What the devil are *you* doing here?"

Sett Rao peered in surprise, then laughed. "You'll find another of those restchairs in the room behind me. Bring it out and sit down."

It was no wonder I had not recognized him. The last time I had seen him, with Rud, he was the immaculate bureaucrat of New Delhi, wearing well-cut Western clothes. Now he wore a long white shirt and a dhoti, and instead of shoes he wore leather sandals. But he still smoked excellent cigars, and his Oxford accent was unchangeable.

I gave him a brief account of my adventures. "I'm damned hungry," I concluded.

Sett Rao rose, and presently returned with sandwiches and a bottle of whisky.

"I generally carry my own rations," he said. "The villagers are hospitable, but their food is awful. By the way, these men who directed you here are *my* men; I shall commend them highly. You shall have eggs for breakfast, for I told the bearer to get some, somehow. But I'm afraid you will have to breakfast alone, for I must be off long before daylight."

"What are you doing here?" I asked again.

"New Delhi wants to put an end to the dacoits. They don't

fit in with the second Five Year Plan. As you may remember, I learned a little about guerilla warfare in Kashmir a few years ago."

"But you aren't a policeman, or a regular soldier. Isn't it a job for the police, or the army?"

"It is. But it's also a political matter. Awkward questions are being asked in Parliament. The government recently put up a number of new resthouses in this district. Nobody dares use them. Government officials come back to Delhi with terrible tales. Congress Party members from this district daren't travel in the ravines, even in daylight, except under armed escort. I was sent to find out what is actually happening."

"I thought that after Man Singh was killed, the dacoits were well on the way to being liquidated."

"That's what the officials and the M.P.'s thought. Unfortunately Man Singh has a successor. Her name is Putli."

"Putli! The wife of a sultan?"

Sett Rao was amused. "Well, her boyfriend was called Sultan Gujar. It's quite a romantic story, if also a little sordid in parts. Putli comes from a Moslem family of traditional songstresses and concubines. She was a streetsinger. In 1950, when she was about twenty, she was hired as a professional entertainer at a village wedding. During the wedding the village was attacked by Sultan Gujar and his gang. Sultan took a fancy to her, and apparently she took a fancy to him also, for she rode off with the gang. In due course Putli bore Sultan a son, but motherhood did not soften her. She played a full part in the murders, robberies, and kidnappings committed by the gang, and she is known to have shot at least one unfortunate policeman dead at Dholpur. Eventually, however, she and Sultan quarreled; she became furiously jealous when he began paying attention to another girl. Putli offered to betray Sultan to the police, if they would give her a free pardon, and the reward. She asked for the reward in advance, and got it; so she returned to the gang, tipped off the police where to find Sultan—he was duly ambushed and shot—then formed a liaison with another bandit called Luhari. She kept the police money, of course."

Sett Rao puffed contentedly at his cigar.

"Luhari didn't last long. I must say he didn't show much sense, for a girl who betrays one dacoit leader isn't to be trusted by another. Not long after she had taken up with Luhari, she murdered him and joined forces with a third dacoit, called Pahara Gujar, who is a cousin of the late Sultan. She and Pahara are still together. She has an infant daughter by him, and she also had a daughter by Luhari."

"What does she look like?"

"According to the police reports, she's no beauty. She's under five feet, and rather fat. She wears her hair short, and dresses like a man. She wears a gold chain round her neck, and a gold ring on her finger inscribed 'Sultan-Putli.' They say she fights on horseback, with a gun in one hand and her infant daughter in her other arm."

"Do you think you will catch her?"

Sett Rao sighed. "The ravines have been in dacoit hands a very long time. Every stranger who passes through the villages is automatically suspected of being either a spy of the dacoits or a spy of the police. On the whole, the villagers prefer the dacoits. They've got used to them. Did you know that Aurangzeb, in the seventeenth century, appointed a governor of this district, specially for the purpose of trying to control the dacoits? In those days, the chief stronghold of the dacoits was a place called Ater; today, Ater is still a dacoit-controlled village. You foreigners constantly forget what a very old country India is, and how very slowly things change here: if they change at all. Some of our own people sometimes tend to forget it. . . . As I told you and your friend in Delhi, the problems are huge, and many of the anachronisms remain. Dacoits are an anachronism in a country that calls itself civilized, nevertheless we still have dacoits.

"But I for one don't despair. There is good even in dacoits. In the second world war, this area"—he gestured toward the silent ravines—"gave the British Raj one hundred thousand soldiers; and *all* the dacoits joined the army. Of course, they didn't do so out of love of the British; they did it because they like to fight. But courage is also a virtue. Too many Indians lacked courage, and so India became a nation of slaves. The dacoits at least have never been slaves."

He rose, yawned, and threw away his cigar. "Shall we catch Putli tomorrow? I don't know; probably not. But we shall try and, if we fail, try again. Poor Putli! She's doomed, anyhow, in the new India of heavy industries which Mr. Nehru is determined to create. Lady bandits can't coexist with steel plants. Anyhow, I'm going to bed. I shan't see you in the morning, for I'll be up long before you are. Good-by and good luck."

"Good luck to you," I said.

Tall, lean, and handsome, Sett Rao smiled. "Wish all of us Indians luck, the whole three hundred and seventy-odd millions of us," he said. "We shall need it."

He kept all his promises, for in the morning he was gone, and the bearer brought me fried eggs, without spices, fresh bread, and hot tea. On my way to Lucknow I passed through Bhind without being challenged, and in that sullen village saw many signs of police activity, but no sign of captured bandits. In a little teashop, hardly more than an open booth by the wayside, near the white Shiva temple, a broad-shouldered man in a white turban and with immense white mustaches, who might have been Man Singh himself, brewed me scalding-hot tea and, squatting on his bare brown heels, fried me some *chapattis*. Outside in the street, hot with dust and glaring sunlight, policemen with *lathis* were halting villagers, making them dismount from their bicycles, and questioning them. They seemed to be getting few answers. The broad-shouldered man with the white mustaches brought me my tea and golden *chapattis*. He was chuckling.

"Did you hear the news?" He jerked a contemptuous thumb back at the policemen. "They've been looking for Putli, the little bandit queen. Of course, she got away."

V

LUCKNOW:
THE MURDEROUS POLITICIANS

In Lucknow we have entered the realm of lunatic fantasy.

O. H. K. Spate

In Bhind I bought an astrological almanac put out by the state government. It accompanied me on many of my further travels, and became dog-eared with constant use. It ranks in my opinion as one of the most fascinating documents ever published by any government information agency. Until I read it I did not know that it was a sign of good fortune if a bat fell from the ceiling into one's lap—but not if it fell onto the back of one's neck—or that seeing a Brahmin first thing in the morning was an omen of good luck, while seeing a widow, or a woman carrying a water pot, spelt a disastrous day ahead.

I found Lucknow in a state of public uproar. Past the long dead nawabs' florid tombs; past the "European-style" castle, complete with turrets, battlements, moat, and drawbridges, and now used as a girls' high school; past the railroad station, with its fantastic fluted columns, cupolas, and vast parapets; past the Drug Research Institute, housed in a former palace, and with a gilded umbrella suspended over its dome—through the crowded streets and alleys of Lucknow—there swarmed endless processions of angry demonstrators carrying banners of protest. Public buildings had been stoned; several people had already been killed in street clashes.

The cause of all the hubbub was a lost dog. A Nepalese visitor to Lucknow had brought with him his pet dog, which he led about on a silver chain. One day he found the dog gone: either it had strayed or, more probably, someone had taken a fancy to the silver chain, and stolen both. The bereft owner advertised his loss in a local newspaper. He described the missing animal, offered a reward, and explained that the dog answered to the name "Mahmud."

Rioting automatically followed. Furious Moslems, of whom there are a great many in Lucknow, surrounded the newspaper office, howling for blood. To pacify the mob, the police arrested the dog's owner. It was in vain that the unfortunate man explained that, in calling his dog "Mahmud," he had intended no affront to the Prophet; "mahmud," he declared, was merely the Nepalese word for "power." But there are a variety of ways of spelling the Prophet's name. "Mahomet" is one; "Mohammed" is another; and "Mahmud" is a third. To prevent the dog's owner from being lynched, the police wisely smuggled him out of the city jail, and secretly sped him back over the Nepal border—without his dog, which remained untraced. When the mobs discovered that their prey had eluded them, their fury increased. There were fresh riots, and more stone-throwing. The police had a busy time.

The least perturbed man in Lucknow was Dr Sampurnan-and, the Chief Minister of Uttar Pradesh State, of which Lucknow is the capital. He was occupied with an experiment in hydroponics, the growing of vegetables in a solution of mineral salts instead of in soil.

He hoped that India might be the first country to succeed in dispatching space ships to the stars. "The space-fliers," Dr. Sampurnanand explained, "will have to depend on hydroponics for their fresh vegetables, for, on such long voyages, soil would deteriorate." Long devoted to vegeterianism and astrology, India was seeing her destiny in the galaxies.

When the Russian leaders Bulganin and Khrushchev visited

Uttar Pradesh, Dr Sampurnanand insisted that they stand on a specially woven carpet embroidered with yellow hearts and red flowers, with a lotus in the center: he explained to them that, according to the astrologers, this would draw forth their full powers of oratory. The Russian leaders were also greeted by five girls (according to the astrologers, five is a most auspicious number), wearing saffron-colored saris, and blowing conch shells. Uttar Pradesh is India's third largest state. Dr Sampurnanand presided over it, assisted by 260,000 officials. None of them dared to make a decision without first consulting Dr Sampurnanand; and Dr Sampurnanand seldom authorised any action until he had consulted the stars.

In Lucknow I asked my friend Mulk Sangh to introduce me to an astrologer. Mulk Sangh said he would ask one to tea. He said it nonchalantly, and I said: "All right, just let me know when he's coming." If I had asked him to produce a yogi, a poet, or an atomic physicist, he would have treated the request in the same casual way. Mulk Sangh is the son of a wealthy man, and one day he would inherit his father's fortune. Meanwhile he and his pretty wife lived in a small but elegant apartment and earnestly studied economics and sociology, in order, Mulk Sangh explained, to fit themselves for strenuous living in the new India. He was reading the works of Professor G. D. H. Cole and she was a member of the All-India Family Planning Association (they had no children). They made a hobby of collecting odd characters and their apartment was usually full of them, talking, eating, drinking, and listening to gramophone records; the last time I had visited them, the chief guest of the evening had been a British left-wing biologist who wore a dhoti and explained that he proposed to spend the rest of his life in India, because Britain had been reduced to an outpost of American imperialism by oversexed American troops who were permanently garrisoned there. "There is not a virgin left in England," he kept saying gloomily. "Not one."

Mulk Sangh's wife, Adi, had urged me to visit the Drug

Research Institute. She was a demure-looking girl with hair like black silk and very long black eyelashes over warm brown eyes. "There's a man who's trying to make an oral contraceptive from peas," she said. "And they're also doing very fine work to combat adulteration of drugs by laying down minimum standards." So I made my way cautiously through the hot turbulent streets to the Drug Research Institute. The demonstrators over the dog Mahmud were still taking out processions with banners and flags, but neither the Moslems, who were demonstrating, nor the Hindus, who feared that the Moslems might start more communal riots, were interested in a white foreigner. I reached the Institute without incident, and a polite young man in a white coat, with a science degree, showed me round. He seemed somewhat oppressed by the magnitude of the problems that the Institute faced. "*Everything* is adulterated," he said hopelessly. "We try to bring the unscrupulous druggists to book, but they are always finding new loopholes. And the Drugs Act is very difficult to enforce: we have so few qualified inspectors. Only the other day in Bombay an unfortunate unemployed man decided to end his family's sufferings: he, his wife, and their seven children were all starving. He spent his last few rupees on arsenic, and the wife mixed it in the food. After taking this last meal, they said their prayers and lay down to die. But in the morning they woke up, perfectly unharmed. The 'arsenic' the man had bought was adulterated." The young man looked at me mournfully. "*That* is the sort of scandal we are trying to put a stop to."

In the roadway outside the Drug Research Institute a large crowd was being fiercely harangued by a snarling little man in a red fez. He employed all the practiced venom of the professional agitator, and he was putting the blame for the dog incident on Dr Sampurnanand and the Congress Party government of Uttar Pradesh. The Moslems who were listening to him cheered lustily. I had seen the man before, in Delhi; but then he had been a member of the Congress Party, which welcomes Moslems into its fold. I was intrigued, to put it mildly.

Mulk Sangh rang me up to say that, true to his word, he had found an astrologer, who was coming to tea that afternoon. I went round to Mulk Sangh's apartment, and was introduced to the astrologer. He was a Hindu refugee from Lahore. At the Partition millions of Hindus fled to India from Pakistan, and half a million of them settled down in Uttar Pradesh. The astrologer had long, sensitive hands, fine dark eyes, and spoke in a gentle voice. He was plainly a highly intelligent man, and I asked him to tell me, seriously, if he really believed there was a place for astrology in the modern world of mechanics, meson particles, and A and H bombs. He considered the question carefully, then said in his mild, deprecating voice: "I think we Indians have gone too far. We consult the stars too often, and on too many trivial matters. I think some of our leading astrologers are very wise men; but they are, after all, only mortals, and mortals should not presume to too much knowledge. I believe the masses have come to expect miracles from astrology. It is time we faced the facts, and realised our limitations." He paused, regarded me steadfastly, and then said gravely: "We should frankly confess that, despite all our striving after perfection, astrology is not yet an exact science."

Over an excellent meal of *biriani pillau*, which consists of rice cooked with meat and cunningly mixed with nuts and spices, and which is a Lucknow specialty, I asked Mulk Sangh if he could explain the seeming riddle of the man in the red fez whom I had seen haranguing the Moslems.

Mulk Sangh was amused. "It's very simple. There are solid blocks of Moslem voters in Lucknow, in Kanpur, in Bareilly and Aligarh, and in many of the other cities of Uttar Paradesh. The Moslem vote is one of the keys to political power in this state. The Communists, the Socialists, even the Hindu *Mahasabha*, believe it or not, are all trying to win over the Moslems.

134

This dog business may seem utterly stupid to you, but the Moslems take it very seriously. So it's a golden chance for those who want to pose as the Moslems' friends and who are trying to stir up trouble for the state government."

"But this man was claiming in Delhi to be a member of the Congress Party."

"So he probably is. But the Congress Party in Uttar Pradesh is split into two opposing factions," Muld Sangh explained. "Dr Sampurnanand's faction is in power and the other faction is trying to oust him. This man has obviously been bought over by the anti-Sampurnanand faction. His being a Moslem is what makes him valuable to them."

"You are a cynic," said Adi accusingly. "But I am afraid you are quite right," she added despondently.

"We have worse things than hired agitators," said Mulk Sangh, cheerfully. "In Uttar Pradesh we have hired assassins. You can hire a professional assassin here for as little as five rupees—only one dollar. Many of the politicians do. Fortunately, the assassins, like the politicians, believe in astrology, and will not commit a murder until they have consulted the stars. If the stars are in the wrong conjunction, no fee, however high, will tempt them. I know at least one Congress Party member of the Legislative Assembly who owes his life to that fact."

"You're pulling my leg," I protested, laughing.

"On the contrary, I am quite serious. Shall I prove it to you? There is a district near Lucknow called Bara Banki, with a town of that name. The district is under a reign of terror. There have been four political assassinations in six weeks."

A few days later Mulk Sangh came to see me. I had forgotten this conversation, but he had not.

"You didn't believe me," he said. "Well, what do you think of this?"

It was a report in the *Lucknow Herald*. It described how two Socialists had been murdered in the village of Badripur in the Bara Banki district. They had called a meeting of villagers, and were making speeches about the land reforms, when a gang of armed men invaded the meeting. Some of the gang held the villagers at bay with spears and clubs, while the others proceeded to beat the two Socialists to death. The villagers had to look on helplessly, unable to prevent the killings. The gang had then burned the two bodies, and departed. The newspaper report added that the Legislative Assembly in Lucknow was in an uproar.

"I'd like to visit Badripur and talk to the people," I said rashly.

"Very well," said Mulk Sangh promptly. "I promised to travel with you for a few days, and that would be a good place to begin. Let's go by all means to Badripur. But we had better start as soon as possible." He smiled cynically. "The police are there already. If they cannot find the assassins, they can always arrest the villagers. If we do not go at once, there may be no villagers left for you to talk to!"

In Uttar Pradesh we have achieved a bloodless land reform that Russia might envy. NEHRU

WE TOOK a crowded train to Bara Banki. The distance from Lucknow was only eighteen miles, and we squeezed thankfully into a second-class compartment whose wooden benches were occupied by cheerful unshaven men in striped pajamas. Four were eating mangoes and bananas which they took from a large wicker basket. One was carefully paring his toenails. Two were poring over a tattered copy of a Hindi newspaper. We sat for a long time, for the train was an hour and thirty-five minutes late in starting. But we dared not leave our seats, for the platform was crowded with people still hoping to get on board. When we did start, the more daring of them leaped on to the footboards of the coaches and squatted there, hanging on precariously to the doors and windows.

The men with the Hindi newspaper started a political discussion. In Nagpur a rickshaw-puller, presumably half-witted, had attempted to stab Mr Nehru with a clasp knife.

"He will have been put up to it by the *Jan Sangh*," said one of the men, darkly. "They hate Nehru because he wishes to destroy caste."

"It is the work of the Moslems," said the other man.

"No, the Moslems would not dare, and anyhow they are afraid of what may happen to them when Nehru dies. It is the *Jan Sangh*, which is run by Brahmins, who denounce Nehru as an enemy of the Hindu religion."

Bara Banki is a railroad town, and looks it. A gloomy pall of smoke hung over its mean streets, and it smelled like an oven. We did not linger long in it, for we had to catch the bus to Badripur. The train was so late that Mulk Sangh feared the bus might have already left. He need not have worried; the bus was late, too. Passengers' baggage was still being roped into place on the roof. But the bus, like the train, was crowded, and Mulk Sangh and I were perforce separated. He found a place in the rear; I got a seat just behind the busdriver, and beside a wispy benevolent gentleman with a ragged gray mustache. He courteously made room for me, with a smile that showed a few yellow teeth.

The bus finally started. Its aged engine roared, the gears shifted protestingly, and the whole chassis shook, making the windows dance a violent jig. We lurched out of Bara Banki in clouds of dust and choking, acrid engine fumes. The driver was a huge man, with vast hairy arms that wrestled valorously with the bucking steering-wheel. He wore only a cotton undervest and a dhoti, but soon his face ran with sweat, as if he had just sluiced himself with a bucket of water. The narrow twisting road overflowed with bullock carts, water buffalo, and herds of goats. The bus kept up a continuous hooting. We were thrown from side to side, and bounced on broken springs toward the roof. My seat companion, still smiling benevolently, approached his gray mustache cautiously toward my ear, and unexpectedly bawled in English: "Good morning!"

He was a village schoolmaster, he explained between lurches. He had been teaching for twenty years, and his salary was forty rupees a month—about eight dollars. Often his words were totally lost, with the violent motion and the engine's uproar. But he continued to talk, to smile, and to nod. I could only smile and nod back, and try to look comprehending.

He looked out of the window, nudged me with a sharp elbow to secure my attention, and pointed out a curious sight. In a field, close to the road a man was walking round a small fire of twigs; he appeared to be chanting aloud.

"He is praying for rain and good crops," the village schoolmaster bawled. "He must walk round the fire until he has recited a sacred verse 3,000 times. It says so in the astrological almanac."

We passed through a village whose single street was so narrow that the bus seemed to brush the stalls, which were piled high with gleaming brassware, several kinds of spiced meat, several kinds of freshly baked bread, and stacks of colored prints of Hindu gods. Women in saris of bright yellow, red, or green were walking toward the village well, carrying pots of clay and brass balanced on their heads.

We stopped, for some of the passengers had expressed a wish to drink tea. When we had all finished doing so, it was discovered that the driver had disappeared: his aunt lived in the village, and he had gone to visit with her. The refreshed passengers, showing no surprise and no annoyance, sauntered idly up and down the village street. Mulk Sangh and I looked over the religious prints. Some depicted Ganesh, the elephant-

138

headed god, who is a popular deity in Uttar Pradesh; others showed Krishna chasing the milkmaids. One print represented Vishnu reclining gracefully on the body of a many-headed serpent; out of his navel there grew a lotus on which sat Brahma. There were also prints of fat Indian holy men, who sat cross-legged, left foot on right thigh and right foot on left thigh, the soles of their feet turned upward, solemnly looking down at their monstrous paunches. There was a print of Gandhi, emaciated, spectacled, wearing only a white loincloth and striding sturdily along a dusty road, holding a staff. And, a startling incongruity among all these, there was a colored photograph of Stalin, wearing one of his wartime field-marshal uniforms, his chest gaudy with medals.

Presently the busdriver returned, smoking a *bidi* cigarette, and we all clambered back on board the bus, and lurched and roared on our way.

Outside the village we passed a group of men, women, and children, trudging along in the dust of the roadside, followed by heavy-laden pack-oxen. The women wore a queer headgear: a sort of shawl which was raised well above the head, supported on what looked very like a pair of wooden horns. My friend the schoolmaster pointed them out excitedly. They were, he said, *lambadi*: a wandering gypsy tribe with an evil reputation for the buying and selling of stolen children. I thought of Meerut, and the children who had disappeared at the *mela*.

Badripur at first glance was a dismal disappointment. I did not know quite what I had expected, but certainly something more impressive than eighty sparsely distributed mud huts set down in a baking open plain and surrounded by wretched little fields, each hardly bigger than a suburbanite's lawn. There seemed to be hardly any people about—which, considering the appalling heat, was perhaps not surprising—but those we saw looked furtive. The place had a ghostly air. The huts were raised off the ground on mud platforms. Steps had been molded in the mud, but were worn to a smooth, sagging shape by much use. Outside the huts cattle disconsolately panted: painfully gaunt beasts, whose ribcages showed clearly through the emaciated hides, matching with uncanny and pathetic exactitude the curves of the worn baked-mud steps.

"But there is a government resthouse," said Mulk Sangh. "We shall find the police chief there, for since the murders the police have taken charge of the village—and of the villagers," he added, rather grimly. "We'd better go and see him."

Mulk Sangh was quite right. Outside the resthouse which, though only a bare bungalow, was larger than any of the village huts, police guards patroled lethargically up and down. On the veranda of the resthouse sat the police chief in his pajamas. He was a small unhealthy-looking man with very hard brown eyes, like stones. He sat upright in a wooden chair, and was being shaved by an attendant.

"The attendant is a member of the government-resthouse caste," Mulk Sangh explained, as we approached. "Yes, it is true," he said impatiently, when I rashly smiled disbelief. "There is a caste which exists to light the resthouse lamps, carry government officials' baggage—and shave the officials, also."

We waited until the police chief had had his shave, and then walked onto the veranda.

While we explained ourselves, the police chief sat perfectly still, his hands crossed on his stomach, his hard brown eyes looking over our heads, unblinkingly—apparently straight at the glaring sun. When we had finished talking, he said in good English: "But there is nothing now for you to see in Badripur: law and order have been restored." He seemed inclined to dismiss us out of hand.

"But," I said, "what about your investigation?"

"It is proceeding."

"You mean you have some clues to the murderers?"

"It is very difficult," the police chief complained. "The villagers' stories are confused. They say they cannot identify the men. We do not know what happened at all."

"But two men *were* murdered?"

"We found some traces of two bodies having been burned," he said grudgingly.

Mulk Sangh said gently: "People find those murders, in this district, very disturbing."

The police chief said loudly: "Law and order have been restored. It is not true there has been serious deterioration in the crime situation in this district. That is very exaggerated, what the papers are saying."

He was beginning to talk like an official report.

"Then why were the two Socialists murdered?" I asked.

The police chief looked directly at me, and for the first time his eyes blinked. "The Socialists," he said simply, "were agitators."

Then he looked at his watch, which was strapped tightly to his wrist, under the sleeve of his pajama coat. He said, more cordially, but with an evident determination to end the interview: "I am expecting an important Uttar Pradesh official here, very soon. Why don't you come back later, and talk to *him?*"

We said we would, thanked him, and withdrew. He proceeded with dignity to scrutinize some papers, bending diligently over a small wooden table that the attendant of the government-resthouse caste had brought onto the veranda for the purpose.

"Now we shall go and visit a man who is the leader of the Socialists in this village," said Mulk Sangh. "I was given his name in Lucknow."

On the way to the Socialist's house we passed a hut which was part residence, part store. Outside it there hung a cage, in which a large green parrot preened its feathers and cocked a beady eye at us. "That is the home of the village moneylender," Mulk Sangh explained. "He charges 25 per cent interest: about 60 per cent of the villagers are in debt to him, and will remain so all their lives. Most of them are born in his debt, for the debt is passed from father to son."

The village Socialist, contrary to my expectations, was a

merry man, with a broad, laughing face and bare, brawny arms. His hut's single room had a mud floor smeared with cow-dung mixed with water. It contained three upright wooden chairs, a wooden bench against one wall, a rope-bed against another wall, and a number of brass pots and brass trays. He greeted us cheerfully, and his smiling wife gave us *namasthe*, pressing the palms of her hands together. "You must be very hungry!" he exclaimed, after he and Mulk Sangh had talked a little. As if the words were an understood signal, his wife rose and bustled outside. The village Socialist nodded after her. "She is a good woman," he said, "and a brave one, for she married me. We defied custom together, for she was a goldsmith's daughter, and I am only a blacksmith. That was against all caste laws. I am a Socialist, and it is my business to break caste law. She is not a Socialist, nevertheless she broke the custom for my sake. Therefore she is braver than me."

I told him, with Mulk Sangh interpreting, that we had come to Badripur to find out why the two Socialist speakers had been murdered.

The broad-faced man reflected a while. Then he said: "There is great bitterness in this district between the Congress Party people and the Socialists."

"And the Communists?" I asked.

He shrugged. "In this matter of land the Communists are with us, certainly. But there are not many Communists."

"The Congress Party claims to have made very great land reforms in Uttar Pradesh."

He grinned. "Well, it all depends on the point of view. This is how we see it. The Congress Party set up a *Zamindars'* Abolition Fund: all was to be done legally, and there was to be no confiscation of land. So, in order to get possession of the land that they worked as tenants, the people had to pay to the *Zamindars'* Abolition Fund a sum which is ten times the rent they pay the *zamindars* annually. Only about 20 per cent of the peasants could afford to do this, and then only if they had good crops, and also by putting themselves in debt to the money-lender.

"But the *zamindars* were still not satisfied. The law said that, if the tenants found the money, the *zamindars* had to accept it, and had to part with all of their land, except that part which they personally cultivated. With the help of corrupt officials, the *zamindars* falsified the land records to 'prove' that most of their land was under their 'personal cultivation.' "

He paused. "Let me give you a figure. The Congress Party's own Committee on the Consolidation of Landholdings in Uttar Pradesh recently admitted that they had investigated and had found 3,576,853 'wrong entries' in 7,082 villages!"

The statistics rolled glibly off his tongue, but this did not surprise me, and I did not doubt his word; I guessed that, like most literate Indians, especially politicians, he had a phenomenal memory for figures.

"Well," he proceeded, "what happened next? Armed with the falsified land records, the *zamindars* and their bribed officials started mass evictions of peasants, who had for long been their tenants but who they now said were unlawful squatters on the *zamindars'* 'personally cultivated' land. This, however, was not enough; for the government passed a law to protect people against mass evictions. The law was based on the tenants' period of occupancy of a piece of land; even if they were so-called 'squatters,' they still could not be evicted under this law. But then the *zamindars* simply moved the tenants about, from one piece of land to another, and *then* evicted them. The law said nothing about that; and the tenants, most of whom cannot read or write, were too bewildered to understand what was happening."

While he had been talking, several people had come quietly into the cool semidarkness of the hut and had sat down. The village Socialist nodded to them, but otherwise paid them no attention. They were dark, earthy-looking men, mostly wearing only loincloths: they sat, listening intently, but saying nothing.

"Well!" said the Socialist, good-humoredly. "Now we have in this village a *panchayat*, or village council. Perhaps we should raise those matters in the *panchayat?* But the landlords have traditionally been the bosses of the *panchayat;* and they remain so. All that happens there, in the *panchayat*, is that the rival leading castes fight among themselves for mastery over it. But all are landlords, and usually Brahmins as well. The people have a great awe of the high-caste Brahmins, and dared not oppose them.

"This village also has a co-operative: perhaps the people should try to gain their rights through the co-operative. But the rival high castes fight to control that also. These castes seek support among the rich peasants. The membership of the co-operative has grown to almost twice what it was. But the members are only pawns in the game played by the rival leading castes. One caste has been very clever. It has maneuvered the other caste into leadership of the co-operative. That seems to you to be a strange thing to do? But see what happens. The other caste, the one that has apparently surrendered the co-operative to its rivals, urges the peasants to apply to the co-operative for loans. The loans are grudgingly granted, because the peasants are egged on to make threats that if they do not get loans, they will burn the crops. Then the peasants are ordered on no account to repay the loans. So, the caste that was maneuvered into taking over mastery of the co-operative is disgraced; but in the process the co-operative itself is made bankrupt. Then the landlords nod their heads wisely, and say: 'In India there can be no co-operatives, for the peasants are too ignorant to make them work; the co-operative is merely a plant held in position by government, but its roots refuse to enter the Indian soil.'"

He looked up. "Ah! Here is your food."

His smiling wife had come back into the hut, and she began briskly to serve a feast. We ate *kakori kababs*, cigar-shaped bits of meat that melted in the mouth, and they were followed by melons and mangoes. The blacksmith did not eat, saying laughingly that he had already had his dinner. Mulk Sangh and I discovered that we were famished. The silent peasants watched us placidly, and seemed pleased that we showed a good appetite. Badripur, I thought, might be a wretchedly poor place, but its hospitality was princely.

"Tell me," I said, with my mouth full of *kabab*, "who is the government official who is coming here today?"

All the peasants laughed. One of them explained: "He calls himself the chairman of the 'Grow More Food' Committee. He is very officious and knows nothing, being from Lucknow. To us, he is only one more Yama, to add to our other burdens —these being the tax collector, the police, the vaccinator, and the *patwari*." Everyone laughed again, more uproariously than before: Yama is the Hindu God of Death.

"The *patwari*," the blacksmith Socialist explained, "is our village headman. He is also the land-record officer and the revenue officer. Besides that, he is a nephew of the moneylender."

One of the peasants said violently: "Give him an anna, and he will denounce his own father as a bastard; I hope he drowns in a tankful of maggots."

The blacksmith said: "He is very superstitious. Last year when the floods came and the village well was defiled, because of a corpse being found in it, he ordered cow's urine to be poured down the well to purify the drinking water."

Another peasant said: "He also fixed a day for the whole village to go to the shrine of Pochamma to pray to avert smallpox. Very few people went. They are as superstitious as he, but they also hate the *patwari*."

"Where is the shrine of Pochamma?" I asked.

"It is next to the new post office that the government built."

"Poor Nehru!" I thought.

"What are the police doing about the murders?" Mulk Sangh asked.

"What d'you expect them to do? Bullying the villagers—or

trying to; our people are rather tough. Sucking up to the land-lords. I was not there when it happened," said the blacksmith. He glowered fiercely. "I mean when our two comrades were murdered. I wish I had been."

"They would have killed you, also, *baba*," said one of the peasants.

"Perhaps: but I would certainly have killed some of *them*. Cowards, to murder two unarmed men!"

"The Congress Party men who were murdered in Bara Banki were also unarmed," said Mulk Sangh, mildly.

The blacksmith looked disconcerted. "Yes, that is true. The whole business is perfectly horrible." He let his eyes widen, and slapped a vast hand on his thigh. "You don't think we Socialists had anything to do with the Bara Banki killings, do you?"

It was a singularly unconvincing show of innocence. Mulk Sangh remained silent. The squatting peasants looked thought-fully up at the thatched ceiling. It was an awkward moment. Mulk Sangh ended it by rising and saying: "My friend and I would like to speak to the *patwari*. You have made us curious about him."

"May he be forced to spend his time in hell drinking his own urine," said one of the peasants.

The blacksmith directed us to the *patwari*'s house. His amia-bility had been fully restored. All the same, he seemed relieved that we were taking our departure.

The *patwari* occupied a little dark hole of a house inside a mud compound at one end of the village. Also inside the com-pound, but built some distance from the main hut, was a smaller hut, made mostly of straw. From this smaller hut, as we walked past it, low moaning noises were coming; I thought it must be an injured animal that was confined there. As we ap-proached the larger hut, a young man came out of it, carefully carrying a small bowl that contained rice and milk. Mulk Sangh stopped him and spoke to him, then watched him walk past the smaller hut and out of the compound, still carefully carrying his bowl of food. "He is the *patwari*'s son," Mulk Sangh said. "He is taking that rice and milk to an anthill where a cobra lives. He takes food there for the cobra every day at this time, he tells me; he is a believer in *nagula panchami*—cobra worship." Mulk Sangh added: "One day, of course, the cobra will bite him. Then there will be one superstitious fool the less in India." Mulk Sangh woefully lacked the proper spirit of objective anthropological inquiry: his tone was contemptuous.

We had to bend our heads low to enter through the door of the *patwari*'s hut and, once inside, we found ourselves almost in darkness. I dimly made out the figure of a man, dressed in white and seated cross-legged on a rope-bed. He rose slowly as we entered, and pressed the palms of his hands briefly together. From the peasants' talk, I had expected to meet a repulsive-looking old man; I had imagined a wrinkled skin, shifty eyes, and a rapacious mouth. Instead, the *patwari* seen at close quarters proved to be a very dignified man, elderly but still handsome, with a well-cut gray beard, a powerful hooked nose, and eyes that seemed full of wisdom. He was the very picture of a village patriarch and might have walked out of a documentary film about the new India. He motioned us to be seated, and sank back on the rope-bed. Mulk Sangh began explaining in Hindi who we were. The *patwari* listened with grave courtesy, stroking his beard: I got the impression that he already had learned all about us, and privately thought of us as interfering busybodies. But his outward manner gave no hint of this. While Mulk Sangh talked, I let my eyes wander round the interior of the hut. Gradually, as they adjusted themselves to the lack of light, I began to make out objects. There were rather a lot of them. In one corner stood a large grandfather clock in a wooden case with a glass panel. Its brass pendulum was motionless, and presently I realized that the clock-hands were missing. A number of wicker baskets hung from the rafters. On a small wooden shelf there were two china mugs, one

147

containing pencils, the other holding toothbrushes. A saw hung on the wall, and a scythe lay under it. Several bulging grainbags lay on the floor. The walls were decorated with the familiar, garish-colored prints of Hindu gods. The corner facing the grandfather clock had been made into a sort of alcove, and in it there stood a curious figure. It was made of wood, and was painted. It stood about three feet high, had three vividly painted eyes, and seemed to have several sets of arms. I longed to know what it was supposed to represent, and was soon to learn.

Mulk Sangh stopped talking. The *patwari* looked at us, and stroked his beard. Then he said: "Gandhi preached the way of nonviolence. But men's hearts are evil, and they are tempted by devils to do wicked things. The land reforms have proved very troublesome. They were to do good, and they have only bred wickedness and greed. The villagers are children, and are easily led into wrongdoing. They no longer obey the Brahmins as they used to do. We are being punished for forsaking the old ways of our fathers."

I thought it a disappointingly sententious speech.

A girl entered the hut. She approached the *patwari*, averting her face from us. Sinking to her knees, she touched his feet. The *patwari* paid her absolutely no attention. She rose and, still with her face averted from us, went to the other end of the hut and poured water from a large brass pot into a smaller one. "She is his daughter," Mulk Sangh explained in English.

I asked the *patwari*: "You yourself then are a follower of Gandhi?"

He nodded gravely.

"And a member of the Congress Party?"

"Of course! I am the *patwari*. The Congress Party knows I am to be trusted."

"Do you think the Congress Party is carrying out Gandhi's plans for India?"

"That is very difficult to do. Gandhi was a saint. We are only mortals. The Mahatma has left us, and we do the best we can.

Gandhi," said the *patwari* simply, "has ascended to heaven, and there he sits with the gods, attended to by hundreds of servants, and enjoying the very best food."

It was scarcely, I reflected, the sort of divine reward for services on earth that the Mahatma himself would have approved; but the *patwari* seemed to think it eminently suitable.

The girl walked across to the alcove with the small brass pot in her hand. There, after kneeling briefly, she rose and proceeded to lave the image.

"It is Ellamma, the goddess of boils," Mulk Sangh said in English. "She is giving the image its daily bath."

The *patwari* listened uncomprehending to the foreign words, and gave us a vague smile.

"Perhaps you could tell us why the land reforms have proved troublesome," I said.

"I will tell you," the *patwari* nodded. "I myself am a Brahmin. The peasants, and other people of the lower castes, used to respect and fear the Brahmins. They knew their position. We Brahmins, though twice-born, treated them almost like members of our own caste. The low castes were grateful for such favors from us. But now everything is changed. The low castes demand more land: *our* land. We dared not refuse, for the government has passed those laws. Yet the peasants are not satisfied. They demand *all* our land. When we do not give it to them, they burn the crops, and threaten to kill us. And the Socialists encourage them and lead them. I hope the police will arrest all the Socialists in this village, for they are wicked men who have turned against Gandhi's teachings of nonviolence; I do not think they even believe in God."

In the alcove the girl finished bathing the image. She filled a small brass dish with food, and laid it reverently at the foot of the image.

"The food is laid before the goddess every day," Mulk Sangh said. He added ironically: "The *patwari* is a very religious man."

We rose, and said our good-bys. The *patwari* did not this

time get up from the rope-bed, but he bowed very low. I suddenly realized that he was complacently pleased that we had visited him. He felt flattered.

As we walked out of the compound past the smaller straw hut I heard the moaning sound again. It was louder and more anguished than it had been.

"What is it?" I asked curiously. "A sick animal?"

"Oh, no," said Mulk Sangh. "I asked the son, as we came in. It is the *patwari*'s wife. She is in childbirth and therefore, being unclean, must be kept segregated from the rest of the family. She would defile the hut and her presence would displease Ellamma, who might give them all boils."

We walked slowly back to the government resthouse. The police chief was not there, but the official from Lucknow who was in charge of the "Grow More Food" campaign was. He was a plump and smiling man, and he greeted us effusively.

"You have had a talk with the *patwari?* I hoped you would, when I heard you were in the village. He is a grand old man. With his help, we are doing very fine work here—which the Socialists, of course, are trying to destroy. We have the village *panchayat* going nicely, and we have managed to put new life into the co-operative: the membership has recently much increased. I think we have finally got the peasants to understand what we are doing, and to appreciate our work. Yes, they are really co-operating."

He beamed at us, then waved a hand toward the village at large: the 80 wretched mud huts, the gaunt beasts with their ribs showing, the bare little fields, and the moneylender's house and store, with the green parrot in its wicker cage, hanging outside the moneylender's door.

"These little village republics, as I might call them: they have begun to play a most vital role in the great task of nattional reconstruction. In their fight against poverty, ignorance, and disease lies the greatest hope for our future!"

Chandni Chowk, the famous bazaar street in Old Delhi. Many of the shops belong to gold and silver merchants. The car is covered against the pervasive dust, but the spices and foods of the sidewalk vendors are not.

ABOVE: A typical Indian garden party, with musicians, dancers, and numerous servants. BELOW: Nehru and Vinoba Bhave (right, bearded) join in mass spinning demonstration on anniversary of Gandhi's assassination.

Jodhpur: Untouchable women selling wood and dung fuel in the market place, while cows gather in front of temple.

Jodhpur: Sacred cattle lord it in narrow street of old city; fortress rising above.

ABOVE: Mud, mud, mud ever where in northern India and this typical unsanitary village the Sind, Pakistan. Here mud hu are straw-covered to withstand rai which left pools in the foregroun LEFT: Primitive winnowing wi the wind. Landscape is characte istic of vast central plain ne Delhi.

OVE: Wooden plow is almost universal. Village in the background, ilt of mud bricks locally made, is a slight rise to escape floods—haps. RIGHT: A somewhat larger ngali village near Calcutta which asts a temple. Huts are mud and iw; notice erosion in foreground.

WOMEN OF INDIA

ABOVE LEFT: A tribeswoman from northern mountains. ABOVE RIGHT: An untouchable laden with silver jewelry, which is the family bank. BELOW LEFT: A Kashmir woman resting at the roadside in her large robe. BELOW RIGHT: Near Jaipur a Rajput beauty, inured to hard work, can carry great weight on her head.

VISIBLE FROM THE ALLEYS OF BOMBAY

ABOVE: A silver merchant and his wares. BELOW: A small native restaurant; kitchen borders the alley so that prospective customers need no menu.

Pathetic escapes from the drabness of life. LEFT: In Benares a primitive hand-turned Ferris wheel, and a festival at the temple in background. BELOW: A Jain procession in a Punjab town. Bullocks in silver harness draw a silver cart containing Jain deity, in honor of woman who fasted for six days.

Bathing ghats stretch for great distances along the Ganges at Benares. Buildings are temples and hostels charitably provided by maharajas for their pilgrims. The devout drink the filthy water as well as bathe in it; for reasons unknown, its microbes die in 24 hours. Tin sheds are for women bathers, although many manage to change wet for dry saris modestly in the open.

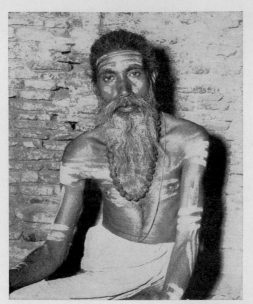

BENARES

LEFT: A pilgrim with yellow caste marks.
BELOW: A narrow street in old city,
which thrives on pilgrims' purchases.
Cows roam at will, and trade hums in the
small shops raised above street level.

ABOVE: A Hindu holy man, head buried in sand, attracts pilgrims come to bathe in the Ganges. He is supposed to have discarded all earthly desires and possessions, but each hour he raises his head to rest and collect coins from the begging-bowl at his side. BELOW: Hindu holy men parading along the Ganges; they have renounced all possessions including clothes.

BOMBAY: TRACES OF THE BRITISH RAJ

ABOVE: The decline of Victorian splendor (modified for the Indian climate) in this downtown scene. The upper sign reads: "Great Punjab Hotel"; the lower, more recent sign: "Great Punjab Lodging and Rooming House." LEFT: A once British, now native street in the business district

Entrance to the great temple at Madura. Its representations of Hindu gods and goddesses are well preserved. At right, lowest level, is many-armed Vishnu, the Preserver god; at left is Ganesh, the elephant-god, symbol of worldly wisdom.

ABOVE: Moslems at prayer at the Jamma Masjid mosque, Old Delhi. LEFT: Cattle feeding undisturbed on refuse in Clive Street, in the financial district of Calcutta.

ABOVE: A student health worker says good-by to a poor family in New Delhi after teaching them modern baby care. But the handprints remain on the wall to protect the child from evil. BELOW: A candidate electioneering on the broad, leafy streets of British-built New Delhi. The camel, easily recognized by illiterate constituents, is his election symbol.

ABOVE: The basket is universally used for bulk carrying where even wheelbarrows are a luxury. Here women carry salt from an open mine in Baroda. BELOW: Bakshi Gulam Mohammed, Prime Minister of Jammu and Kashmir, watches children marching in his honor at village not far from Srinagar.

VI

BENARES: HOLY INDIA

Brahmins rule Benares still. KIPLING

ALL DEVOUT Hindus hope to die in Benares and have their
ashes cast into the sacred Ganges.

I entered Benares with Rudyard Jack, to whom I had
written from Lucknow. We drove into the city along a dusty
road crowded with pilgrims. One man was walking behind a
cow and was holding the animal's tail. He had killed a cow
by accident and was making a public show of his remorse.
"Killing a cow is held to be as great a sin as killing a Brahmin,"
Rud explained; "for cows and Brahmin were created on the
same day."

Rud was thinner than when I had last seen him in Delhi.
He told me ruefully he had had a bad go of dysentery. But his
pale blue eyes, under the sandy lashes, were as alert and
friendly as I recalled them. He was studying at the Hindu
University in Benares. He had shaved his head because of the
heat, so that his reddish hair was only a stubble, and he wore
a loose white shirt and leather sandals in the Indian fashion.
This and his shaven head ought to have made him look like a
Brahmin or a Buddhist priest. Instead, his freckled cheekbones
and blue eyes made him look more American than ever. Altogether he was a queer figure to find in Benares.

I told him so, and he grinned. "I don't pose to be a swami
or a guru, though some of the foreigners who come to study

151

at Benares seem to tend that way. But I'm learning a great deal, and in spite of dysentery and other discomforts I'm really enjoying myself. I don't propose to spend much more time here, though. Benares is a place one can have enough of."

The sun blazed in a blue sky that shouted for the relief of monsoon clouds; but Benares itself was under a pall of smoke, from the burning ghats where the corpses were cremated. Out of the smoke there loomed gilded *sikharas*, the conical pinnacles of Hindu temples; and there was a constant sound of bells and temple gongs.

The Ganges was crowded with bathers and boats. Broad flights of steps descended steeply to the water's edge past the flanks of riverside palaces, like tributaries of stone. On the way down I counted 17 *lingams*. All were monuments to Shiva and fecundity; for the *lingam* is the penis of the god. Some were of smooth-polished stone, others were badly weathered and eroded. But only the rankest imagination could have found them obscene. Stubby pillars with rounded tops, they looked like pillarboxes: one instinctively examined them for the slit through which to drop letters. Anyone who did not know what they were meant to represent would scarcely have given them a second glance. To the outward eye at least, they were as decorous as sundials.

At the foot of the steps bathers stood waist-deep in the muddy water of the river, which was the color of bad coffee and which smelled of bilge. The bathers plunged their heads under the surface, rinsed their mouths, gargled, and spat. On the lowest flight of steps great masses of Hindus were grouped. The men wore dhotis, or only simple loincloths. The women wore ankle-length white dresses and had cowls over their heads. All were barefoot. Some had spread carpets to sit on, and rested in the shade of huge straw umbrellas, for the day was very hot. Most of them seemed to have come in family groups. Infants crawled and gurgled on the carpets. Small boys in white shirts and knee-length pants and small girls with swinging, glossy

black pigtails chased one another merrily up and down the
steps and round the *lingams*. Everyone looked cheerful. For
these families, at any rate, an afternoon beside the Ganges was
the equivalent of a day at the seaside. For the genuine pilgrims, there were the temples, and for the mourners, the burning ghats.

Rud proposed to hire a boat and go for a row on the sacred
river. The boat was a gondola-like affair, with a canopy, red
side-curtains, and dirty cushions. The boatmen wore loincloths
and had a professional air. The Indian families at the water's
edge politely made way for us, and we gingerly embarked. The
boatmen pushed away from the bank, and poled the boat
slowly into midstream. But for the *lingams* and the loincloths,
we might have been in Venice.

Leisurely, Benares unfurled its four-mile riverfront for our
inspection. It was an astonishing sight. Behind a forest of tall,
thin bamboo poles fringing the river's edge, and a shifting
curtain of thin blue smoke from the burning ghats, great walls
of crumbling stone reared up like sheer cliffs. These were the
walls of the eighteenth-century palaces of the Mahratta princes.
Their tops formed a serrated skyline of turrets and towers,
interspersed with clusters of slender minarets, like exclamation
marks. At some places gaping holes had been torn in this fantastic stone façade, showing where the Ganges, rising in flood,
had torn away entire palaces and temples, like teeth wrenched
from a jaw. But these devastations of nature merely heightened
the effect of ruined grandeur. Behind its shifting curtain of
corpse-smoke Benares was a holy city under a burning sun, like
something seen in the fever of a delirium-haunted dream.

The tiers of steps transformed the riverfront into a vast amphitheater. And the amphitheater was crowded. The day was
not an especially holy one. There was no lunar or solar eclipse,
or any of the other phenomena that the great *melas* are held
to celebrate. But stretched along all the four miles of riverfront, there must have been at least a million people. They

were massed thickly on the broad steps, on the stone platforms of the bathing ghats, under the straw umbrellas that sprouted like giant mushrooms on the stone terraces at the water's edge. And the river was full of the bobbing heads and brown bodies of the bathers, swimming from the bank or from boats.

Every tier and terrace had its rows of *lingams*, and its trumpeting elephants, its bulls, and its placid sacred cows, carved in stone or cast in brass. On one ghat there towered an idol with two sets of arms. One hand held a trident, a second a flower, and a third a club; the fourth hand was empty, but was thrust out toward the river, the palm uplifted. Another ghat was dominated by a figure representing Durga, one of Shiva's wives: she had ten arms. Sprawled on its back over a whole flight of steps was the huge clay figure of one of the legendary Pandava brothers. The idol was painted, and had splendid curving black mustaches, arching black eyebrows, and great black astonished eyes. Stretched there with outflung arms, the figure had a look of comically dismayed surprise, like a man who has fallen down and finds he cannot get up again.

Meanwhile, from the 1500 temples of the city there came all the time the solemn booming of gongs, the clanging and tolling of innumerable bells, borne to us on the sullen, smoke-laden air.

We went ashore at the Manikarnika ghat. There were many *sati* stones, commemorating the fiery deaths of pious Hindu widows. Near by, boats with furled sails rocked lazily on the muddy stream, in which people were washing clothes or collecting water for cooking. On the brick-laid surface of the burning ghat, several corpses lay stiffly stretched across twisted branches and boughs, ready for cremation. The bodies were tightly swathed in white or red cotton shrouds. Most of the faces were covered. Wrapped in their cotton cocoons, the heads seemed unnaturally large and round, like footballs. Here and there a naked foot protruded rigidly, as if its owner were a sleeper who had been laid on a bed that was too short.

Children, with tangled black hair and running noses, paused in their play to look curiously at the bodies. Grownups walked past without a second glance, busy with their own affairs. The whole scene had a casual air.

A small girl approached the corpse of an old woman whose head was uncovered, and peered closely and inquisitively into the aged face, whose jaws were locked in a death-grin. A man called impatiently to the child, who obediently ran after him and accepted his hand. The man and the child walked off.

"Some children love to watch the cremations," Rud said. "The skull is usually the last thing to be burned. Sometimes it collapses with a loud pop, like a balloon bursting. When that happens, the children clap their hands."

We walked from the ghat to the near-by Charanpaduka, to inspect the miraculously preserved footprints of Vishnu: they are visible, in marble, on top of a stone pedestal. A few high-born families have the privilege of being cremated at the Charanpaduka instead of on the ghat.

Higher up the steps from the Charanpaduka, pilgrims to Benares were filing patiently into the Siddha Vinayak, the temple to Ganesh. They had to queue up to receive the certificates which testified that they had not only visited the sacred city but had completed the 36-mile circuit of it, which is called the Panch Kosi. It takes six full days to go round the circuit, for many temples and shrines have to be visited on the way. Those who make the trip are automatically absolved of all sins, and are born into a higher caste in their next incarnation; while those who are fortunate enough actually to die within the magic crescent of the Panch Kosi are not reborn at all, but become one with Brahma. Given this belief, it is not difficult to understand why many aged people make the pilgrimage to Benares, and linger hopefully along the Panch Kosi. Inside the temple the pilgrims who had received their certificates were performing *puja* before the elephant god, whose trunk is made of silver.

We walked on and found ourselves in an area of narrow lanes linking the ghats. The lanes were so narrow that even the most intrepid of tonga drivers could not have maneuvered his vehicle into them. But this did not deter the cyclists, who whizzed up and down the crowded lanes with a wild shrilling of bicycle bells, and who shot round corners and charged straight at the pedestrians that blocked their path in a solid mass. Nobody paid the slightest attention to them or seemed to make way for them; but somehow they got through and disappeared in the crowd, still briskly ringing their bells.

The lanes were crammed with little stores and overhung with balconies that almost touched. Shops and houses were painted a deep, dark red, and on the crimson dusky walls were outlined the figures of bulls, gods, monkeys, warriors, priests, and holy men in various attitudes of profound meditation. The sharp angle of a building sprouted a winged figure with flowing hair. From the top of another, sharply and fleetingly outlined against a patch of glimpsed blue sky, the monkey god extended his paws. The pavement and sidewalks were painted with gaudy yellow flowers and realistically hissing red cobras. Amid this startling profusion of decorative art the crowds went placidly about their business, in a dense but orderly swarm, like bees in an ornate hive.

Coppersmiths hammered and blew. Woodworkers made lacquered birds. Giant wooden looms clacked, weaving rich brocaded silks. A Brahmin priest in an orange robe strode past, looking neither to right nor left. Two sharp white teeth protruded over his lower lip and the whites of his eyes showed horribly: he seemed to be in some sort of walking religious trance. Nobody heeded him. Sacred white cows shouldered their way ponderously through the throng, occasionally pausing to put down their heads and lick rice from the bowls of uncomplaining beggars. And all the while, the trick cyclists continued to shoot round sharp corners like bullets, violently ringing their bells and swerving wildly to avoid collisions by a hairbreadth.

A crowd had gathered at the open door of a temple that was no bigger than a wayside booth. They gaped at what lay inside: a freakish five-legged calf, plainly regarded as being especially holy.

Outside another temple confectioners were selling sugar birds. The bird Garuda is the steed of Vishnu, who conferred immortality on it after Garuda stole the moon. On the way to the moon (which it concealed under its wing) Garuda passed a lake where a tortoise 80 miles long was fighting an elephant twice its size. Garuda seized the tortoise in one claw and the elephant in the other, and flew with them to a tree 800 miles tall, where it ate them both.

In the temple to Garuda a priest stood in front of a stone idol with a silver face and four sets of arms, waving a peacock fan to drive off evil spirits. In his other hand the priest meaningfully held out toward visitors a coconut shell for receiving alms.

"Had enough?" Rud inquired pleasantly.

I was streaming with perspiration, footsore, plagued by clamoring beggars, deafened by the continuous clang of bells and din of gongs: dazed by all we had seen. I said I thought I had had enough for one day.

"If we go along here," Rud said, "I think we can get hold of a tonga. . . ."

Next day Rud was engaged elsewhere. I rambled alone through the streets and lanes of the sacred city, revisiting the ghats and inspecting the Temple of the Moon, which claims to be able to cure all diseases. I saw women praying to Shiva's *lingams*, begging for sons, and I watched crowds of orthodox Hindus shove and push one another to get into the Golden Temple to drink water from Shiva's well. The worshippers all wore Shiva's mark—three horizontal lines smeared across the forehead with cow-dung ash—which is a common sight in the Ganges plain.

Benares is Shiva's city, and no one knows how old Benares

is, for when Buddha visited it, in the sixth century before Christ, it was already ancient. Shiva worship is probably the oldest living faith of mankind. It was practiced in Mohenjo-daro, in the Indus valley, perhaps five thousand years ago. When the Aryans invaded India, legend says, the Shiva-worshippers fled from the Indus valley and settled near the Ganges. Shiva haunts graveyards, and is the lord of ghosts. He married Sati, the granddaughter of Brahma. To do him honor, she leaped into the sacrificial flames—and so started a custom that for centuries has been the curse of Hindu women. Another of Shiva's wives is Kali, who likes human sacrifices. A third, Parvati, bore him a son called Ganesh. One day, in a rage, Shiva cut off Ganesh's head. To conciliate Parvati, he sent retainers into the forest with orders to bring back the head of the first living thing they found. They returned with the head of an elephant, and Shiva clapped it on Ganesh's body, so that today Ganesh is the elephant-headed god of the Hindus. Shiva appears to his devotees in the form of a typical Hindu ascetic, his hair matted, and carrying a skull in one hand and a begging-bowl in the other. The followers of Shiva smear themselves with cow-dung ash, and their holiest men lie on beds of nails, hang themselves upside down from trees, and walk until they drop dead.

The Brahmins ruled Benares until India was conquered by the Moslems. The Moguls were men of the Renaissance who aped European monarchs and built imitations of Versailles. But there continued to exist a vast, turbulent Hindu under-world of yogis and priests, idols and castes. The worshippers of Shiva survived the British. And it seemed to me conceivable that they might survive India's contemporary ruling caste of left-wing intellectuals. Walking through the crowded streets of Benares and listening to the tolling bells of its 1500 temples, it occurred to me that the confident planners in New Delhi had not yet really come to grips with the Hindu mind.

"You must meet Pandit Appasamy," Rud said. "I'll introduce you to him. He's an authority on the Hindu religion, and also he's a big shot in the Hindu *Mahasabha*. I think you'll find him an interesting man."

The Hindu *Mahasabha* was one of India's two right-wing Hindu political parties, the other being the *Jan Sangh*. I had read their manifestoes, which seemed to me to be virtually identical. They bitterly opposed the Congress Party, and particularly Nehru, whom they regarded as an enemy of Hinduism because of his attacks on the caste system. They had had very little time for Gandhi either. The man who assassinated Gandhi was said to have been a fanatical member of the *Jan Sangh*; and both the *Jan Sangh* and the Hindu *Mahasabha* were reputed to be very strong in Nagpur, where a crazed rickshaw-puller had recently tried to stab Nehru.

We drove out along the Durga Kund road, past the Vizianagram Palace. Pandit Appasamy's house was a surprise. He might be a Hindu mystic, but he was no ascetic, for his home was amply furnished in a modern Western style. He was a slim brown man, very good-looking, with the cultured affability of a faculty dean in some American midwestern university. He wore a white turban and a dhoti; but, after greeting us, he sank gracefully into a deep leather armchair. Presently a maid brought in tea, which was served in thin porcelain cups and was poured from a silver teapot.

"Westerners are frequently baffled by Benares," said Pandit Appasamy. He spoke pleasantly modulated English, and made small gestures with his well-manicured hands. "Baffled: and also disconcerted. They are confused by all the gods and goddesses; and, besides, they find the whole place rather smelly!" He gave a jolly laugh. "What they therefore frequently overlook is that Hinduism is a very old and also a very sophisticated religion. Hinduism is full of subtleties and profundities. It has nourished great literature and great art; and it contains very great religious truths."

He threw himself back in his chair, and wagged a reproachful finger at us; it was evident that he had not lectured for three years at Oxford University for nothing.

"All those gods and goddesses that distress you Westerners —they are only *symbols*. Symbols of what, you may ask? Well: first of all, of various manifestations of nature. For in the beginning we Hindus were nature-worshippers. There was Surya, the sun god." He quoted. " 'Seven tawny-haired mares draw thy chariot, O dazzling Surya!' And there were the rain gods." He smiled, and with considerable relish quoted again. " 'They press the clouds like a breast, they milk amid the roar of the thunderbolt!'

"And Shiva—Shiva was the god of both creation *and* destruction."

Pandit Appasamy paused, and raised a quizzical eyebrow, like a lecturer who waits to see if there are any really bright pupils in the class. He plainly wanted us to tell him what Shiva represented.

I did so. We were, after all, drinking the Pandit's very excellent tea.

"Shiva was the monsoon!" I cried excitedly.

Pandit Appasamy smiled his approval.

"Just so! Shiva was the Monsoon. And in *Bharat* in those days—*Bharat* is what the ancients called our holy land of India, and we hope the name will be revived—in *Bharat* there were many lesser gods, with whom we need not trouble ourselves: Kama, the god of love, for example, who was armed with flowery arrows and who rode a parrot. But all these were merely symbols.

"But, as Hindu thought developed, they ceased to be simply symbols of crude natural forces. They became—they are today—manifestations of different aspects of Truth." Pandit Appasamy smiled triumphantly, and again shot out a finger at us. "You of the West did not think of that, did you? But wait! The Hindu mind delved still deeper! For human souls also appeared as parts, or aspects, of one universal, divine substance, or Truth—whom we call the Brahma. Yes: the Brahma. With, of course, each soul undergoing countless transmigrations, reincarnations, and so forth.

"It was to meditate on this Truth that the yogis retired to the forests. And after much deep and profound thought, this is what they came up with."

The Pandit leaned forward, and ceased smiling. Impressively, he announced: "Everything that lives, dies; and nothing that dies, dies forever. That is what they came up with."

He shook his head solemnly. "In the 'Mahabharata,' our great epic poem, Krishna says: 'That which is born is sure to die, and that which is dead is sure to be born.' There you have the essence of the Hindu view of life."

I thought of the women praying before the *lingams,* the five-legged calf, and the man who had killed the cow. I also thought about the caste system, and the 50,000,000 untouchables.

"Pandit Appasamy," I said, "which aspect of Truth does the caste system represent?"

"Order," said the Pandit immediately. "Symmetry. Harmony. The caste system, I fully realize, is not appreciated by Westerners. But that is because they have not studied it properly. What has preserved the Hindu way of life through many millennia of vicissitudes? Why are we the oldest civilization on earth? The answer is: the caste system. In that system, every man knows his place, because he is born into it. Lower castes respect higher castes: higher castes respect lower castes. This has been the secret of our immense stability. Destroy the caste system, and you destroy *Bharat.*"

"But suppose,"—I paused delicately—"suppose *you* had been born an untouchable, instead of a Brahmin. Wouldn't you feel the arrangement was rather unfair?"

"Not at all," said the Pandit gravely. "For, by resolutely casting out sin and obeying the Brahmins, an untouchable may himself hope after several reincarnations to become a Brahmin; and a sinful Brahmin risks being reborn as an untouchable."

It appeared to be time to change the subject.

"Turning from religion to politics," I said, "how do you and your friends in the Hindu *Mahasabha* feel about the situation in India today?"

After so urbane a philosophical discourse, I had little hope of getting specific answers. Another few yards of the silken eloquence in which Pandit Appasamy seemed to specialize would, I expected, be unrolled for our admiration. But in India it is always the unexpected that happens.

In a twinkling he was transformed. Urbanity dropped from him like a cloak, and his eyes flashed.

"*Bharat* is still not free!" he cried. "Already the glow of illusory freedom has vanished from the hearts of the people. Under Congress Party misrule, we live amid the reek of corruption. True Hindus are more vilely oppressed than they have ever been before in their history. Nehru and the Congress Party spurn Hindu ideals and the Hindu way of life. They are trying to make *Bharat* a mere carbon copy of the West. Worse! They are traitors. *Bharat* is a living organic whole. It was not shaped by human hands. It has a culture that is one and indivisible, which has flowed down to us in an unbroken stream from the *Vedas*. Yet the Congress Party conspired with the Socialists, the Communists, and the British Imperialists, to cut *Bharat* in pieces to appease the Moslems."

I asked him what his party, the Hindu *Mahasabha*, proposed to do about it.

"The Partition was a crime," he said forcefully. "It must be revoked. A sacred duty lies upon us to protect the cruelly oppressed Hindu minority in Pakistan. First, we must take steps to recover the thousands of Hindu women who were forcibly abducted to Pakistan by Moslem rapists. Then we must work and fight for a reunited India: a revived *Bharat*. There must be undivided allegiance to *Bharat*."

He leaned forward. "In order to achieve this, we must get rid of Nehru's misconceived notion of democracy. It can never inspire the masses; and it gives full scope to the machinations of the Socialists and Communists, to the detriment of the nation.

"Co-operation must take the place of riotous individualism. There must be discipline. Military training will be made compulsory for all young men up to the age of twenty-five. Arms will be given freely to the inhabitants of all areas bordering on Pakistan. We shall resolutely oppose Moslem brutality and trickery, and fight Congress Party persecution. India will be developed as a national home for Hindus, where the sublime qualities of Hinduism can at last find fulfilment. We shall establish a Hindu Raj.

"Sacrifices will have to be made by all. Monopoly capitalism will be curbed. Capital will be compelled to accept the laboring masses as an equal partner. Both will function under the direction of the state. All strikes and lockouts will be forbidden.

"We shall restore the village as the centre of Hindu life. The Hindu system of medicine, Ayurveda, will also be restored. The killing of cows will again be sternly punished as a crime against our religion.

"In time state compulsion will become unnecessary. The state's bureaucratic machinery will be replaced by bands of voluntary workers inspired by the ideal of service to the nation. The free peasants will go cheerfully about their work, gaily singing the Vedas. Thus Bharat will recover its soul, which under Congress Party tyranny it has meantime lost."

I reflected that, between them, the Hindu Mahasabha and the Jan Sangh claimed the political allegiance of some 5,000,000 Indians. That was perhaps not very many, in a country of over 370,000,000 people. But Hitler and Lenin had started with less.

Rud and I got tactfully to our feet, and prepared to take our leave.

bhoodan movement, for distribution to the poor. "Ah, well,"
said Mahalingam cheerfully, "that is more than you Bihar landlords ever gave to Buddha, who asked for land for the same
purpose, and got nothing. But I bet when Vinoba Bhave comes
to inspect your gift, he will find it consists mostly of barren
rock or unusable jungle." In high dudgeon, the landlord moved
into another compartment at the next halt, and Mahalingam
roared with laughter.

Bihar is about the size of Missouri, and its 40,000,000 people
are the poorest in India: poorer even than their 65,000,000
neighbors in adjoining Uttar Pradesh. Bihar has only one crop,
rice, which is sown at the end of the monsoon and harvested
in January. In the intervening six or eight months, the peasants
have literally nothing to do, and when they have sold or eaten
their rice crop, they subsist on onions and peppers. They are
deeply in debt to the village moneylenders, and grievously
oppressed by the landlords, who have a reputation for tough-
ness unusual even in India. Yet Bihar could be rich, for it pro-
duces 35 per cent of the world's mica, and under its granite
skin lie 3,000,000,000 tons of high-quality iron ore. The firm
of Tata has created a modern steel town at Jamshedpur, and
the Nehru Government has vast irrigation schemes for Bihar,
which include two barrages and a dam higher than Boulder.
Meanwhile, however, 82 per cent of the people of Bihar scratch
a sub-living from farm plots.

Mahalingam was a cheerful traveling companion; he explained, with a loud laugh, that his name meant "Big Penis,"
then proceeded to relate the results of his researches into the
government's land reforms.

The government was establishing community-development
schemes, embracing blocks of villages: each village was supposed to have a "multipurpose" worker, and each block a
development officer.

Mahalingam glanced out of the coach window. "You ought
to see an 'unimproved' village, then compare it with an 'im-

proved' one. If you care to break your journey, I could show you both."

We left the train at the next station. With cheerful proficiency, Mahalingam secured a taxi which, though it had admittedly seen better days, had four wheels and was swifter than a tonga; soon we were rattling along a dusty potholed road in aching and blinding heat.

The village to which he took me crouched low on the stony ground, as if to avoid the heat; there were few sheltering trees. It was, however, superior to the village I had visited near Lucknow, for it had five shops, a telegraph office, and, unfortunately as it turned out, a village headman who was the proud possessor of a telephone. He was an anxious-looking man, with rheumy eyes and a stained gray beard, who spoke English with a plaintive Welsh accent.

"This is not a good village to see," he complained. "We are not yet in a development scheme. You should go to the improved village. Sri Sewa is there today; he is the development officer. There is nothing to see here."

Mahalingam, however, was equal to the occasion. The taxi-driver, hitherto silent, revealed that his wife's brother lived in this village, and offered to take us to him. Soon we were talking earnestly to a typical, if "unimproved," tenant-farmer of Bihar.

A friendly but painfully unloquacious man, he had, after all, little to tell us. He grew rice, but the landlord got most of it, and the village moneylender most of the rest. The village land was cut up into tiny strips—one landlord claimed no fewer than 200 of those pocket-handkerchief-size patches—and there was a great deal of confused litigation over who owned what.

"But what about the government's land reforms?" Mahalingam demanded. He sat with his thin cotton shirt hanging outside his pants, smoking a cigarette and impatiently rocking one thin knee, like a vengeful prosecuting-lawyer. "Hasn't the government offered more land to you people yet? Hasn't it fixed ceilings on land, so the landlords must surrender some of theirs to the tenants and the landless laborers?"

Zamindars, the taxi-driver's wife's brother meekly replied, had not yet been abolished in Bihar: even when they were, they would have to be paid compensation for the "surplus" land, after ceilings had been placed on the land they could retain. The tenants who wanted to acquire land would have to pay either the market value of the land, or fifteen times their present rent, whichever was less.

"Compensation already paid to *zamindars* in the five states where landlords have been abolished has come to over $1,000,000,000," Mahalingam explained to me. He turned back to the tenant-farmer. "Are you going to buy some land, then, when the time comes?"

The man shrugged. "How can I afford to do that?" His total income from the five acres he worked as a tenant was only $154 a year; and he owed the moneylender $70, a sum which remained constant from year to year, for he was always having to reborrow.

"Now we shall go and visit the 'improved' village," Mahalingam said.

When we arrived there, it was evident that our visit came as no surprise. The villagers indeed were waiting to greet us, patiently lined up in the village street in the broiling heat. When our taxi appeared, they even raised a feeble cheer. As soon as the taxi halted, a man sprang forward to open its door for us. "My name is Sewa." He briskly gave us a *namasthe* greeting. "I am the development officer. I shall be very happy to show you everything. We are rather proud of our work here. Here we are really building up the new India."

I had not seen this particular set of smooth jowls before. But I had seen plenty of jowls like them; also the well-laundered shirt of the right kind of khaddar cloth; also the carefully adjusted dhoti. Here was a professionally devout Gandhian, a true "Congress wallah."

Inexorably, we were taken in hand; with practiced efficiency, we were conducted round. We passed along a narrow lane lined with new brick cottages, through whose open doors we glimpsed infants suspended from the rafters in swinging wicker baskets. Everything was neat and tidy; even the usual *pi* dogs and goats had been, temporarily, cleared out of sight, though we could hear the dogs' frustrated barking from behind the cottages. "You will observe," said our guide, "that this little lane has been *paved*. Yes; paved! Truly a revolution in the lives of those poor people." It was true: down the middle of the lane, where the sewage normally ran, a fresh line of bricks had been rather erratically laid. From their doorways the villagers respectfully peered and, when they caught the development officer's eye, bowed.

We were swept on to the village's new school. As we approached it, the fresh clear voices of children poured, not very spontaneously, through the open windows. Teachers bowed and smiled. The well-drilled children rose smiling from behind their desks. One by one, they were picked out to sing for us carefully rehearsed songs; one boy also made what was evidently a set speech prepared for such occasions. He was a thin little boy, with large, sad eyes, and he was painfully polite. As soon as he had finished, small girls rushed forward with ready-made garlands to hang round our necks.

Only when we visited the hot tiny office of the village's "multipurpose" worker did the routine break down. The multipurpose worker was a very old man, and he had evidently been dragooned into the job, without quite understanding what he was taking on. He still did not understand it. He produced, with pathetic eagerness, several large, crayon-colored charts which purported to show how far the village had advanced, in hygiene and in farm techniques, since its "improvement" had begun. But the charts made little sense, for the figures that they contained contradicted one another in several instances. When Mahalingam pointed this out, Mr. Sewa fidgeted, and the old man gaped, with his jaw dropping, and then firmly repeated his mechanical exposition.

"But how," Mahalingam insisted, "can the amount of land you say has been brought under irrigation be greater than the amount that you say is irrigable?"

The old man blinked his eyes, and looked as if he were about to weep.

"There may have been some slight error in the returns," said Mr. Sewa smoothly. "The land records that we took over from the British were not, I'm afraid, in all cases very accurate. This project covers 10 villages altogether, and each village has some 600 people. The work is rather new to him, and most of the peasants are of course illiterate." He swept us out, leaving the unfortunate multipurpose worker brooding over his charts, but not before casting at him an ugly look which boded ill for his future.

On the way back, however, Mr. Sewa recovered his spirits. Had we not liked the children's singing? Was not the school a great achievement? "What you have seen is just a little bit of India's Plan," Mr. Sewa cried. "The plan is to set free the creative energies of the people so that they may by their own efforts build a better life. . . ." The speech rolled smoothly on. "Creation of popular representative organs . . . multipurpose co-operative societies . . . complementing the machinery of government by community efforts based on self-help . . ." Then we were at the taxi, and Mr Sewa, deciding that *namasthe* was not enough, was shaking hands. "I hope you will not be too hard on us; there is so much to do, and so few qualified people to do it; but we have really begun to build. . . ." He was begging for a word of praise, a pat on the back.

Suddenly I thought of Mr. Sewa as, probably, the only man for miles who read a book, or even a newspaper. Once, certainly, he had been, not a smooth-spoken Congress wallah, but an idealistic young man, his head stuffed with John Stuart Mill, dreaming of a great Indian awakening. And I wondered what I would do, if I were to be put in charge of a community-development project and instructed to change the lives of some 6,000 people, who were only one small part of 300,000,000 people whose lives it was proposed to change. Shaking hands, I said: "You have a tremendous problem; I certainly hope you will succeed in building a new India." Then we drove away, leaving him standing there, in his khaddar shirt and his neatly tucked dhoti.

As we bumped our way back to the railroad station, Mahalingam said: "Nehru claims there are 100,000,000 peasants already included in community-development projects. But half the villagers don't know the name of their 'multipurpose village-level worker,' and about a third of them don't even know they are supposed to be living in a project area. All that most of the peasants know is that suddenly they are being taxed more; this is called a 'voluntary contribution.' The development officer is usually just the tax collector under another title. The Community Projects Administration claims that thousands of acres of lands have been 'consolidated' or 'reclaimed,' and that new roads are being made and wells are being dug. But compulsory consolidation of holdings is called 'public participation,' and the road-making and the well-sinking have become command performances."

"Well, what's the solution?" I demanded.

"Ah!" said Mahalingam, grinning. "You'll have to ask the Socialists that. You'll find them in Gaya."

Stalin had a useful start. Asoka Mehta

Gaya. The place is named after a demon, so holy that all who saw or touched him were immediately admitted to union with Brahma. But it is also where the Buddha meditated and preached under a fig tree. A few yards from the famous tree, there is a temple where Hindu monks worship an image of the Buddha—as an incarnation of Vishnu.

But I had come to Gaya to see the Indian Socialists at work. Their choice of Gaya as the place to hold their annual party conference was unfortunate. Gaya is normally too hot even for Indians' comfort. An influx of politicians in addition to the usual throngs of pilgrims threw an intolerable strain on the little town's totally inadequate resources of drinking water and sanitation. Gaya panted like a suffering beast. Its mean, narrow streets were packed to suffocation with animals and humans. The oxen that wearily pulled the creaking carts were ghastly caricatures of skin and bone, and the people all seemed to be dressed in dirty rags. Everything and everyone smelled strongly of perspiration. The thermometer was stuck at 112 degrees F., for the temperature did not vary even between high noon and midnight. It was a mockery to try to rest, for going to bed simply meant lying wide awake in darkness on a charpoy, stark naked, while sweat oozed out of every pore. When in the morning you drew aside a curtain, or opened a door, the new day's hot breath rasped on your skin. It was like living permanently in a stokehole. People fell down in the street, with heatstroke, as if they had been poleaxed. Dysentery was rife, and there were grave rumors of cholera. After a day and a night or two, one's vision became blurred and blood-red, one's brain felt like a sponge that was being inexorably squeezed, and the hot walls of panic-breeding claustrophobia began closing in.

This unhappy atmosphere strongly tinged the Socialists' conference. The main meetings were being held in a very large tent, which irresistibly recalled the more raucous sounds and rankest smells of the circus. The leaders were grouped on a platform, where they squatted on sweat-stained mattresses. They had left off their shoes, and wore white cotton Gandhi caps and thin white cotton tunics. This is the customary wear of all Indian politicians, but the Socialists somehow managed to look aggressively proletarian; perhaps because they were all

lean and even cadaverous men, like hungry Cassiuses. Their
state of mind matched their appearance, for there was no doubt
that they regarded Nehru, with great bitterness, as a usurping
Caesar. They proclaimed as much, at considerable length, into
the platform microphones whose fat black cables trailed in
confusion across the mattresses, getting in the way of the
speakers' bare feet. The big tent reverberated with their tinny
protests and accusations. Squatting below the platform, on the
bare ground or on little straw mats, the Socialist groundlings
stoically endured the heat, and frequently applauded their
leaders. They looked even hungrier than the men who harangued them, for they seemed to be mostly of student age:
lean and tattered representatives of the millions of semiedu-
cated young men whom India's schools and colleges tirelessly
turn out, year after year, but who cannot find jobs.

"In close liaison with the landlords and moneylenders," a
Socialist speaker bawled, "the Congress Party led by Jawaharlal
Nehru is circumscribing the liberties of India, jeopardizing
democracy, shooting down the workers and systematically pul-
verizing all its opponents!"

Out of the loudspeakers, unnaturally magnified, poured the
vitriolic words; down below the platform, knees rocked in an
agony of concentration, heads nodded rapidly, and hands
smacked together in approval.

According to the Socialists, no fewer than 17,000 "martyrs"
were currently undergoing severe hardships in the Nehru Government's jails for having opposed the Congress Party's capitalist dictatorship and its attempts to suppress the workers and
peasants. In the eyes of the Socialists, Nehru had clearly replaced the British Raj as the source and mainspring of all the
evils afflicting Mother India. In the fetid atmosphere of Gaya,
and with all this fevered oratory besieging one's ears and one's
heat-squeezed brain, it was very difficult to take other than the
gloomiest possible view of Mother India's future.

Unhappily it rapidly became clear that the Socialists were
far from being united even among themselves. A severe schism

173

existed, between the Praja Socialists assembled at Gaya, and another group of Socialists, led by Ram Manohar Lohia, who had taken themselves out of the Socialist Party and gone off to Hyderabad to found a new, purified Socialist Party of their own. The Praja Socialists denounced the Lohia Socialists as undisciplined deviationists; the Lohia Socialists denounced the Praja Socialists as persons who were simply out for personal power and who did not really have the interests of the masses at heart. Both continued to attack the Congress Party as the deadly foe of all Socialists, if not of all mankind.

The most intelligent of the Indian Socialists seemed to me to be Asoka Mehta. He was a slight and sensitive man, who wore a beard which made him look like Jesus Christ, and who had the manners and accent of a Cambridge or Oxford don. "South and East Asia," he said in his precise, very English voice, "represent the ultimate cesspool of poverty, where wants are truly raw." In Gaya, this appeared to me to be only too true. "In the final analysis," Mehta continued, "factories cannot work if the men in them starve. And that is where our true quarrel with Nehru lies. Nehru, like Stalin, wants a form of Socialism that will put all the emphasis on the rapid creation of heavy industry: on the multiplication of factories. But in India this cannot be achieved without totally estranging the peasant; for who is to pay for the building of the factories, except the peasant, who manifestly can't afford to let them be built out of his sweat? Stalin had a useful start. Even as far back as 1913, Russia's steel output was over 4,000,000 tons a year, and her population was only a third of what ours is now. India's steel production today is barely more than a quarter of Russia's in 1913.

"Nevertheless," Mehta pointed out, "Stalin only achieved 'industrialization' by ruthlessly squeezing the Russian peasants. How does India hope to attain industrialization, except by a similar squeeze? Even China's task is easier, for she is leaning heavily on Russia. As for Yugoslavia—didn't Tito make his break with Stalin precisely because he shrank from squeezing his peasants to the point that Stalin demanded? Just because of this historic refusal, there's at least a chance of Yugoslavia becoming an interesting example of a Marxian mutation. But Nehru, who goes about saying that Marxism is obsolete, is preparing to tie the Indian peasant to the Stalinist flogging-machine. Why? Because he wants to have more factories; wants India to imitate Russia, to imitate the West. But for Asian countries to achieve the visage of Russia, or of the industrialized West, is just not possible, except at a price which is far too high to pay—a political dictatorship that will bend the peasant to make him fit the shape of the economic Plan, instead of adjusting the shape of our planning to meet the needs of the peasant.

"By quite modest means, India could increase its food output by 50 per cent in 20 years. Wouldn't that mean a great increase in the happiness of Indians—of the Indian people? I don't oppose small industries, which mean giving employment to the people, not squeezing them. But we cannot imitate either industrialized Russia or the industrialized West. Nehru is in love with his Five Year Plans; with gigantism. To push his plans through, he will either have to borrow massively from abroad—which means opening India's doors either to Soviet domination or to a new Western colonialism —or he will have to squeeze the necessary capital out of the peasants. There is no other way. And, if he tries squeezing the peasants, they will resist, and then he will have to become a dictator, like Stalin."

According to another Indian Socialist, Jaya Prakash Narayan, Nehru had become a Stalin-type dictator already. In an impassioned speech, Narayan attacked Nehru for developing a "cult of personality" around himself, and accused him of "shooting down more Indian workers than the British ever did."

It was strange to hear those bitter charges being hurtled at Nehru by Narayan; for many Indians had long supposed

Narayan to be Nehru's most likely successor. A tall and strikingly handsome man, with gray eyes and a formidable jaw, Narayan was the son of a poor peasant. He had worked his passage to California and spent eight years in the United States, where he studied economics and science at five universities (including Berkeley and Wisconsin) while earning his keep by working as fruit-packer, farm-laborer, waiter, and factory-hand. He returned to India unconverted to capitalism and dedicated to Socialism, and in 1932 was jailed by the British. Out of prison, he formed a railroad workers' union, with a million members, and launched the Indian Socialist Party. The British jailed him again in 1939, for they regarded him as a desperate agitator. He went on a 51-day hunger strike, then escaped from prison by scaling a 20-foot wall, and hid in the jungles. In 1946 after having led his Socialists into the Congress Party, he led them out again and, after organizing a big rail strike, was chiefly responsible for gaining 11,000,000 votes for the Socialists in free India's first elections.

In spite of his vigorous appearance, he suffered severely from anemia and diabetes, and he disliked the Communists as much as he had come to loathe the Congress Party. Referring to the Communists, he passionately declared: "We must hurry, or else those who believe in violence will step to power over our dead bodies." Nevertheless, he dismayed the Socialists by suddenly quitting the party, and dedicating himself to Vinoba Bhave's *bhoodan*, or land-gift, movement.

Narayan stood out strikingly amid his Socialist comrades, for his tall figure was swathed in white cotton garments that seem to have been tailored almost to a Dior design. But, despite his new-found dedication to the strictly nonviolent methods of Gandhism, he appeared to be even more bitter about Nehru than they. "One can only hope," he said, with a handsome sneer, "that the 'socialist pattern' about which Nehru now talks will end the paradox of the few idle rich wallowing in luxury, while the masses sweat for a loaf of bread." The sneer eloquently indicated that, in fact, he entertained no such hope.

Yet Narayan, in his Dior-like dhoti, did not give the impression
of being one with the sweating masses. And, when the party
leaders rather pathetically appealed to him to return to the
fold and do some hard work for the Socialist cause, his answer
was prompt. "It is my irrevocable resolve," he declared solemnly,
"never again to take part in party politics, for my life belongs
to *bhoodan*." Like the Socialists, I could not but feel that this
was a highly unsatisfactory answer. It also appeared to me to
make nonsense of his vigorous onslaughts on Nehru and the
Congress Party, and to greatly weaken his alleged fear of
what the Communists would do to India, if nobody bothered
to fight them. The unhappy, split Socialists, who badly needed
a leader, were presumably as baffled by Narayan as I was.
After further appeals, and more firm refusals, he swept out
of Gaya, in his elegant dhoti, to return to his *ashram*, or
saintly sanctuary, where doubtless he will continue to meditate
in a sneering sort of way on the folly and vanity of all human
beings save Jaya Prakash Narayan.

I was glad to be able to leave Gaya myself—so glad, that I
rashly launched on a long journey by rail and road to Nagpur in
central India: a journey that I was to look back upon with a
considerable degree of horror. Unlike an *ashram*, it afforded
few opportunities for meditation. But one thing was clear in
my mind. For some time to come India would continue to be
ruled by the Congress Party, for the very simple reason that
India showed no signs of producing any alternative to it. In
spite of the undoubted intellectual eminence of one or two of
their leaders, the Socialists could not rule India, for they could
not even agree among themselves. The Communists despite
Nehru's admiration of Russia were unlikely, while Nehru lived,
to be able to do much more than hang on to his coattails, and
the *Jan Sangh* and Hindu *Mahasabha* belonged (one hoped)
to the past rather than the future. But the Congress Party, in
effect, *was* Nehru, so what would happen to it, and to India,
when Nehru was no longer there?

VIII

NAGPUR: CHRIST VERSUS GANESH

We advocate Socialism and cling to caste. NEHRU

The structural basis of Hindu society is caste: if and when caste disappears, Hinduism will also disappear. M. N. SRINIVAS

O N THE railroad platform a woman rested against an iron pillar, breast-feeding an infant. Bells clanged and red-turbaned porters padded about with bare feet. Children begged for annas. The hands of the station clock pointed to fifteen minutes after midnight.

In the compartment two small fat men were undressing and talking in Welsh-English. I caught only snatches of their conversation.

". . . onion-skin for a nosebleed, and . . ."

"*Achya!* That is indeed interesting. But once, I tell you, when I was just about to seat myself on the commode . . ."

The other passenger was a thin man with a shining, bald brown head. He was wrapped in a thin brown shawl and his spectacles had slid to the tip of his long nose.

I had been traveling southwest from Gaya for what seemed days. The roads were bad, the food fly-blown, the water scummy. Everything smelled of sweat, cinders, scorched earth, and cowdung. Hotels were nonexistent and the so-called "resthouses" were rat-ridden and snake-infested. The heat-rotted strings of the charpoys broke and the moldering wood concealed armies

178

of bedbugs. I was sick of unending poverty, the bare squalor of mud huts, and the swarming alleys of fetid towns.

When I awoke it was daylight, and the two small fat men had gone. Big drops of rain crept down the windows of the coach, tracing little rivers in the dust. Everything smelled of wetness.

The thin man gave me a solemn friendly smile. "*Achya!*" he said. "The monsoon."

His name was Vasagam, and he was an inspector of untouchables. The Nehru Government is striving to abolish untouchability. "But this cannot be done simply by issuing an order from Delhi," Vasagam said. "I have been in villages where untouchables may not draw water from the well. On this tour I visited a place where forestry officials were using the untouchables for slave labor."

We left the train at Jubbulpore. The streets were ankle-deep in mud, and gangs of bedraggled men wearing fezes were roving about, shouting menacingly. A tonga drawn by a starving horse took me through the rain to a hotel. Outside its gate a man in dirty rags was boiling eggs. The hotel proprietor had a hooked nose and thin black hair plastered over a sloping skull. "I am a Moslem," he said, "and so are my waiters. They are out taking part in the rioting."

He saw I was puzzled.

"It is over the dog of Lucknow. It was called Mahmud. The Moslems will not tolerate this. There were riots in Lucknow. Now there are riots here. News travels slowly."

I asked if there had been much damage.

"A few Hindu stores destroyed," he said carelessly. "And ten killed; or it may be fifteen. Let me show you the rooms."

The first had a strong smell and no window. The second contained two beds piled on top of each other, several trussed-up carpets, and five lampstands with no lamps. "I do not think this one is quite ready," he said.

I finally settled for a room that had for a bed only a flat

179

wooden board laid on trestles, but which looked comparatively clean.

The dining-room was large and gloomy. I was the only diner. The proprietor brought me four hard-boiled eggs, and I had eaten three of them when a memory began to haunt me. I quietly followed him when he went for bread and my suspicions were confirmed. My supper had come from the man in dirty rags who kept the foodstall at the hotel gate. "The cook has joined the rioting also," the proprietor said.

I went to bed, using a shirt filled with rolled socks for a pillow. But I had hardly stretched out on the wooden board when the hotel exploded into cheerful noise. In adjoining rooms lightswitches were snapped on, furniture was dragged about, people laughed and talked loudly. This went on all night. More people kept arriving and joining in the talk. At half past three in the morning the early risers got ready to leave. Charpoys scraped across stone floors, and water splashed into tin basins. At half past four, I decided I, too, would make an early start. It was still pitch-dark. The hotel proprietor, wearing white cotton pajamas and a fur hat, offered me boiled eggs, which I hastily declined.

A car splashed into the hotel courtyard, and out of it stepped Mr. Vasagam. He greeted me warmly. "I am delighted you are up and about to leave. I am driving toward Nagpur and wondered if you would care to keep me company."

The way to get to know India, I reflected, was to travel on Indian trains and meet the right people.

We left Jubbulpore behind and drove southwest through a dark wet countryside over roads slippery with mud. The headlights showed only heavy rain falling and the gleaming eyes of bullocks. Then the night lifted, and we could see fields and houses, rich, black cotton-growing soil and in the distance, to the south, the fringes of considerable forests.

"Once all this area was thick forest," Mr. Vasagam said, "inhabited by Gonds and other Dravidian tribes. These tribes

still form a fifth of the population of central India, but they
have been gradually pushed into the remnants of the forest.
They are the 'tribals.' "

Mr. Vasagam wished to send a telegram, and we stopped in
a village street outside a mud-walled telegraph office. An Indian
with a red cloth tied round his head offered us hard-boiled
eggs sprinkled with black pepper. I was hungry enough to eat
them. While we breakfasted the man in the red turban told
us about himself. He had traveled widely and spoke French
and Spanish as well as English. He talked wistfully of Paris and
Madrid, like an exile condemned to live out his life in a strange
place. He wore rags and had not shaved for a week. "It is a
great pleasure to me to talk with civilized people once in a
while," he declared. Travel had made him a snob.

Near Nagpur was a village Vasagam wanted to inspect. We
were looking for the resthouse when we were overtaken by a
flaxen-haired young man and a red-haired girl in an ancient
Ford. The young man wore a check shirt and the girl wore
blue jeans. He hailed us in a hearty voice with a midwest accent.
"I am the Reverend Billy Jowitt and this is my wife, Alice."
He addressed himself to me. "Sir, are you in this neck of the
woods on the Lord's behalf?"

When I said I was not, he looked relieved. "Then we still
have this vineyard to ourselves, Alice!" he exclaimed. "Did you
see the Tabernacle, gentlemen, as you came in? It is the little
church we have just finished building unto the Lord. We are
the first pentecostal invasion team to hit this area." He looked
rather defiantly at Vasagam. "We are militant evangelists out
to capture the villages for Christ. Our goal is '600,000 villages
in 10 years.' "

"What do the Brahmins say?" I asked, and the Reverend
Billy Jowitt's brow darkened.

"Did the priests of Baal welcome the messengers of the Lord?
We are here to bathe lost souls in the blood of the Lamb."

At the resthouse we were greeted by an obsequious official.

181

Mr. Vasagam's telegram had been received. Lamps had been lit and rooms freshly swept. Bearers padded about with hot water and towels, and a meal awaited us.

Thin and solemn, his bald head shining and his spectacles sliding down his long nose, Vasagam asked sharp questions. Did the untouchables have access to the village well? Could they freely enter the temple?

He evidently found the official's answers evasive, for he proceeded to issue peremptory orders.

"You tell me the untouchables may enter the temple only on special occasions. Summon them, for I myself will lead them to the temple this very evening."

The village untouchables were summoned by the beating of a drum. The drummer, an untouchable sweeper, was a short man with a grizzled mustache. The drum was large and black, and he walloped it with vigor, producing an awesome booming. The untouchables obeyed the summons, holding aloft bedraggled black umbrellas and looking apprehensive. It was difficult for them to believe that a summons by a government official meant anything but trouble.

Mr. Vasagam had put on a clean white shirt and dhoti. With his thin brown shawl pulled over his head to protect it from the rain, he looked like a taller Gandhi.

"I come to you from the Government of India, which is trying to carry out the reforms promised by Gandhiji," he said gently. "In the new India there are no longer untouchables, or such a thing as untouchability. If you wish to enter the temples, you need not break down their doors, or chase away the priests. No man may try to prevent you. You must send your children to school, and there they will sit freely beside the children of your neighbors. You may use the village well in the same way as others do, and all public places are open to you."

Vasagam led his motley throng of butchers, tanners, and cobblers through the village toward the temple. The street was lined with curious spectators, all holding umbrellas. They showed neither hostility nor enthusiasm. I had no way of knowing what they were thinking. Caste is rooted in Indian village life, but the poverty of the people makes outward signs of class distinction almost impossible. The people who lined the street were barefoot and their simple cotton clothes were little different from the untouchables: even their umbrellas were the same. Vasagam's action was possibly having an earth-shattering effect; or perhaps they were accepting it philosophically as just another bit of the incomprehensible behavior of the new Raj in Delhi.

At the temple the untouchables left their umbrellas outside. Candles lit the dim interior. There was a strong smell of incense. The deities of this village were represented merely by a number of stones, shapeless and of no imposing size. Some were smeared with ocher, and all had garlands of marigolds and halves of coconut shells laid before them. Standing before the crude idols, the untouchables reverently raised their hands to the level of their foreheads, and began to perform *puja*.

A man in an orange robe appeared and cast a garland round Vasagam's neck. He pressed vermilion paste on Vasagam's forehead with his thumb, gabbling in Hindi. The untouchables he ignored.

Outside, the drum began to bang. Obediently, the untouchables filed out of the temple. The procession started back to the village. Vasagam irritably rubbed the mess from his forehead. "That was the temple priest," he said. "He thanked me for the visit and said he would remember me in his prayers." His tone was ironical.

Vasagam led the way to the village restaurant. Wooden benches flanked trestle tables. In a dark cubbyhole at the back, a man squatting on bare heels attended to cooking-pots simmering over a fire laid on the bare earth floor. But the untouchables grinned hugely and, when the food was placed before them, thrust eager fingers into the steaming mixture of rice and scrawny chicken bones. The restaurant-keeper, a fat man with a greasy look, hovered anxiously in the background. When he caught Vasagam's eye he bowed so violently I expected him to topple over on his face.

I found myself seated next the drummer. He turned out to be half-witted but amiable. He had two cows, two wives, and four children all under three years of age. Both his wives were pregnant, he told me proudly. I reflected that there were 50,000,000 untouchables like him.

When the last splinter of chicken bone had been gnawed, the untouchables rose. One of them had slipped out, and now he returned with two garlands. One was draped round Vasagam's neck and the other, to my embarrassment, round mine. Then they shyly gave us *namasthe* and passed out into the rainy darkness, clutching their bedraggled black umbrellas. Vasagam paid the bill. Twenty rupees, or slightly over $4.00, had bought a meal for over 30 persons. On our way back to the resthouse, Vasagam said: "We cannot hope to win 600,000 villages away from untouchability in 10 years; we can only hope to make a start."

Before I fell asleep, I thought of Vasagam, traveling endlessly about the vast, hot countryside of India, scolding backsliding officials and leading untouchables into village temples. He had told me that in the course of his work he traveled 30,000 miles a year. Here, I felt, was at least one truly devoted man.

In the morning it was still raining. We breakfasted frugally off boiled eggs, and departed. On our way through the village we saw a remarkable sight. Outside the restaurant where we had eaten, the ground was strewn with smashed crockery. Inside, down on his hands and knees, the fat restaurant-keeper was frantically scrubbing the floor with milk instead of water. Already scrubbed until they shone, the wooden benches and trestle tables stood on end all round the walls.

I stared, uncomprehending.

"He has broken the cups and plates we used, because the untouchables defiled them," Mr. Vasagam explained. "He is scrubbing his restaurant with milk to purify it, and also by way of penance for having been in contact with untouchables."

I had nothing to say, but Vasagam laughed quietly to himself all the way out of the village.

"We Indians are a remarkable people," he said.

Do mission hospitals stock poisons? OFFICIAL QUESTIONNAIRE ADDRESSED TO CHRISTIAN CHURCHES IN INDIA

THE RAIN was still tumbling down when I reached Nagpur. A shrine to Ganesh had been erected opposite the Anglican cathedral. It was garish with electric lightbulbs, and a wheel of light whirled behind the god's elephant head, like a halo. The worshippers of Ganesh paraded through the streets, led by men who wore tigers' tails and had painted their naked bodies with yellow stripes. There was much chanting and beating of drums.

The state government had set up a commission to investigate the Christian missions. Outside the Nagpur Assembly Hall was a white statue of Queen Victoria. Inside a picture showing Gandhi and Nehru together hung on the wall. There were rows of wooden benches and a scattering of spectators. The members of the commission sat on a raised platform behind a large table. At a side desk a clerk hammered loudly and inexpertly on an ancient typewriter, drowning out the words of the witnesses.

The commission was cross-examining an American missionary. He was a Quaker from Ohio. He had thinning ginger hair and wore a thin white cotton shirt and trousers. The soles of his thin sandals were cracked.

He explained he had been doing mission hospital work in India since 1940. The hospital staff were all Indians.

"But they are all Christians?"

"Yes, they are Christians."

"And the patients: are *they* Christians?"

"No, sir," said the Quaker. "In the villages where we do our work there are no Christians whatever."

"*Achya*, but you try to convert them?"

"No, sir," said the Quaker. "Our duty is to tend the sick. It has never entered my head to try to convert sick men."

"But isn't it true that a mission doctor may offer up a prayer before treating a patient who is seriously ill, even though that patient is a Hindu?"

"Yes, sir," said the man from Ohio. "We do."

"But isn't that," his interrogator asked triumphantly, "an insult to the Hindu's religion?"

He darted a sharp glance at the clerk, who immediately hammered industriously on his typewriter.

A sullen-looking young Indian with a shock of black hair testified that the missionaries in his district had a secret radio transmitter. "It is for broadcasting India's secrets to the foreign powers!" he cried.

Another young man described, with a lecherous leer, how the missionaries abducted Hindu girls for immoral purposes. A third declared Indian Christians were taught to sneer at Indian culture.

At the testimony of a fourth, I pricked up my ears, for he swore solemnly that the missionaries were self-confessed agents of foreign governments, boasting that they were paving the way for India's conquest. "I have heard them say it themselves," he cried. "They call themselves soldiers, and say they are going to capture all the villages." I remembered the brash words of the Reverend Billy Jowitt with his talk of "invasion teams."

The people who filled the wooden benches listened in a sort

186

of perplexed apathy. Most of them were poorly, but neatly dressed, and it suddenly occurred to me they were probably Indian Christians. When the day's proceedings adjourned, they rose and drifted forlornly out into the rain. They were careful not to look at the missionaries.

The Ganesh worshippers were still prancing through the streets. Some were carrying umbrellas. A man was beating monotonously on a drum outside the elephant god's well-lit shrine. The Anglican cathedral was dark and silent.

Next day I called on one of the missionaries. "The modern fakirs of the middle west have discovered India," he said gloomily. "The Gandhi glamor had a lot to do with it. I've noticed that Gandhism seems to attract people with rather odd minds. The roads of India are filled with Jehovah's Witnesses, Holy Rollers, and, if you'll pardon the expression, God knows what. They play into the hands of the Hindu extremists."

Then I called on an Indian Christian minister. He was a large listless man, with dark pouches under his eyes, and big, broken-nailed hands. He invited me on to his veranda, and we sat side by side, looking out at dripping orange trees. His daughter, a plain girl in a black dress, brought us cups of weak tea.

"I was an untouchable and have worked all my life among them," he said. "But recently they have lost interest in the church. Very few come to see me, and my congregation has dwindled to a handful. The young men say they have no use for religion and that everything must be done through politics. Some support the Congress Party and others the Communists, but they are all against the West. They say the church is a fraud, and that it is rooted in colonialism. They have a great admiration for Russia and China."

"There must be many who still seek religion," I said. "Which way do you think they will turn?"

He looked at me with his dark-pouched eyes. "I think they will find a third path."

187

From Nagpur, I planned to fly to Bombay. On the way to the airport I passed a large procession of men and women, led by two priests with shaved heads and wearing saffron robes. There must have been a thousand people, and they looked as if they knew where they were going.

"They are untouchables," my taxi-driver explained. "It is a mass conversion. They have decided to become Buddhists."

The untouchables of Nagpur had found the third path.

IX

BOMBAY: CITY IN FLOOD

Two monsoons are the life of a man. BOMBAY SAYING

I FLEW from Nagpur to Bombay in a little Dakota. A sign in English and Hindi warned the passengers not to smoke, for the plane was not fireproofed. Liquor was not permitted either, for Bombay is a dry state. Presently a pretty Anglo-Indian hostess in a dark blue uniform handed each passenger a cardboard box containing a frozen chicken leg and two hard-boiled eggs. Lunch had been served.

My seat companion was an Indian businessman. He had just come from the Delhi trade fair. India's biggest manufacturing company had devoted part of its fair pavilion to an exhibit pointedly praising private enterprise, in contrast with the "public sector," and had invited a Cabinet Minister to a preview. The Minister promptly ordered the exhibit to be closed down.

"India is now on a Socialist path," said my businessman. "We capitalists are guiltily conscious that in the past we have behaved badly. We must accept Mr. Nehru's goal." He was a fat, froglike man, and he said it with froglike solemnity. I could detect no irony in his tone.

Bombay, almost twice the size of Oregon, is India's largest state, and has 48,000,000 people. It is also the richest state, for it has both the cotton mills and the rich black soil of the cotton-growing areas. We had a bumpy ride, for the monsoon

189

was at its height. The plane flew on shuddering wings through vast, billowing gray clouds. We were still in a gray murk when we began to nose our way down. Then suddenly we were under the clouds and over a great bay, with solid blocks of apartment houses looking out to sea. The glimpsed city heeled away, and we passed over tightly packed rows of shanties. The plane skimmed over those slums and dropped neatly on to a runway of the Bombay city air terminal.

Torrential rain was falling and a taxi-driver in a ragged cotton shirt grabbed my luggage. With a clash of rusty gears, we were off. The taxi plunged into a rutted lane between smoke-blackened houses that were falling apart with damp and woodrot. We raced through a maze of wretched lanes, hitting submerged potholes. Great waves of muddy water broke over us. The taxi's windshield-wipers were not working, but the driver never slackened speed. An elderly man skipped agilely out of the way, and three women ran screaming.

We skirted a vile-smelling swamp and came out on a main highway. Suddenly the world was filled with whizzing cars and charging trucks, hurtling through the monsoon. A train roared past, perilously overhanging the road. It was packed, and white-clad figures also clung on outside.

We whizzed along the rim of the bay. On our right the sands of Chowpatti beach were crowded with people despite the rain. They were carrying placards and banners and flags. "They are taking out a procession against the Portuguese Fascists in Goa," the taxi-driver explained. Farther along the beach two rival meetings had clashed, and people were hitting one another with sticks. "It is the Maharashtrians and the Gujeratis," the taxi-driver said. We passed the new Bombay Secretariat, and he pointed. "Ah, there is more trouble, I think." Ragged young men were fighting with policemen in the courtyard and were heaving stones through the windows. They cheered as the glass crashed. "They are Maharashtrians," the driver said.

He made a startling U-turn and, after ricocheting off a rickshaw, came to an abrupt halt.

"The hotel," he said proudly.

I paid him off with shaking fingers.

Four bellhops escorted me to the elevator and then along a passage to my room. The hotel had an immense cathedral-like roof with plaster ice-caking. But the walls of the passage had succumbed to dinginess and damp, and the lock on the door was broken.

The bathroom contained no soap or towels. The ceiling-fan was loose and made a screeching noise. The cupboards, lined with pages torn from the *Times of India,* smelled hideously of old varnish and new green mold. The floorboards sagged, and a large damp patch spread over one wall. On the back of the door was thumbtacked a notice:

"Persons residing in this hotel are requested to allow any drinking party in their rooms only after satisfying themselves that all persons participating in the drinking are permit-holders of the following classes: (1) special permits to visiting Sovereigns; (2) foreign visitors' permits.

"In the case of health permit-holders, such a drinking is not permissible unless and until the said permit-holder brings his own drink and participates same under his permit.

"A tourist's permit entitles holder to one quart of spirits or three of wine or nine of beer.

"The permit-holder shall not get drunk in any public place."

Having no permit, I went for a walk. The streets were filled with jostling crowds carrying black umbrellas with bamboo handles. The men all wore white shirts without neckties. Hawkers stood under archways, selling ballpoint pens, celluloid combs, nail-scissors, spectacles, keyrings, bottles of hair-oil, bottles of ink, imitation-leather briefcases, plastic cigarette cases, pencils, erasers, notebooks, rubberbands, matchboxes, and betel nuts. People paused to light their cigarettes from smoldering bits of tarry rope obligingly hung outside booths. Beggars whined, and an old man thrust out a bandaged leg fantastically swollen with elephantiasis. A vast sweating warehouse of a bookstore displayed numerous copies of the *Kamasutra*, the Hindu "Art of Love." The book urges newlyweds to bite one another's flesh and leave lotus-shaped marks. Grooms are abjured to bite their beloveds playfully, gently, and in the highest moment of passion reverently: but never lustfully.

The rain became more torrential. A tram that went past with a melancholy clanging of bells seemed to float like a great metal barge, with water lapping it on all sides. To cross the flooded street I removed my shoes and socks and rolled my trousers above the knee. The street was full of similarly minded waders, their hands full of sandals. I bought a pair of black rubber boots and a black umbrella with a bamboo handle.

Jamsetjee Janah had made a dinner appointment with me. He arrived three quarters of an hour late, in the Bombay fashion. "Let us have a drink," he said. I pointed to the notice tacked to my door. "Nonsense!" said Janah, and rang the bell for a bellboy to whom he spoke in Maharashtrian.

"Bombay seems to be having trouble," I said.

"Yes, it is the fault of the Gujeratis. Because they are rich, they think they own Bombay. In fact, Bombay is Maharashtrian. We and the Gujeratis have nothing in common. You foreigners think all Indians are alike but you are wrong. Maharashtrians and Gujeratis speak different languages. We eat meat, they are vegetarians. We are as different from each other as Germans and Frenchmen."

Almost half the 3,000,000 people of Bombay city are Maharashtrians. The Gujeratis are only a third of the remainder. But the Gujeratis are merchants and cotton-mill owners, while most of the Maharashtrians are poor mill workers, living in wretched tenements called *chawls*. The Gujeratis had long been in effective control of Bombay city, but were now being challenged by the Maharashtrian proletariat, led by

Communists and also by a few ambitious Maharashtrians who had become rich.

"At least, you all agree about Goa," I said.

"Certainly," said Janah, with an air of injured surprise. "We are all Indians, aren't we? Goa belongs to India, and the Portuguese must get out. The Goans would have thrown them out already but for this madness of prohibition. The Goans want to be citizens of India instead of slaves of Portugal; but they also want to be able to take a sip of wine when they feel like it. There is no prohibition in Goa. Prohibition in Bombay State was of course a Gujerati idea. It will be the ruin of Bombay. That is why we Maharashtrians must oppose the Gujeratis with all our strength."

There was a knock on the door and an old man with a swollen leg came in. He was the beggar I had seen in the street who had elephantiasis. Janah closed the door, and the old man unwrapped his swollen leg. Taking off the wrappings revealed not a hideously diseased limb but only a wooden one. It was hollow and from it the old man produced a bottle of whisky.

"One must resort to such subterfuges," said Janah. "It is so hard to tell which policemen can be bribed and which can't."

After a while we left the hotel and drove to the Royal Turf Club. Janah had the use of his father's Cadillac and his father's chauffeur. His father was a Maharashtrian industrialist who had started from scratch. Janah was a slim-waisted young man with a silky black mustache that he liked to stroke with a well-manicured finger. He flirted with politics and for a time had been a member of the Bombay Communist Party. But the Communists, he said with scorn, were "low-caste men who have married rich women and go to party meetings in their wives' limousines." Janah quit the party and joined the Committee for the Liberation of Goa.

"Sadenand Dass is dining with us," Janah said, as we sailed along past hurrying shoals of black umbrellas. "I must warn you he is aggressive. He is a brilliant writer but he does not like the West. Actually, he does not like anyone."

The writer was waiting for us, seated at a table and biting his fingernails. He was a squat man with bulging eyes. He wore no necktie, and he sneered at our white jackets.

"Dass wants you to get mad and call him a Communist," Janah said. "Then he will accuse you of McCarthyism. He is very impressed by the Russians."

"I loathe the Russians," said Dass promptly. "But at least they do not arm the Pakistanis to attack India, as America does. They do not ally themselves with the Portuguese Fascists." He folded his arms and glared at me. "Why are the Americans building air bases in Goa? Do they have colonial designs on India?"

"If you do not unfold your arms you will not be able to eat any dinner," Janah told him. "Besides, it is rude."

"I do not mind being rude," Dass said. "I am not bourgeois."

"He is determined to defy the British-club atmosphere," Janah said. "This was where the cream of Bombay white society enjoyed themselves. Indians were not admitted. His blood boils when he thinks of the sahibs."

It was a large dining-room, but there were very few diners. The waiters stood about yawning and inspecting their frayed cuffs. The walls were stained with damp and the tablecloths were not very clean. A creature that was either a large mouse or a small rat skipped out from behind a heavy, old-fashioned sideboard and ran under a table. A waiter flapped at it half-heartedly with his napkin.

"The Russians are barbarians," Dass said suddenly. "I will tell you how I know. I visited Russia with a good-will mission. We were never left alone for an instant. Guided tours here, guided tours there! They also gave us cameras and expensive watches. The Russians are very crude.

"But the worst thing happened in Leningrad. We had a handsome, young woman guide. She appeared sympathetic, and she and I became friendly. One evening I suggested we should slip off by ourselves. She agreed. I was delighted. We dined and strolled in the park. There was a beautiful moon. And then," said Dass dramatically, "I tell you, the mask was torn from the face of Bolshevik Russia, revealing the hideous lack of culture that lies behind it!"

"What happened?" I asked.

"She said if I believed in astrology then Indians must be very backward people."

"I am thirsty," said Janah. "We cannot get anything to drink here but lemonade. Let us go elsewhere."

Dass rose with alacrity.

Janah told the gaudily sashed doorman to call his car. The doorman stood on the step and bawled, but no car came.

"It is that chauffeur," Janah said, half annoyed, half laughing. "He has gone off somewhere—perhaps to attend a party meeting. We shall have to take a taxi."

The obliging doorman produced a very small taxi. In addition to the driver it contained the driver's brother, a thirteen-year-old boy with a witless look.

"We cannot all ride in this," Janah told the driver impatiently. "You must tell your brother to get out."

The driver removed the boy, and we drove off. It was a twenty-minute ride and the driver seemed determined to avoid the slightest bump. We drew up outside a large office building and I had my hand on the door of the taxi when it was opened from the outside by the driver's brother. "I put him in the trunk," the driver explained.

The building seemed deserted but Janah confidently pressed the button for the elevator. At the top floor we stepped into a different atmosphere. From behind closed doors came sounds of gaiety, and a waiter passed us carrying a tray loaded with bottles and glasses.

Janah ordered drinks, and presently we were joined by the younger brother of a Cabinet Minister. The Minister was a

Maharashtrian who was campaigning to take Bombay out of
the control of the Gujeratis. Other people kept dropping in,
and the party grew rapidly.

Someone prophesied there would soon be serious trouble
over Goa. "It is not really an urgent problem," he explained,
"but a diversion is very much needed. After the first flush of
liberty, the Indian masses are disillusioned. They have discovered that as far as their every day life is concerned they are
no better off."

"That is cynical," Janah protested. "Goa must be set free."

"If the Gujeratis can use the Maharashtrians to free it and
kill off some of them in the process, they will be happy to
agree with you," said the Cabinet Minister's younger brother.
He turned to me. "You are Scottish. If an Irish minority controlled Glasgow, would you like it? That is the position in
Bombay."

Janah looked at his watch. "Goan patriots are giving a concert to raise funds for the freedom fighters," he told me. "I
think you should see it."

"I am sure they will strike terror into the hearts of the
Portuguese with their song-and-dance recitals," Dass said sarcastically: he was again in a revolutionary mood.

We drove through the wet streets to a large concert hall.
There were many empty seats. On the stage a number of young
girls were going through the motions of a slow dance and
singing plaintive songs. Slowly churned by large fans, the humid air gave one a sensation of drowning.

When the concert finished everyone applauded politely,
gathered up their umbrellas, and left the hall. Opulent-looking
automobiles were waiting to take most of them home.

"Let us walk," said Janah. He was in an expansive, but
serious mood. "I feel very keenly about the sufferings of the
people in Goa," he said. "They are kept in ignorance and
poverty. Most live wretched existences, always on the verge of
starvation. It's intolerable that such conditions should exist so

close to Bombay. That is why we say Goa must be set free."

Many children were roving about the streets, though it was very late. They went in bands, both boys and girls: furtive little ragged figures, the oldest about ten and the youngest three or four.

"Who are all those children?" I asked.

"They are the slum children of Bombay. There are many thousands of homeless waifs. They beg during the day."

"And at night?"

"I do not know," said Janah, perplexed. "I suppose they sleep somewhere: under railway bridges perhaps; or at the railroad stations. Really, something should be done about it."

"Tell me, Janah," I said. "How does your friend Dass manage to drink so much, when there is supposed to be prohibition? He can't spend all his time at that club, or always be sending out for bootleggers with wooden legs."

"He is a health permit-holder. A health permit-holder," Janah explained, "gets his doctor to testify that he is a chronic alcoholic. Then he can buy as much liquor as he likes. There are many health permit-holders in Bombay."

As I rode up in the elevator, through the gloomy decaying splendor of the hotel, to my shabby room under the wedding-cake roof, I reflected that Janah had unwittingly put his finger on the solution to the problem of those Goans who wanted Goa to become part of Bombay State but who disliked Bombay's prohibition laws. All they had to do was to become health permit-holders.

Next day I visited a clinic of the Family Planning Association. Bombay is not only the center of the gospel of prohibition; it is also the center of the gospel of contraception.

One of the clinic's doctors was forcefully eloquent on India's urgent need to control births. "One Indian is born every four seconds," he said. "India adds 5,000,000 to her population every year. The population threatens to double every century. There are 9,000,000 Indian wives under the age of fourteen."

"When we opened this clinic," he went on, "we had a lot of people coming to us who thought we were going to advise them how to have *more* children. The more children a man has, the better a Hindu he feels himself to be. Also, the men fear that contraceptives would come between them and the pleasures described in the *Kamasutra*," he added sarcastically.

I left him to his problems and set out to find a taxi. None was in sight, and I hurried through the rain. A small car passed me, then stopped. The driver wound down his streaming window, and beckoned me. He had a face as round as a brown moon, and his teeth were badly stained with betel-nut juice. He offered me a lift, and I eagerly accepted. To my dismay, he turned his head and said something in Hindi, and the car's curbside rear door popped open and out of the car trooped a stout lady in a sari and five children. "Please to come in now," said the moon-faced man cheerfully. "They will wait here for me."

We left his wife and children standing uncomplaining in the rain, under umbrellas.

"You are a stranger in Bombay?" he asked, as we drove along. "You study our politics? I myself am a businessman. Politics I find very boring." He dismissed politics. "It is probable that you have heard of me. I am Nagwajan Narayan."

When I confessed I hadn't, he looked honestly perplexed.

"That is strange. I thought everyone had heard of me. I am a genius, you see," said Nagwajan Narayan. "I—I alone—invented the world-famous remedy. I alone manufacture it, from my own secret recipe. And I alone distribute it. Millions have found it beneficial, and every day they call out blessings on my name."

"What does it cure?" I asked.

"Everything," said Nagwajan Narayan confidently. "Anything. It is the most powerful sovereign specific remedy ever invented. If you have ulcers, it will cure ulcers; if you have stones, it will dissolve them; if you have lost your sexual vigor, it will restore it. There is *nothing* that my world-famous drug will not cure." He gave me a sidelong glance. "You are doubtful. You are hesitant. You are a foreigner and do not understand. I will convince you. It is a miracle-working paste, and its ingredients include diamonds, pearls, emeralds, rubies, and sapphires. Of its absolutely genuine authenticity I give you my personal word. Here we are, at your hotel. Try my cure at once. It costs only five rupees a box—seven rupees twelve annas for the larger size. Sir, I am glad to have been of small service to you."

"Mr. Narayan," I said, climbing with difficulty out of the small car, "I am extremely grateful to you."

"It is my humble duty."

I hesitated.

"Mr. Narayan," I said, "do you know a gentleman called Kaviraj Lal? He is in your line of business."

Across the moonlike face there flitted an expression of strong distaste. I could have sworn that the words "That charlatan!" trembled on his lips. Then he recovered himself. "No, sir," said Nagwajan Narayan, magnificently. "I have never heard of him."

I watched admiringly as he drove away; perhaps he really was a genius.

Janah took me to a meeting of the Committee for the Liberation of Goa. We went through pouring rain to a hall that was decorated with banners and Indian flags. At the entrance we were challenged by young "freedom fighters," wearing white shirts and white cotton Gandhi caps, and khaki shorts and brown sandals. "He has come to see Peter Alvarez!" Janah cried, and the young men were greatly impressed.

"Which ones are the Goans?" I asked Janah, in a whisper.

"Oh, there are no Goans. These are all Maharashtrians."

"But you said 40,000 Goans lived in Bombay."

"Yes, but it was decided it would be wiser for them not to attend our meetings. Their families still living in Goa might suffer."

A hollow-cheeked man came up to us. He had large spectacles, one lens of which was cracked, and the thinnest face I ever saw. When he spoke his jawbones clacked like knitting-needles. He brought his face close to mine and a spray of saliva assaulted me.

"The Portuguese Fascists and the imperialists are allies," he hissed. "The Americans are building airfields all over Goa. They want to bomb Bombay, isn't it?"

Freedom fighters gathered round. He stopped spraying me and began spraying them.

"The Americans and the Portuguese Fascists are allies," he said.

"*Achya!*" the young men said, shaking their heads, meaning "Yes."

"The Pakistanis have also made a shameful alliance with the Portuguese Fascists."

"*Achya!*"

"By a great coincidence, the Pakistanis are also in the pay of the Americans," said the spitting man, sarcastically.

"*Achya!* That is right!"

"The Americans are arming the Pakistanis with atom bombs for attacking India in the north, while the Portuguese Fascists attack in the south."

"*Achya!*"

"The Government of India is blind," he said angrily. "It cannot see its own danger. The Fascists must be chased out of Goa. The Pakistanis must be driven back from Kashmir. The American plot must be exposed!"

Then the leaders arrived, and everyone scrambled for a place near the platform.

Peter Alvarez was a man of about fifty. He wore a white Gandhi cap and at first glance looked startlingly like Nehru.

It was a resemblance that he seemed at some pains to cultivate. The other leaders formed a white-capped frieze behind him. They were mostly plump, professional Congress Party wallahs, and they looked bored.

Peter Alvarez described the atrocious conduct of the Portuguese in India from the fifteenth century onward. It took him a long time. His speech got only perfunctory applause from the Congress Party men on the platform, but was received with wild acclaim by the freedom fighters. One freedom fighter hung a garland round Mr. Alvarez's neck and the others formed a guard of honor to escort him from the hall.

On his way out we came face to face, and he looked at me with considerable interest. I introduced myself and said: "Perhaps we shall meet in Goa."

It seemed to me that an expression of acute alarm passed over his face.

"I mean," I hastened to explain, "if Goa becomes part of India."

He looked relieved, but not pleased. "Goa *is* part of India," he said severely. "Goa will be under Indian rule before the end of this year."

The end of the year was not far off. It was high time to go to Goa, if I wished to see it while the Portuguese still occupied it. I caught the night train from Bombay.

X

GOA: GUNS IN THE JUNGLE

The regime in Goa will collapse. NEHRU

I⟧T WAS dark when we clanked into Poona: dark and, of course, raining. Poona was for about a century the parade-ground of fire-eating British Blimps. Now there is a brand-new Defense Academy where Indian officers are trained. On my last visit I had lunched with an Indian general and his smart cadets, in an elegant messhall round whose walls ran rather indecent friezes of sportive Indian gods and goddesses.

In the station restaurant I met a Sikh army captain, a handsome young man with a neat black beard. "India will not attack Goa," he said. We have an army of 400,000 men and could overrun it. But the terrain is difficult, all hills and rivers and jungle. It would not be worth it."

He turned to other problems that interested him more. "The Sikhs are the backbone of the Indian Army but the Hindus do not trust us. The most revered Sikh in India is Master Tara Singh, but Master Tara Singh is in jail. Yet the Sikhs are called on to do all the dirty work. If there is serious trouble in Bombay between the Maharashtrians and the Gujeratis, they will call in the Sikhs. If there is a war with Pakistan, it is the Sikhs who will have to defend India."

The Indian Army is kept well out of sight, except in Kashmir. A fairly large force is stationed in the jungles of Assam, engaged in a little-publicized guerilla war against the Naga hill headhunters, who resent Indian rule as much as they formerly resented British rule. But the average Indian likes to believe his country relies exclusively on peaceful coexistence and soul-force.

Next morning I woke as the train clanked into Castle Rock. Everyone had to get out for customs inspection. The luggage was piled on wet wooden trestles on the platform. The customs men, wearing dhotis, drank coffee and read the newspapers. We were voluntarily entering Goa, therefore we were either fools or Fascist spies. Suitcases were roughly opened: two passengers were loudly bullied for not declaring their wristwatches. When my turn came the customs clerk was tolerably affable. "Report the truth about the horrible conditions of exploitation under the Portuguese," he said. "Do not repeat Fascist lies about India."

The train crawled on into Goa. Portuguese customs officials boarded it. All copies of Indian newspapers, including my *Times of India*, were confiscated. A Portuguese in a dark green uniform said: "You will be expected to report the existence, which you will see with your own eyes, of democratic freedom and religious toleration in Goa. Do not repeat Indian Communist lies."

Goa is about the size of Rhode Island. Occasionally the rain mists parted to reveal roaring waterfalls and dizzy glimpses of sheer cliffs and dense green jungle. The train did not go farther than Margao. A bus would take us to Panjim, another twenty-five miles. Old women wearing torn gunny sacks to protect them from the rain carried the luggage to the bus. It was an odd vehicle, for it had brass sides and carved wooden seats. The last passenger was wedged in and the door slammed. The driver appeared twenty minutes later and we lurched off. Along the way other passengers were picked up, some with goats. The bus soon smelled strongly of goats and of Portuguese tobacco.

Panjim, the capital, was a small port with wide streets and imposing official buildings along the quay. We drove past the rain-blurred statue of Affonso d'Albuquerque, who conquered Goa for Portugal in 1510, and drew up at the Mandovi Hotel.

The pretty dark-haired girl at the reception desk gave me a form to fill in in triplicate. Two young men who had been loitering near the desk peered over my shoulder as I wrote. When I had finished, one of them took one of the copies and went off to deliver it to the secret police. The other also pocketed a copy, then said gravely: "We welcome you on behalf of the Government of Goa, which asks only that you report truthfully on what you find. There is by the way absolutely no censorship: that is one of the calumnies of the Indian Communist Government."

The hotel, subsidized by the state, was a large and splendid establishment. In the red-plush-and-gilt-mirror cocktail lounge I was joined by a thin elderly man with sad brown eyes. He looked like a cross between Don Quixote and a harassed professor accused of liberal sympathies. I offered him a glass of port wine, and he accepted with gratitude.

"I have been here fifteen years," he said, and sighed. "Time passes slowly, for I have nothing to do. I had my own law firm in Lisbon, but here I cannot practice." He lowered his voice. "You see, I am a political exile. I criticized the regime in Portugal, and was deported. My only friend for a long while was a Goan doctor: a man of considerable learning and very popular among the people. But he is no longer here. *He* criticized the regime, and was deported to Portugal."

Before going to bed I took a stroll in the town. Only a few stores were open, but all of them were well stocked with imported goods. Only newspapers and magazines were lacking. The only newspapers obtainable were the two that were printed in Goa. One was called *Heraldo* and the other *O Heraldo*. They contained only official communiques and speeches by Dr. Salazar.

Next morning I was joined at breakfast by the two young men. They wore identical brown suits and pointed brown shoes. "I would like to interview the Governor-General," I said. They exchanged triumphant glances. "An interview has already been arranged for ten o'clock," they said. "It is now nine forty-five. Let us go."

We drove to the quay in a large motorcar which bore large stickers that said in Portuguese: "Defend Goa! We defy Nehru!"

The Governor-General of Goa was a small, alert man who exuded self-confidence. We sat under oil portraits of all Portuguese Viceroys of Goa since the year 1520. "We are here and we mean to stay," said the Governor-General. "Goa is not India's affair."

I asked him what would happen if unarmed Indian *satyagrahis* crossed the border.

"If Indians illegally cross our frontier we shall naturally take all measures permitted by international law."

"What political rights do the 600,000 Goans have?" I asked. "Do they elect some sort of assembly?"

"There is naturally an assembly."

"Is it in session?"

"Ah, no," said the Governor-General, smiling. "There is no need for it to meet. Everything is calm."

The young men were waiting. "There is time before lunch to go for a drive," they said.

We drove to the Church of the Good Jesus to see St. Francis Xavier's jasper-and-marble tomb. Then we visited the Cathedral, walking across the great square where the autos-da-fé were held. "After lunch, we shall visit some coconut plantations," the young men said.

I had other plans, but thought it wiser not to say so. I watched them out of sight, then went to find a taxi. First I drove to the telegraph office, where I cabled a brief report of my interview with the cocksure Governor-General. Then I told the taximan to drive as near as he could to the Indian border.

The road wound through soaked jungle. There were small villages of mud huts, and all the villages had white Hindu temples. The Portuguese claim that almost half the people are Catholics, but Christianity seemed to be confined to Panjim and its immediate surroundings. In one village I was hailed by men drinking beer on a veranda. A party was in progress. The host was an enormously fat men, half Portuguese and half Goan. He had a rifle laid across his knees and, tapping it, he said, "We are getting ready to shoot tigers."

Everyone roared with laughter.

"Mr. Fernandez has shot many tigers," said one of the men.

"Twenty-three," said the fat man complacently. "But I am waiting for the tigers from over there." He pointed toward the Indian frontier.

"There are people who would like to welcome the Indians and throw out the Portuguese," said Fernandez, and the men around him looked uncomfortable. "But I know who they are. They will all go to prison." He drank down beer amid a sudden unhappy silence.

"People are afraid of that Fernandez," said the taxi-driver, when we were out of earshot of the happy little group. "It is not only tigers he has shot, or Indians either. He is too fond of other men's wives."

Beyond the village was a frontier guardhouse. On the Indian side of the frontier there was only empty and very damp jungle, but I did not like the look of the guards, who were very young and plainly nervous. Their officer was a strutting blue-chinned man who wore a heavy revolver and binoculars. He peremptorily waved me back.

I suggested we return to Panjim by a different route, and the driver agreed. It turned out to be a lucky choice, for presently we came on a large military encampment. It bristled with artillery: the Portuguese were taking Peter Alvarez seriously.

I was made welcome and led to the officers' mess. In a twinkling, bottles of wine were produced, also sardines, olives, bread, meat, and an enormous assortment of cheeses. Someone opened a box of cigars. The Portuguese Army did itself well. They were pleasant young men, and they discussed the situation with professional calm.

"We could not hold Goa against 400,000 men, but we could make the Indians very sorry they attacked," one said. "If we have to take to the ships, the Indians will find they have paid a high price. We have mined all the bridges."

"The Indians say they will not attack," I said.

"Then why have they deployed troops on the border? Why do they have planes in position?"

I said I had seen no troops or planes, and added that the Indians claimed the Americans were building air bases in Goa. They laughed. "The Americans and the British would like us to surrender meekly to Nehru. They wish to placate him. That is their only interest in this affair."

I reached Panjim after dark, and the young men in the brown suits and pointed shoes were waiting for me. Their faces were rigid.

"We are sorry you did not tell us you wanted to go to the border. We would have arranged it properly."

I felt rather ashamed, but not for long.

"There has been trouble about your cable: it will not be sent."

"You told me there was no censorship," I said sharply.

"Certainly there is no censorship. But we reserve the right to refuse to send messages that abuse the head of the state. You called the Governor-General a cock."

"It is a mistake," I said. " 'Cocksure' means something quite different. It means—"

But they would not listen. "Ah, mother of God!" one said bitterly. "You have disgraced us. We shall lose our positions."

"You had no right to hold up my message," I said. "I shall return to India and send it from there. There is no censorship in India," I added.

"You cannot leave Goa tonight," one of them said. "Tomorrow perhaps you can explain matters to our superiors." He stalked off, but the other young man lingered. "It was *very* rude to call the Governor-General a cock," he said reproachfully.

The taxi-driver had been an interested onlooker. When the

young men had gone, I asked him: "Is there no way of getting a train out of here tonight?"

"There is one that leaves Margao, but you have barely an hour, and the road is very bad."

"Would you be willing to try?"

"Certainly, if you wish it."

We hurtled down the winding road to Margao with a recklessness that suited my mood. It would not really have mattered, for the train, of course, was late in starting. At the Indian border Portuguese officials came on board for a customs inspection. At Castle Rock the Indian clerk said dubiously: "You have nothing to declare? No American shirts, or Swiss wristwatches?"

"Nothing."

He said joyfully: "It is true then. The Portuguese Fascists are feeling the pinch. Is it correct that there is great famine and panic in Goa, and that the people are reduced to eating dogs?"

At Belgaum a cheerful unshaven man in a badly buttoned waistcoat gave me a large omelet and buttered toast for breakfast, and told me Alvarez's freedom fighters had already passed through on foot on their way to the Goa border. I thought of the nervous Portuguese frontier guards, and the tiger-shooting Mr. Fernandez, and wondered what the effect on them would be of bands of Indians suddenly appearing out of the jungle. "You had better go to Vaki," said the unshaven man. "They may have more news there. My cousin drives a taxi and he will take you." But when I reached Vaki the freedom fighters had already gone on toward the border. The unshaven man's cousin drove me to where the road ended at a muddy river bank. A large canoe poled by a nearly naked man was waiting. "You must cross in the canoe," said my driver. "The border is not very far. I shall wait for you here."

Across the river a narrow track wound through thick jungle. It was raining. I had walked twenty minutes when I came on two men. They made an odd pair. One carried a black bag and wore pajama trousers and a white cotton jacket. He covered

the ground with swift strides, though he went barefoot. The
other, who panted to keep up with his companion, carried a
camera.

"My name is Sitana," said the man with the camera. "I am a
Poona newspaper correspondent. The doctor is here to treat
those who will be wounded."

The doctor had strode on without sparing me a glance. We
hurried after him. It turned out to be a long march. The track
was often under water, and there were places where we waded
waist-deep. We clawed our way up cliffs and slithered down the
sides of steep ravines. The doctor continued to pad along barefoot. He never said a word to either of us.

I had left the taxi a little after noon, but it was growing dark
when the doctor halted at a ruined white Hindu temple. The
place was filled with freedom fighters and women were stirring
giant cooking-pots suspended over blazing fires. They ladled out
steaming rice, with banana leaves for plates, and gave each man
as many *chapattis* as he could eat. The rice we ate with our fingers. I was ravenously hungry and found the meal delicious. But
we had scarcely finished it when there was a stir, and Peter
Alvarez was in our midst, wearing a glistening wet raincoat and
a white Gandhi cap.

He made a speech; and then the men unfurled Indian flags
and marched out of the temple, shouting: "*Goa India ek hai*"—
"Goa and India are one." Sitana and I followed. It was now
completely dark and the column moved without lights. We
stumbled through tall wet grass, and ahead there was a roar of
rushing water. I almost fell into the river, but a man caught my
arm. "Only the *satyagrahis* cross; the rest of us wait at the temple," he said. We could hear them splashing across the river,
but the splashing finally stopped and there was no other sound.
"*Achya!*" said the man who had halted me, with satisfaction.
"They are all across and into Goa." On the way back to the
temple I found myself marching in step with Alvarez. He peered
at me, and I reminded him we had met in Bombay. He must

have guessed my unspoken question for he shook his head. "No, I am not crossing with them, for I have other work to do tonight."

Alvarez did not wait at the temple. "Many *satyagrahis* are crossing into Goa at different places," a young man explained. "He is going farther along the border."

I myself was too weary to stir another step. In the temple the fires had died to a ruddy glow, and the women were unhooking the cooking-pots. Everyone stretched out on the hard stone floor to sleep. At midnight a group of men staggered in with a wounded comrade. They had brought him back across the river, they explained, for the Portuguese had attacked them. The wounded man had a broken leg, and his face was bloody. The doctor with the black bag suddenly appeared out of the shadows and knelt at the man's side. "Elsewhere there has been much shooting," one of the men said. "Many have been killed by the Portuguese." The doctor put a splint on the broken leg.

It was still dark when Sitana shook me awake. "It is all over here," he said. "We should make for Vaki, for there there will be more news. It is a long walk," he added unnecessarily.

Our guide was a small man with an extraordinarily wizened face topped by a mop of white hair. He looked decrepit, but he was as agile as a squirrel. He led the way, carrying a small oil-lamp. He was a remarkable guide, for he sang songs in a high-pitched voice, and frequently burst into shrill cackles of laughter. The night shredded into a gray dawn, and he extinguished his lamp and left it beside the path. Leaning on a borrowed staff, I limped after the others, feeling stiff and sore. My shoes had shrunk with the wading, and my feet were badly blistered.

The guide's name was Joshi. From time to time he dropped back from the lead to walk beside me. He would shoot me quick, squirrel-like glances, then clap me heartily on the back and sing one of his preposterous songs. When I lagged too much, he would dance mockingly ahead of me, and once out of sheer exuberance he turned a number of brisk cartwheels. It was a fantastic sight, for he had the face of a senile man. He came back to my side and proceeded to imitate my painful hobble, shouting with glee. I decided the man was some sort of village imbecile, and angrily quickened my pace.

We came at last to a tiny jungle hut, and Joshi halted us. "It is my aunt's house," he said. Inside, I collapsed on a strip of coconut matting spread on a bare earth floor. A withered old woman was bending over me and holding to my lips a brass cup filled with scalding tea. When I had drunk it, she fed me slices of coconut. "We are just going outside, to smoke a cigarette," Joshi said, and he and the others vanished.

After a while I looked at my watch, and quickly sat up. Our progress had been painfully slow. Joshi with his antics had kept me going for fully seven hours. Left to themselves, he and the others could certainly have traveled much faster. But they had never complained. I hobbled outside. There was no sign of the men, and they were gone a long time. Then they appeared with Joshi leading, and he was pushing a bicycle. "It is my cousin's," he said. "I borrowed it for you. It is not far now to the river, and the path is not bad." I had dismissed him as a village idiot!

I had another surprise: on the other side of the river the taxi I had hired in Belgaum was still waiting for me. The driver opened the door for me as casually as if I had been gone only a few minutes instead of over twenty-four hours.

Joshi put out his hand. "I must return my cousin's bicycle," he said. "Good-by, my friend." We shook hands. He gave a shrill cackle of laughter. "When you come to the Goa jungles again, be sure your feet are in good condition!"

But I never went there again.

At Vaki they told us the Portuguese had shot 22 *satyagrahis*, and wounded or captured scores more. In Bombay mobs rioted, demanding war on Portugal. The Bombay police opened fire and shot 85 of the rioters. But India did not go to war, and nothing was achieved. The Portuguese remained in Goa. As for me, I lost some of my toenails, and was compelled to hobble about painfully for many weeks.

XI

TRIVANDRUM: THE RED SOUTH

I incline more and more to a Communist philosophy. NEHRU

On a road near Mysore city I met a young man of overpowering holiness called Krishna Subrabrahmavishnu. He had removed his shirt while he mended his bicycle, which had a flat tire, and he wore looped over one bare shoulder the sacred thread of the twice-born. He was so holy that he had covered the saddle of his bicycle with deerskin (which is pure and sacred) to avoid coming into contact with leather (which defiles). All this he explained to me with great solemnity.

When in Mysore city I mentioned this wayside encounter to a friend, he laughed cynically.

"Yes, he is so holy he will not drink tapwater, complaining it passes through a leather washer. Actually he is no Brahmin but belongs to a left-hand caste. Even untouchables of a right-hand caste would refuse to eat with him. The left-hand caste people are worshippers of Kali. Their wedding processions are not allowed to go through streets where right-hand castes live."

Caste is a constant preoccupation in South India, despite a literacy rate of 52 per cent, compared to the Indian average of 16 per cent. There are also serious language divisions. The majority of the 19,000,000 people of Mysore State, which is slightly smaller than Nebraska, speak Kannada. Their next-door neighbors in Kerala, which is half the size of Maine, speak Malayalam. The people of Madras speak Tamil, and the people of Andhra speak Telugu. All are afraid of being compelled to adopt Hindi and therefore cling to English as a lingua franca.

I moved south by easy stages, pausing frequently to rest and bathe my still tender feet at pleasant inns. The hill country around Ootacamund is still full of English influence, and there are still English-owned tea plantations there. It is the last place in India where Indians have not yet defiled the English caste system by demanding admission to English clubs.

In Kerala I was in a country of palm-thatched mud huts, banana groves, and sharp-prowed wooden boats loaded with rice and coconuts. Kerala seemed to consist more of water than of land. There were moldering wharfs and mangrove swamps, and the roads were green tunnels through black mud.

The communists were very busy in Kerala. I met their propaganda carts everywhere. The carts were like boats, for they had tall bamboo masts aflutter with red flags, and nailed to the masts were pictures of Communist leaders. In the villages the Communists put on open-air plays, watched by peasants who came from miles around on foot and by bullock cart. The plays were all about wicked landlords. Between the acts pretty girls sang Communist songs in Malayalam.

The peasants found this propaganda more palatable than that of the Congress Party. The Congress Party speakers, many of whom were big landlords, said: "The Communists offer you land, but that is impossible, for there is no land, unless the Communists can bring it from Russia."

In a crooked backstreet in Trivandrum I came on a tiny bookshop. I looked inside with no expectation of anything but a wooden box filled with secondhand paperbacks, a few copies of the *Times of India*, and a tray or so of ballpoint pens.

But there were shelves of books, and I went inside to examine them. They were in English and had been printed in Moscow and Peking. Some were illustrated with pictures of smiling workers and peasants and none cost more than thirty cents.

"Because of his being a Communist," my informant explained. "The Communists get the best jobs. Communist bridegrooms are becoming a caste of their own."

It seemed to me a moot point whether Communism would conquer India, or whether India would, if it had to, simply absorb Communism, by adding Marx to its already huge pantheon. Nehru has said: "In India, when we want to kill something, we deify it first." Marx has not been dead a century: the caste system has been in existence two or more millennia. The Marxists might end by wearing special caste marks.

XII

MADRAS: MARX AT THE FAIR

How are you better for smearing your body with ashes? An ass can wallow in dirt as well as you. SEVENTEENTH-CENTURY SOUTH INDIAN POET

THE MAIN road into Pondicherry was lined with hundreds of Madras State police wearing red and blue helmets like cardinals' hats. Flowery gateways arched over the road with inscriptions that read in English: "Welcome, Jewel of Asia!"

There was only one man in India for whom such a display could be intended. Presently an open, powder-blue Cadillac swept by with Pandit Nehru standing up in it, dressed in dazzling white and with a red rose in his tunic. In the car with him was the new Indian High Commisioner of Pondicherry, a Punjabi who had formerly been Indian Consul in Lisbon.

The Pandit was looking pleased. The Portuguese were still entrenched in Goa, but the French had handed over Pondicherry, which they had held for three hundred years.

But his pleasure was short-lived, for at the Pondicherry railroad station the organizers had botched their job. Six special trains had come from Madras, but when Nehru arrived the crowds were all looking the wrong way. The Pandit shook his swagger-cane in a rage, and exclaimed: "The people are being kept from me."

He was hurriedly garlanded, and then his car swept on, past the Place Dupleix and the statue of Joan of Arc, to the mayor's

217

palace. Children were grouped under an arch inscribed, this time in French: *"Nehru, l'ami des enfants."* Fresh green palm boughs strewed the road over which the Cadillac would pass. But the spectators squatting under large white parasols raised only feeble cheers. Perhaps they were intimidated by the fact that close behind the Jewel of Asia followed a bright blue bus filled with Madras police.

At the mayor's palace, Nehru got a more enthusiastic welcome from a brass band and claque crying "Welcome, light of the world!" The claque had been imported from Madras. Baskets filled with paper flowers hung from glass chandeliers that tinkled in the breeze from the blue Indian Ocean, which could be seen through the palace's open windows. Nehru made a speech from a dais, with his back to a huge mirror that filled all of one wall.

Then the Pandit drove through Pondicherry's sweating and malodorous streets to a meeting in a jungle clearing. His route took him past mud and straw huts, and the hut-dwellers' political convictions were not in doubt, for every hut wall was daubed with a crudely painted hammer and sickle.

A Pondicherry Indian explained the political situation to me. "The French were talked into handing over Pondicherry by the Socialists. The Indian Socialists were very powerful here. But now the Socialists are being forced to make way for Congress Party men. The Congress Party is not popular, and in the end the Communists will be the only gainers."

Nehru made a speech welcoming into the Indian fold the people of Pondicherry, Karikal, Mahé, and Yanam: an addition of 190 square miles and 400,000 people to India's territory and population. The audience consisted mostly of cows, whose horns had been painted green and purple for the occasion. No great man fails to make a fool of himself at least once; I suspected this was Nehru's day for doing it.

I left before he had finished speaking, and returned to Pondicherry. The Café Mendès-France had been renamed the Nehru

Restaurant, but there was still a French Club. The 60 members had gone off to the beach to swim and drink champagne. "There will be no more champagne," said the French-speaking bartender morosely. "Madras State is dry, like Bombay."

Madras State is somewhat smaller than Alabama, and has about 30,000,000 people. I took the train from Pondicherry to Madras city in time to see U.N. Dhebar, the Congress Party president, arrive at the railroad station in a powerful aura of Gandhism. He had traveled from Delhi in a hard-class coach, as Gandhi used to do; but from the station he drove to the Congress Party offices in a bright yellow Plymouth convertible with the Congress Party colors painted on the side. "Mr. Dhebar likes to back into the limelight," a local wit remarked.

The Congress Party offices in Madras were in a dingy two-story building, with a concrete public lavatory on one corner. A vast crowd wearing Gandhi caps jammed the street outside. Opposite was a fire station and the firemen had mounted their ladders to get a better view. Mr. Dhebar remained closeted with his Madras colleagues for several hours. Then they all came out and drove away in large limousines, with the yellow convertible in the lead.

A man in a dhoti tugged my sleeve and led me up a narrow steep stair. It was covered with a red strip of carpet and was cumbered with potted plants all the way. At the top of the stairs was a room with a large white mattress and a score of crumpled pillows. The windows were closed and, as it was a hot day, it must have been a stuffy session. My guide pointed to one of the pillows. "That is where Mr. Dhebar sat," he said solemnly.

The Madras streets were filled with incredibly thin coolies. Naked to the waist and dripping with sweat, they hauled enormous carts. I could only hope the distressing sight had not caused too much pain to the Congress Party dignitaries sweeping past the coolies in their large limousines.

A big Congress Party meeting was being held some distance from the city, near a temple to Shiva. Vast crowds trudged into a huge arena, through an enormous gateway that outshone Shiva's temple. The gateway had been built for the occasion by one of the Madras film companies. It shimmered with gilt. In the center of the arena was a great raised mound covered with masses of flowers. Amid the flowers a tent the size of a circus big top dominated the scene. Facing the crowds was a platform supported by two wooden elephants with jeweled tusks, and protected by a canopy. Loudspeakers boomed out the speeches that were being made from this platform. The crowds sat patiently listening in the hot sun. Mr. Dhebar finally appeared on the platform and modestly clasped a microphone. "The Congress Party is a tear dropped from the heart of suffering humanity," he began.

In Madras itself, the Congress Party was sponsoring a big fair to coincide with the meeting. The fair was intended to show the progress India was making under the Five Year Plan. But someone had blundered, for the exhibit that was drawing the second largest crowd was put on by the Madras Communist Party. The Communists were selling quantities of Marxist books printed in Moscow and Peking, and had on display pictures of smiling Russian and Chinese toilers operating vast machines. These pictures clearly fascinated Madras's half-naked and malnourished coolies, and were in sharp contrast with the humble pots and baskets and other products of Indian cottage industries which were all that the Congress Party's fair had to offer.

The exhibit drawing the biggest crowd, however, was that of the Madras Public Health Department. Outside a large white tent a young man like a circus barker cried: "Fight venereal disease! Have your stools and urine examined, free of charge. Be tested today and we guarantee you the answer tomorrow!" Eagerly hitching up their dhotis, the crowd shuffled past him into the white tent.

XIII
HYDERABAD:
PROPHETS AND MARTYRS

*The difference between me and a Communist is the difference
between a living man and a corpse.* VINOBA BHAVE

FROM MADRAS I flew to Hyderabad, the capital of Andhra
Pradesh, in another of India's little, unfireproofed Dakotas. Andhra Pradesh is larger than Colorado. Its 32,000,000 people
speak Telugu, which, next to Hindi and Bengali, is the mother
tongue of the largest group of Indians. Hyderabad is really two
linked cities, the other being Secunderabad. Outside Secunderabad white-hot sunlight rippled over vivid green ricepaddies,
where women with red skirts kilted above their knees bent to
their work; and a white temple was reflected in the still water
of a little lake. In Secunderabad I dined at a Chinese restaurant
called The New Peking and surrounded by garish cinemas. On
the walls of The New Peking were big, scowling photographs of
Mao Tse-tung and Chou En-lai; but an enormous radio was
pounding out American jazz.

Hyderabad was formerly the capital of the Nizam of Hyderabad. Outside the Mecca Masjid, the city's principal mosque, a
very ancient motorcar drew up, and a very old-looking, small,
shrunken, lean-shanked man got out of it. It was rather like
watching a tortoise get out of its shell. He wore a very faded coat
and cap, and very shabby red slippers. It was His Exalted High-

ness the Nizam—for the Indian Government, while depriving him of all power, permitted him to retain the title. He had come to visit the graves of his ancestors, who are buried in the quadrangle of the mosque. In Hyderabad an Indian bitingly remarked to me: "There were some enlightened Indian princes: the Nizam was not one of them." In the days of the Raj he was scolded by Hyderabad's British residents—the Raj's watchdogs in the princely states—for absolutism and neglect of his subjects. Even after India achieved her independence, and the princely states were absorbed in the Indian Union, the Nizam continued to draw revenues from land amounting to £2,500,000 a year, and had a privy purse of £500,000 a year. But that was the least part of his huge fortune: it was said that in his white marble palace in Hyderabad, the Nizam kept jewels estimated to be worth £35,000,000, and that the vaults were crammed with boxes filled with gold bars. Despite this wealth, and his possession of a fleet of automobiles including Rolls-Royces and Cadillacs, the Nizam preferred to ride around in an old Ford and to dress like a Moslem beggar.

Alone among Indian princes, the Nizam forcibly resisted the incorporation of his 81,000-square-mile state in the Indian Union. He had surrounded himself with a militia of ragged cutthroats, who opposed the Indian Army for a few days. This little civil war was shortly followed by a bloody Communist uprising, directed not against the Nizam but against Nehru. That also was suppressed, and the Congress Party took over the reins of government. The Nizam never had any popular support, but I gathered that the people were finding Congress Party rule bewildering. An old man told me: "Once the Nizam arranged to have the palace nightingales sing for George the Fifth. But when the King of England visited the palace, the nightingales did not sing a note. Today we are like the Nizam's nightingales, for we do not know the Congress Party tune. 'Work, work!' comes the call from every Minister sitting in Delhi. But where is the work? We are all unemployed. 'You must sweat and toil,' say the leaders. Again the question is, where to sweat and toil, and at what?"

The Socialist faction led by Ram Manohar Lohia had turned up in Hyderabad to capitalize on this bewilderment and discontent. Mr. Lohia, who looked like a dark frog wearing spectacles, delivered a 20,000-word speech, in which he complained: "In India, under the Nehru Government, phrase-making and speechmaking are increasingly becoming a substitute for action." But it was difficult to discover what sort of action he wanted. "No democratic government in the history of the world," he declared, "has opened fire on its own people as often as the Indian Government." But the people, he hinted, were equally at fault. "The people on their part," he chided, "should realize that the rigorous discipline of civil disobedience does not admit of their throwing stones and burning buses. In this country, the government and the people behave toward each other like murderous parents and irresponsible children."

The Indian Socialist Party, whose members I had heard declaiming at Gaya and from whom Mr. Lohia and a few followers had recently broken away, were in his view even worse than Nehru. "These Praja Socialists," he cried vehemently, "have themselves violated all the principles of democracy." It transpired that what this meant was that the Socialists had objected to Mr. Lohia remaining a member of their party and continuing violently to assail all the party's policies and all of the other party-leaders. "Discipline," said Lohia mysteriously, "should mean the long arm of free speech and the strong fist of controlled action." I concluded that Mr. Lohia was simply a windbag, but was intrigued by his final bit of political analysis. "No opposition party," he said, "ever does its job well if it yearns for power and office. The Socialist Party should not be dependent on the fleeting mood of the people. If the people do not listen, it does not matter." A tolerant friend of Lohia's explained: "He likes being in opposition: his role is to be against the government—*any* government."

Another reformer was on his way to Hyderabad. Rudyard Jack wrote: "As far as I can figure—this outfit does not plan much ahead and stays resolutely hazy about times and places —the best place for us to meet would be at a village called Hanpet, which is a little southeast of the city. We travel fast but irregularly, and nothing is sure. The old man's English is perfect, and he speaks several other languages, including Arabic. Despite this gift of tongues, he is not exactly communicative. But, if you can make it, I think you would find this bunch interesting." I thought I detected in my friend's spidery handwriting a note of tempered enthusiasm.

Vinoba Bhave, India's fast-walking saint whose disciples hailed him as a second Gandhi, was a Maharashtrian Brahmin of the same caste as the fanatic who assassinated Gandhi. At the tender age of twelve, he took a vow of chastity. He was studying in Benares when he first met Gandhi. The Mahatma had just returned from South Africa. Vinoba Bhave promptly joined Gandhi's *ashram* at Sabarmati in Gujerat and devoted himself to opening new *ashrams*, or saintly sanctuaries—one was for village women, and another for sick and aged cows. Gandhi preached the dignity of manual labor: Bhave helped villagers dig wells, and with his own hands cleaned out laborers' latrines along a stretch of railroad embankment. He also took part in Gandhi's civil-disobedience campaign against the British and spent three terms in prison; his last sentence, imposed in 1940, was for five years. In jail he learned Tamil, Telugu, and Malayalam, and read the *Koran* seven times to improve his Arabic.

Despite those accomplishments, Bhave was little known in India until 1952, when he was fifty-seven. In that year he demanded 50,000,000 acres of land for his *bhoodan*, or voluntary land-gift movement. His argument was simple. In India, he said, there were 300,000,000 acres of cultivable land, and there were 60,000,000 Indian families living off the land. If the total were equally divided, each family would have five acres. But there were in fact 10,000,000 families without any land who were employed by other peasants as farm laborers. Bhave, insisting that "every family should have five acres, no more and no less," therefore demanded 50,000,000 acres for distribution to the 10,000,000 landless families. When it was argued that this crude redistribution would only mean "distributing poverty," Bhave retorted that farming families in Japan had an average of just over two acres per family, but that Japanese farmers nevertheless had a far higher living-standard than Indian farmers. He complained that the Nehru Government's land reforms not only did not make any provision for people without any land, but that the much-publicized abolition of landlords was little better than a fraud. The former landlords, Bhave said, had simply turned themselves into government officials, collecting state rents from the state's tenants, to be handed over to themselves in the form of "compensation." Bhave declared: "The peasants find they are paying the same rents as formerly, to the same people as before." When he was asked how he proposed to get his 50,000,000 acres, he staggered everyone by announcing that he would collect them in person, walking from village to village throughout the length and breadth of India and demanding "land gifts."

I set off for Hanpet and on the road I passed caravans of camels, loaded with bales of cotton, and bullock carts driven by men with large white mustaches and large white turbans. Their wives, wearing bright saris, peered inquisitively at me from the carts. The fields were scarlet with pepper, and the road was lined with thickly corded, muscle-bound palms growing at odd angles. In the villages women went about with small brass pots balanced on their heads, and small girls wore shell-pink pajamas and their raven's-wing black hair was glossy with oil. At one place women road-menders were down on their knees, filling baskets with loose stones. They were clad in rags, but wore silver bangles and had jewels in their noses.

Before leaving Hyderabad I had called on the Communists. A Communist member of the State Assembly received me in

wheels, traditional symbols of Indian piety, I had expected; but not the tape-recorders, the microphones, and the portable power plant for the loudspeakers. Vinoba Bhave might be an Indian saint, but he was also a twentieth-century one. One cart contained rucksacks and, also, a much-traveled, battered suitcase covered with travel labels, which I recognized as Rud's. Rud himself came limping behind the cart accompanied by two young Indian men, and all three looked footsore.

I waved to him, and he came over to me after a word with his two companions, who nodded and followed after the cart. He sank down on a rock and grinned at me. "We've been up since before dawn. I guess I've walked a hundred miles in the last week. The old man is tough, for although he is over sixty he always seems to be as fresh as a daisy."

"Where is he?" I asked.

"He'll be along presently. He likes to give them time to set things up." Rud kicked off the dusty sandals he was wearing and ruefully squinted down at his blistered feet. "He talks like Christ, but sometimes he behaves like a touchy prophet out of the Old Testament. I've seen village untouchables crowd round to touch the hem of his garment and powerful landlords slink away from him like whipped curs. He likes to believe he is full of humility and loving-kindness, but he has the terrible pride of the truly dedicated man. When he was in Bihar, and giving the government hell, Nehru sent a message inviting him to Delhi to tell the Cabinet what he thought they ought to do. Bhave accepted, but said he might be a little while, as he had urgent business to attend to on the way. He walked the whole distance, holding village meetings, and did not turn up in Delhi for three months. The whole thing is crazy, magnificent, and rather pathetic. He has a notion he may not have long to live—he suffers from anemia and dysentery, and has a weak chest—but he refuses to eat anything except curds, and he drives himself all the harder. He seems to have no sort of proper organization, and a lot of the land that *bhoodan* has collected is just paper promises

228

so far. When you try to talk to him about that, he looks you in the eye and says gravely that everything is in God's hands, though he adds that God helps those who help themselves."

We walked slowly through the village, to one of the huts that had been set aside for the *bhoodan* people. "India is a queer country," Rud said, "and Bhave may be just the miracle that it needs. But personally I don't believe history repeats itself like that. There can be only one Gandhi. Bhave is highly intelligent and extremely well-read. But he refuses to bother himself with 'political problems,' and he seems to have no understanding at all of economics. Talk about Five Year Plans just goes over his head. Anyway he loathes machines and factories, and his ideal for India is a land of small peasants all leading idyllic existences, owning everything through 'village republics' and going about their daily work singing Hindu and Christian hymns. India's problem of overpopulation doesn't seem to worry him, though he must know that if you aren't going to have periodic large-scale famines you must have dams and irrigation works, and you can't have those unless you have large-scale industry."

Rud shook his head. "Nehru respects Bhave enormously. But Nehru is a practical statesman with a tremendous job to do, and he does not even try to fit Bhave into his plans. I think Nehru is right. The Congress Party is unwieldy, topheavy, riddled with jealousies, and to a large extent corrupt; but it is still the only hope for India, for it does work, and nothing else does. It's true that there is a lot of disillusionment among the masses with the Congress Party; but if it falls apart, the pieces will be picked up not by Bhave but by the Communists, for they, too, promise miracles, but they at least have an organization."

One of the young Indians put his head in at the door. "He is coming," he announced, and vanished.

Vinoba Bhave was a slight man with a short beard and large spectacles. He wore only a hand-spun white dhoti, a thin white shawl, and rubber sneakers. He entered the village with swift, eager strides, looking neither to right nor left, as if he were hastening to a tryst and was already very late. His formidable reputation had clearly preceded him, for, though the villagers crowded the road that they had decorated with mango arches for his coming, they looked shy and abashed. They need not have, for Bhave paid neither them nor the welcoming arches the slightest attention. The road might have been empty, and he a solitary figure hurrying along it. When someone, bolder than the rest, stepped forward and thrust a garland into his hands, he broke it in pieces as he walked, and threw the pieces to the children who also lined the way. It was to a child that he gave his only smile of greeting, and it transformed his face from the stern mask of one constantly preoccupied with lofty matters into a singularly sweet expression.

In the village a hut had been set aside for his special use. When he reached it, he swerved abruptly into it, apparently by divination, for there was nothing I could see that distinguished it from the others. The door was left open, and together with some of the more inquisitive villagers, I peeped in. Vinoba Bhave ignored us. Removing his shawl, he seated himself on the floor. An Indian girl, apparently one of the disciples, sat down also, with writing paper and pencils, and Bhave spoke in a low, quick voice while she wrote industriously. He was evidently dictating either letters or a newspaper article—I learned later from Rud that by dictating in this fashion, at the end of each day's march, he managed to keep up a vast correspondence and to write many articles about the work of *bhoodan*. When he had done, he rose lithely, walked across to the charpoy which was the room's sole furnishing, and in what appeared to be seconds was tranquilly asleep, with his lean brown back turned toward us all. The girl composedly arranged her papers, got up, and left him alone.

Bhave slept for exactly an hour. At the end of that time he rolled off the charpoy, as if an alarm clock had rung in his ear, and came briskly out of the hut. The disciples had been busy arranging a platform at the end of the village street.

He got on the platform and the villagers crowded expectantly round. But instead of making a speech he squatted down, and a girl disciple handed him a brass bowl filled with curds and a glass which, Rud told me in a whisper, contained fresh lemon juice sweetened with a touch of molasses. He drank the lemon juice first, then proceeded to eat the curds, sitting bolt upright, and staring severely at the villagers through his large spectacles, rather like a stern schoolmaster. He sat cross-legged, and suddenly he shot out a thin arm and pointed a finger at a villager.

"What is your name and how much land do you have?"

The man, a thickset, hairy individual who had been eying Bhave rather hostilely, stammered that his name was Deshmukh (which also means, literally, "village headman") and that he owned six acres. He wilted visibly under the saint's steady glare. "I am a poor man, your honor," he stammered, "and I have no land to give to *bhoodan*; for I have five sons, who expect to inherit from me, and I must do justice to them. That is the law of Manu."

While the man talked, Bhave went on eating his curds. I noticed that he carefully swirled each spoonful around exactly eight times in his mouth, before swallowing: it seemed to be a ritual with him.

When the man had finished speaking Bhave said: "You have five sons. But if you had six sons, would each not receive an equal share? For that is as you have just said the law of Manu. Treat me then as your sixth son, and give one acre of your land, for *bhoodan*." He put aside his empty bowl, and got to his feet. The microphone was placed before him, and the loudspeakers that the disciples had rigged up carried his voice, alarmingly magnified, all over the village. "I am the sixth son: the ten million families of India who have no land of their own. There is enough land for all, but only if it is divided properly among all the people who live on the land. God helps those who help themselves. The Government of India has instituted land reforms, but these are not enough. Besides, the Government is far away, and it is busy with other matters that have to be attended to. It is for you, the people of India, to settle this question of the distribution of the land among yourselves. To the rich, I say: 'If you do not give a sixth of your land to the poor of your own free will, the Communists will come sooner or later and will take far more than a sixth from you, by force.' To the poor, I say: 'If you listen to the Communists who tell you that only by force can you get what should be yours, your last state will be worse than the first, for the Communists will take from you the land that you took from the landlords, and you will only have exchanged many masters for one master who will be more powerful than they or you.'" He repeated his simple arithmetical lesson about the amount of cultivable land that there was in India and how, with equal distribution, every family could have five acres. "I agree that five acres is not much," he said, looking at the man called Deshmukh. "It is certainly less than six. But it is more than most Indians now have. And it is better to give one acre than lose all six."

This raised a laugh, as he had no doubt intended; and it also concluded his speech. As soon as he had finished, the disciples began calling for volunteers to give land to *bhoodan*. To my surprise, a score of people surged forward, and they were led by the thickset Deshmukh, who looked like a man who knew he was doing a foolish thing but felt he had no choice. Bhave himself did not wait to see the result of his lecture. He simply got down from the platform and strode back to the hut where he had napped, without a backward glance.

Rud had decided to continue walking with Bhave for a few days, and I rose before it was light to see him off. We waited at the end of the village. Presently some of the disciples came hurrying along, carrying lanterns, with Vinoba Bhave following. He strode swiftly past us, looking straight ahead. Neither Rud nor I might have existed, though Rud had been his close companion for a week. Rud laughed softly. "He'll walk like that until the sun rises. Then, if we're lucky, he may start a conversation. If I'm very lucky, it may even be with me. The last time he spoke to me, we were in the middle of fording a river, and he began a discussion of Persian poetry!"

The carts came past, laden with the disciples' baggage, the loudspeakers, the tape-recorder and the portable power plant. Rud stepped out after them. I watched the carts creak past and the lanterns bob away into the darkness. The smell of dawn was already in the air. I hoped Rud's feet would last out better than mine had done in the Goa jungles.

Bezwada in Andhra Pradesh is a railroad town. Sooty hills bounce back the shrill whistling of shunting trains; the town is bisected by a scummy canal filled with slow-moving barges. Through the town's maze of narrow congested streets go rooting 50,000 large black pigs, Bezwada's only scavengers. The pigs are owned by Yenada and Yeragua tribesmen who collect pig manure to sell as fuel: every pig has attendant on it an anxious "tribal," carrying a small shovel and a large bucket, who follows the animal about with an air of hopeful expectation.

To get out of the railroad station, I climbed a steep flight of iron stairs, pushing my way through hordes of tattered beggars, and walked across an iron bridge. The bridge commanded a view of the canal and the encircling hills, and I noticed that the slopes of the hills were still marked with huge painted hammers and sickles, relics of the recent hotly contested election in which the Communists had been defeated. The most famous man in Bezwada was Varagha Vayya, the gray-bearded president of the Andhra Astrological Propaganda Society. He had forecast a victory for the Congress Party, thus putting to rout the professional fortunetellers. Throughout the election, the fortunetellers squatted on the sidewalk outside the Bezwada post office with packs of cards and a flock of green parrots. For an anna, a parrot would pick a card foretelling the winner of the election: a pair of yoked bullocks to symbolize the Congress Party, a crossed hammer and sickle for the Communists. The parrots had consistently picked the Communist card. "It was nothing," said Mr. Vayya carelessly, when I asked him about it. "I also prophesied the fall of Malenkov."

I walked past the beggars, the pigs, the fortunetellers, and a large statue of Gandhi standing outside a brand-new movie-house advertizing Cinemascope. But when I reached a hotel, I was dismayed to be told it was full. All the hotels were full. I returned to the railroad station and sought a night's sanctuary in the railroad "retiring-rooms": a long gaunt dormitory of cubicles each containing a very large four-poster bed with a mosquito net hung over it. The "retiring-rooms" were built directly over the tracks, and all night long I lay awake under the mosquito net, shaken by the thunder of passing trains and deafened by the screaming of their whistles.

I wanted to see something of the Andhra countryside, and to visit a local raja. In the morning I hired a car and drove out of the town, past green rice fields and through villages that smelled of hay and bullocks, and were crowded with naked children, black water buffaloes, and slow-moving, high-wheeled sugar-cane carts. The village huts were built of dried mud and thatched with palm fronds, and the shops were open-air booths, whose owners squatted cross-legged amid mounds of white rice and pyramids of fresh oranges. I passed a bald-headed man with a big mustache, who was trudging along the road wearing only a loincloth and carrying a large straw umbrella.

And once, in a clearing at the side of the road, I came on an astonishing spectacle. Black-bearded men, wearing crimson drawers with small jingling bells attached to them, were flogging a woman with short, yellow-cord whips, urged on by a musician who blew frantically on a flute. They were holy men, I was told, and they were trying to cure the woman of a sickness. She stood with her hands raised above her head and her eyes closed, as the holy men whirled around her in a mad sort of dance. When they had whipped her until they were exhausted, a very old man with a long gray beard hobbled up, holding an iron ladle filled with ashes, and smeared the ash on

her forehead. Then, as offerings to the local tree deity, a garlanded goat had its throat cut and chickens' heads were briskly
chopped off, and the woman, her eyes still tight shut, was led
away by an anxious-faced man. "He is her husband," I was told.

At Vuyyuru there was a white Hindu temple, its walls gay
with freshly painted statues of gods and goddesses and sacred
bulls, which stood out in sharp silhouette against the bright blue
sky. Around the temple, lying face down on the ground, were
several score of women, whose backs were smeared with ocher.
They were praying. The temple walls still bore election scrawls
in Hindi, urging the people to "Vote for Congress." Near by
the temple and the praying prostrate women a market was in
full swing, and eager crowds were flocking toward a large, flimsy
wooden structure, which periodically shook to shattering roars
from within its own bowels. Inside, a man on an ancient motor-
cycle was driving round and round a "wall of death," and the
people could watch him from an upper platform by paying
four annas.

At Tiruvur the election had been fought between a 58-year-
old Congress Party candidate, Mr. Peta Batayya, and his 35-
year-old son, Mr. Peta Rama Rau, who was a Communist. The
father felt very bitter about the whole thing. "My son went
about telling the people I was a capitalist," he said. "I own 25
acres of land. When my son joined the Communists, he was
unemployed, and I was in a British jail for supporting Gandhi."
When I went to see the son, he just shrugged. "We may have
lost one election," he said; "but the future still belongs to
Communism."

In spite of the election, the villages of central Andhra were
still very much a Communist stronghold. The Communists had
defiantly renamed the villages "Stalingrad," "Moscow," "Leningrad," and so on. On the walls of the village houses there
were still tattered posters, with crude drawings of innocent
peasants being tortured by brutal policemen. One village had
erected a statue of a "Communist martyr." It was a very life-

like statue, for it wore a wristwatch. The villagers treated it with great reverence, for they burned incense before it, brought it offerings of coconuts just as if it were a god, and hung it with garlands of marigolds. A young Communist willingly led me to it. "His name was Narayan Rao," he said, speaking like a priest at a shrine. "He was shot down in cold blood by Nehru's police." The face of the statue reminded me of the wild-eyed young men whose photographs I had seen in the Communist office in Trivandrum. Later I asked an Andhra police official about him. "Before we caught up with him," he replied simply, "he had murdered eight people." The Andhra Communists had a reputation, doubtless fully deserved, for considerable ferocity; they had tried to turn the Telengana district into a sort of Yenan, and there had been much bloodshed. Yet the Communists I met in Andhra showed no hint of this. They were all quietly spoken young men, with mild round faces, looking singularly guileless, with their large horn-rim spectacles, neat white dhotis, and plain leather sandals. I suspected that in their early days of struggle the Chinese Communists had struck many observers in the same way.

A Communist introduced me to an Andhra toddy-tapper. He was a squat, broad-shouldered man, with very thick black hair that hung over his face, and wearing a loincloth. There were formerly 200,000 toddy-tappers in Andhra. Carrying a small jar slung on a cord round his neck, and with a sharp knife gripped in his teeth, a toddy-tapper—who belonged, of course, to a hereditary caste—would skim up a tall palm with professional ease, and after slitting the trunk of the tree near the top, under the fronds, would proceed to pour the sap into his earthen jar. Sugar was then added to ferment it: the result was palm-toddy. But this was before toddy-tapping was forbidden by the prohibition-minded Congress Party. Now the toddy-tappers had been thrown out of work.

I said I would like to taste some toddy, and without more ado the ex-toddy-tapper burrowed in a corner of his hut, and produced a jar. The contents smelled very bad, but to my surprise tasted like a rather fine liqueur brandy. When I expressed my appreciation, the toddy-tapper beamed.

"This man," said the Communist indignantly, "almost starved to death, because the Congress Party took away his livelihood. Now he is employed as a coolie in a rich raja's sugar factory at a wage only a fifth of what he used to earn as a toddy-tapper."

The Communists were, of course, fighting the Congress Party's prohibition law. I tactfully forebore to point out that, judging from the excellent contents of the jar from which I had just drunk, the law did not seem to be very effective.

In the election a raja had defeated a leading Communist. The raja had stood as a Congress Party candidate, which was a remarkable conversion, for before India gained her independence, the raja had been a great persecutor of Congress Party supporters. Moreover, he was ably backed during the election by his own former chief prosecutor, who in the courts had always demanded "severe sentences" for Congress Party members.

I called at the raja's five-story palace. Sheltered behind high thick walls, it was a large and rambling, if rather ramshackle edifice. Green parrots perched on crumbling balconies; black ravens peered inquisitively between the stout bars over most of the windows. The raja was not at home, but I was made welcome by his sixteen-year-old son. We shook hands very solemnly; he was a plump-cheeked youth who looked as if he would like to be jolly but had decided instead to be very dignified. "You must stay the night," he said gravely, and led me through a vast stone entrance hall, decorated with big stone lions, where about thirty men had laid themselves down to rest on straw mats on the floor, under large bad oil portraits of former rajas. We crossed several open courtyards, and then the raja's son led me along a narrow stone corridor and up two flights of stone stairs. We had evidently reached the family living-quarters. There was a large room, containing a dining-table and chairs, and an old-fashioned radio; adjoining this room was a bedroom. "You will want to wash your hands," he said, and a woman servant led me to a tiny washroom off the bedroom. Small brass pots filled with water stood on the stone floor. She picked one of them up, and poured water over my outstretched hands. Then she ceremoniously dried them with a small towel. This feudal duty performed, she went back to laying the table.

It became clear that the raja's son and I were to dine together alone. It was also very clear that he was tongue-tied with embarrassment at the prospect. We consumed soup, fish, a very hot curry, a chicken pie, and a custard fruit tart, in pensive silence. Though the ice can never be said to have been broken, I managed to extract from him the information that he went to school in Bombay. As soon as the meal was finished, he excused himself, and fled. I retired to the bedroom, and was dropping off to sleep when I became aware of a steady drone that rapidly increased in volume. It sounded as if a squadron of planes were circling the palace. But they were not planes, they were mosquitoes. The air was thick with them. Sleep was out of the question. I got up and decided to go for a walk. I tiptoed across the deserted dining-room and down the stone stairs. I fervently hoped I would not blunder by error into the women's quarters, but I reached the courtyard without seeing anyone. In the great entrance hall, the raja's retainers still slept, but not for long. Even while I was admiring their tolerance of the mosquitoes, which hung over them in clouds, the sound of a stricken brass gong boomed and shuddered through the palace. About ten of the men rose hastily, grasping thick staves. They groped their way outside—for the only light came from a clouded moon—and got into a truck that stood ready waiting. The truck roared off. I returned in perplexity to my room. I was halfway there when I met the woman who had washed my hands for me and served the meal.

"Where have the men gone at this time of night?" I asked.

"They have gone to deal with some Communists who are burning a field," she replied simply.

I reclimbed the stairs and paused in the doorway of the dining-room. The raja's son had stealthily returned. He had turned on the radio, and was snapping his fingers and doing steps to a lively dance tune. We stared at each other guiltily.

"I thought you had gone to bed," he stammered.

"I thought *you* had gone to bed," I said.

We stared at each other again. And then he laughed. The ice was really broken this time.

"Do you like jazz?" I asked.

"Very much! I like Duke Ellington and Count Basie and Louis Armstrong and . . ."

We had a most entertaining chat, in spite of the mosquitoes.

Next morning the raja returned home. He arrived in a mud-splattered 1933 Chrysler, with an ancient canvas roof, a spare wheel screwed to the running-board, and a rubber-bulb hooter. The raja was a short, stout man with a brown, bald head. He had a red caste mark in the middle of his forehead, and rimless glasses were perched on his small fat nose. He wore a brown jacket and shapeless slacks, and had a very large diamond and emerald ring on the third finger of his right hand.

He greeted me affably, and explained that he had just concluded a tour of 120 villages, traveling over very bad roads. The people he had been visiting had formerly been his subjects. Since winning the election they had become his constituents. "I am constantly at their beck and call," he said, a trifle despondently.

The raja's right-hand man, formerly his chief prosecutor and now his political secretary, drew me aside. He was eager to explain that the raja, as a good Congress Party man, had voluntarily given up his former vast estates, keeping only a few thousand acres and several sugar mills to himself.

"But he must have received compensation," I objected.

"Ah, yes: the Government gave him a little."

"How much?"

"Only half a million pounds sterling," said the raja's political secretary. "And, out of that, he has to pay all his retainers, and fight the Communists."

I drove back to Bezwada. This time the railway "retiring-rooms" were all full, and I found I could not get a train to Cuttack until the next morning. I went the round of the hotels. One of them had a room—on the roof, directly under a glaring green neon-sign—but, the proprietor explained, it would not be vacant until 11:00 p.m.

"Perhaps I could see it," I suggested.

We climbed a steep outside staircase to the flat roof. A low parapet ran round it: I had another view of the muddy canal, the town alleys, and the rooting black pigs followed by their attendants holding shovel and bucket in constant readiness. The room was one of several tiny wooden structures that had been added to the accommodation to hold overflow guests. The door was tightly shut; I peered through the one small window. Inside, in a haze of cigarette smoke, nine men in cotton vests sat on the single bed and on the floor, playing cards and drinking palm-toddy.

"They will leave at eleven," the proprietor said. "They are catching a train. Then you can have the room all to yourself."

I slept in the open on the flat roof, under the blinking green neon-sign.

XIV

CUTTACK: THE MAD MONK

Why do you have faith in holy men who exploit and rob you?

NEHRU

THE TORN-UP railroad tracks had been relaid, but Puri railroad station, destroyed by the mobs, seemed totally beyond repair. Puri is the scene of the famous annual car festival of Jagannath—Juggernaut, as Westerners miscall it. Jagannath, which means Lord of the Universe, is really Vishnu. The idol—it has a large diamond in its forehead and its arms project from its ears—is drawn through the streets once a year, in a huge 16-wheeled car, 45 feet high and 35 feet square. The idol is attended by 6,000 priests, and 100,000 pilgrims come from all over India to take part in the festival. From time to time a few fanatics throw themselves under the car's wheels and are crushed to death. But the mobs who had destroyed the railroad station had not been worshipping Vishnu. They were protesting against a proposal to take some territory from Orissa State, and transfer it to Bengal. Anarchy had reigned for several days.

In the circumstances I preferred not to linger in Puri, but to press on to Cuttack, the chief city of Orissa. Orissa is somewhat larger than Georgia, and has a population of 15,000,000, of whom 3,000,000 are "tribals," living in remote forests and mountains. It is one of the poorest states in India: which may account for the ferocity of its recurrent quarrels with its neighbors Bengal and Bihar.

When I reached Cuttack, I made contact with a friendly police official. He courteously escorted me to the *kaliaboda math*, or holy place, that I had come to see. We had to drive a considerable distance to reach it, over appalling roads and past wretched villages that seemed to be entirely composed of outcastes' hovels. "The people are very poor and very superstitious," said my police escort, unnecessarily.

The *kaliaboda math* was a formidable fortress. It brooded over the surrounding villages, reminding me forcibly of Dracula's castle. At the time of our visit it was, of course, deserted. We passed through the great main gate, and saw the courtyard where the policemen had been killed. The statues of the founder still dotted the overgrown gardens and orchards, and we inspected the chariot in which he had had himself hauled about by his disciples. Then we visited the archery range, where the wooden targets in the shape of human figures still stood. Under the main building, of solid stone, was a maze of passages and monks' cells; beneath them was the armory, with its steel doors, and the dungeons where the women had been kept. Finally, we visited the founder's private quarters. His bedroom was still adorned with tiger skins, and he appeared to have had a taste for pornographic statuettes.

"A holy man was almost stoned to death near here last week," my guide remarked, as we drove back through one of the villages. "The villagers are very hostile to all *sadhus* now."

The founder of the *kaliaboda math* had been lodged in the Cuttack jail. I was allowed to have a glimpse of him. It was a depressing sight. An incredibly ancient-looking man, with a tangled white beard, he sat in a corner with his arms folded, staring straight ahead of him. But his wrinkled old face still retained some battered dignity. He appeared to be muttering to himself.

"He doesn't give too much trouble," said my policeman. "But

242

he will keep asking for meat dishes. The other prisoners receive only vegetarian diet."

There are about eight million *sadhus* in India. The vast majority are harmless enough. They wander about the countryside with begging-bowls. Indians readily give them alms, partly from piety, partly because they fear a *sadhu*'s curse. But the man who called himself *Pagala Baba*, "the mad monk," was in a class by himself.

No one knew much about his origins, though there was a story that he had taken the vows of chastity and poverty at a very early age, and in his beginnings appeared to have been genuinely religious. For most of his life he roamed the countryside like any other obscure *sadhu*, and he was in his late sixties before he achieved any sort of notoriety. But when he finally did so, it was on an impressive scale.

He first came to prominence when he got up before a gathering in Cuttack, and informed his awed listeners that, in addition to appearing before them, he was simultaneously sitting in a bus that was traveling from Calcutta. He explained that he was able to do this because he was actually an incarnation of Brahma, and that if he cared to exercise his full powers he could easily destroy the universe.

In no time at all the Mad Monk was being worshipped by a large and growing following. His disciples included a couple of Maharajas, and wealthy converts poured money into his coffers. With those offerings, he built the *kaliaboda math*, and filled it with warlike retainers in the guise of monks.

When the crash came the Mad Monk was a venerable eighty. He might easily have died in an odor of sanctity, within his castle walls, if his own and his followers' concupiscence had not gone too far.

The *kaliaboda math* began to acquire an evil reputation. The monks discarded stealth and with increasing boldness sallied out of their stronghold to demand money from the villagers. When their demands were refused, they beat the villagers up.

For years village women had been disappearing, but unfaithful wives who have lovers waiting to receive them are not uncommon in Orissa, and the husbands preferred to nurse their hurt pride in silence. Now the disappearance of the women began to be associated with the monks' forays.

The climax was reached when an eighteen-year-old village bride vanished on her wedding night, and her husband traced her to the very gateway of the *kaliaboda math*. Moreover, there was ample evidence that the girl had not gone willingly. The bereaved groom reported the kidnapping to the police, and demanded action. The police, who had long been suspicious of the *math* and were waiting only for a suitable opportunity to raid it, were only too glad to comply.

Even then the Mad Monk's reputation for miracles and piety produced an extremely odd result. A small party of policemen arrived at the main gateway of the *math* to find themselves confronted with a row of monks on the walls, all armed with bows and arrows. The Mad Monk himself appeared. He explained to the police that, as the *math* was a holy place, they could not be permitted to enter unless they first removed all contaminating objects made of leather from their persons—not only their shoes, but also their belts and revolver holsters.

Astonishingly, the policemen agreed to those conditions. When they had discarded their arms, the great gate was swung open, and the policemen marched in. Immediately they had done so, horn bugles sounded shrilly, and the unhappy policemen found themselves the targets for skillfully directed arrows and thrown spears. The Mad Monk, according to one survivor, sat in the courtyard throughout the battle, clad in animal skins on a lotus-shaped throne, waving a red cloth and crying: "Let blood flow!"

Most of the policemen managed to withdraw. They hastened back to Cuttack and raised the alarm. A troop of soldiers were dispatched to the scene of action.

By the time they arrived, some of the monks had fled. But

the others, including the Mad Monk himself, had taken refuge in their underground cells, and the military had to force them out by using tear gas.

In the armory, behind the steel doors, the soldiers found vast quantities of two-handed swords, tridents, spears, and bows and arrows, as well as piles of slings and sacks filled with stones for use as slingshot. They also found a fortune in gold and jewels which had been donated to the *math* by wealthy followers of the Mad Monk. And, in the dungeons they found eight terrified women, including the kidnapped eighteen-year-old village bride.

At his sensational trial the Mad Monk had the last word. When he was given a sentence of two years' imprisonment, he loftily announced: "I am indifferent to punishment by men, for God's justice is supreme." There was a good deal of tension in Cuttack until it became clear that he did not, after all, propose to carry out his threat to destroy the universe.

XV
CALCUTTA:
"RUSSIANS ARE BROTHERS"

Life is strife, and strife means knife, From Howrah to the Bay
KIPLING

THE FIRST time I visited Calcutta a gaunt policeman wearing
faded khaki and a maroon beret stopped my car and handed
me a leaflet. The leaflet announced that the entire Calcutta
police force had gone on a hunger strike for more pay.

Protesting policemen had barricaded themselves in their
stations. When soldiers driving prison vans were sent to arrest
them, other policemen lay down in the roadway to prevent
the vans passing. Some hundreds of policemen were nevertheless removed to Dum Dum prison, five miles outside Calcutta.
But the Dum Dum prison-warders joined the strike. The policemen and the warders were then taken to Fort William, and
locked up there.

Many fasting policemen fainted in the streets and were taken
to hospitals. At one hospital a nonstriking superintendent
visited his men to rebuke them. Policemen dragged themselves
from their beds and feebly smote him with their nightsticks.

The second time I visited Calcutta, I saw Bulganin and
Khrushchev being mobbed. The Soviet leaders' route from the
airport was lined with poles from which hung red wicker baskets.
An Indian official explained that the baskets represented the
toiling masses. "Laborers normally use such baskets for carrying
sand, bricks, and earth," he said. But the toiling masses insisted

246

on making a personal appearance. Every balcony and rooftop was crowded. Red flags flew in every alley. The Communists had brought 200,000 supporters into Calcutta and had set up soup kitchens. An open Mercedes-Benz had been placed at the Russians' disposal. At the intersection of Muktaram Babu Street and Chattaranjan Avenue Mr. Khrushchev rose in his seat waving his straw hat and affably shouted: *"Hindi Russi bhai bhai"*—"Indians and Russians are brothers." Scores of enthusiastically howling Indians immediately threw themselves bodily on the car, which broke down. Bulganin, Khrushchev, and the Chief Minister of Bengal, Dr. B. C. Roy, were rescued with difficulty and driven off in a patrolwagon. The disappointed masses stripped the abandoned Mercedes-Benz, then amused themselves by pulling mounted policemen off their horses.

On my third visit to Calcutta I landed at the airport after dusk. The air bus jolted through streets that smelled of sulphur, past smoky hovels from which ragged creatures peered at us. My companion on the bus was a man called Banerjee. He had several gold teeth and wore a ring with two rubies in it. He at once began to tell me the story of his life.

"The first Viceroy to reside in Calcutta," he remarked, "was Cornwallis, the general who lost the battle of Yorktown. He had twenty-four successors. The last few, before the seat of government was moved to Delhi, led rather harassed lives. I threw a bomb at one of them, which missed. We young Bengalis were very revolutionary in those days."

Mr. Banerjee escaped abroad and traveled, under several aliases, in Malaya, China, and, after the Bolshevik Revolution, in Russia. "I broke with the Bolsheviks after they shot Radek, who was my friend," he said. "It wasn't that I had ceased being a revolutionary; but they had."

It was a remarkable story to hear from a complete stranger; but almost anything can happen in Calcutta.

"I returned to India and joined the Congress Party," he said. "It was a mistake. We Bengalis never dreamed that Bengal would be partitioned and that India would retain less than half of it. Consequently, when the partition was announced, terrible things happened in Calcutta. We Bengalis are a very volatile people. I myself saw one Bengali, walking up and down the Chowringhee, armed with a meat-hook. He was killing Moslems."

Mr. Banerjee had organized a refugee camp for Hindus streaming into the city from East Pakistan. "I insisted that the people in my care should be vaccinated and that there should be proper sanitation. The Brahmins objected. Nobody was vaccinated, there was no sanitation, and the death rate in the camp rose to 320 a week."

He peered out into the sulphury dusk. The bus had halted in a narrow lane. "I think the bus has broken down," said Mr. Banerjee. He lifted his luggage from the rack. "We had better try to find a taxi."

We left the stranded bus and walked along the lane. One of Calcutta's numerous wandering cows was eating garbage in the gutter. In the other gutter the swollen corpses of several large black rats lay in pools of their own blood. "We have much trouble with rats in Calcutta," Mr. Banerjee said.

At the end of the lane we hailed a cruising taxi and were driven to the Great Eastern Hotel. Ragged beggars roused themselves from the sidewalk and whined at us. Mr. Banerjee brushed them aside. We dined together and after dinner went for a stroll on the Chowringhee. It was an evening of soggy heat, but Calcutta's main thoroughfare was packed with people. Over 2,500,000 people live in Calcutta, and another 500,000 in Howrah across the river. Most of them live in tenements or in hovels called *bustees* and prefer to spend as much of their time as possible on the streets. The crowds poured along the well-lighted Chowringhee in a solid flood: we were swept along irresistibly with them, past garish cinemas, crowded cafés, sidewalk booths, and squatting beggars. Most of the booths sold glittering junk, but some of them called themselves "urinogenital clinics," and, near these, young men in white shirts were displaying pornographic books. India's obsession with fecundity and the organs of reproduction reaches a high tide mark in Calcutta.

"Let us cross the river to Howrah," Mr. Banerjee suggested.

Howrah is Calcutta's factory area. Its tangled streets were jammed with people, buses, bicycles, bullock carts, and wandering cows. The factories looked like prisons, but were solidly bourgeois and respectable compared with the tiny workshops where gangs of children poisoned themselves making matches and *bidi* cigarettes.

We plunged into an unlit lane that cut a muddy, uncertain path between tightly packed hovels. "The people here live five to a room," Mr. Banerjee remarked. "Each room is about ten feet square. Fortunately, the *bustees* are frequently burned down, in communal rioting."

The owners of the *bustees* were also the factory-owners. A Calcutta social worker had recently calculated that in the *bustee* area there were about 8 latrine seats and 2 watertaps to every 400 inhabitants. It was not surprising that Calcutta's infant mortality rate was 673 per 1000 births.

"The death rate exceeds the birth rate," Mr. Banerjee said. "But there is constant immigration from Bihar, which is poorer than Bengal."

A Calcutta factory worker earned 60 cents a day; but only 20 cents of this was his wage. "The remainder is called his dearness allowance," said Banerjee.

"Wages are kept low by the people who come from Bihar and also by the refugees who still arrive from East Pakistan ten years after Partition," he added. "The immigrants and the refugees and the Bengali unemployed fight at the factory gates for jobs."

Before the partition of India, Bengal was as big as Idaho. Partition cut it down to the size of Maine, but it still had to support a population of over 26,000,000. The Bengalis, who have a superiority complex toward other Indians, found this hard to bear. In a flash, truncated Bengal was reduced from an overlord of neighboring states to a supplicant for *Lebensraum*. The jute mills of Calcutta were fed with human flesh from Bihar; but Bengal demanded territory from Bihar as well. The secretary-general of the Bihar Congress Party called Bengalis "Hitlerites"; the president of the Bengal Congress Party talked of "Fascist oppression of the Bengali minority in Bihar"— about 20 per cent. The Assam Congress Party denounced "Bengali imperialism," and mobs chased Bengalis out of Assam. Calcutta had become a giant head on a pigmy body, and Bengal warred verbally with its neighbors. There were times when all that kept it from becoming a shooting war was Delhi's control of the army and the fear by all concerned of Pakistan.

And Bengal went on having labor troubles. Banerjee and I returned to the Great Eastern Hotel, and next morning I read in the newspaper that 50,000 coalminers had gone on strike. The president of the state-run Coal Board announced that all the strike-leaders had been arrested.

Cities are filled with thieves and vicious men. THE *Vishnu Purana*

HE LIVED with his six wives in a large house surrounded by a large garden. He was reputed to be a millionaire, but the big house was in a poor state of repair. Some people said he was the meanest man in Calcutta. He was one of several wealthy Hindus who were devoted to the welfare of the cow. He had built a number of homes for aged cows, and was very critical of the Nehru Government for its refusal to ban the slaughter of cows.

I called on the jute-mill owner by appointment. The double gates of his "compound" were closed, and when I rang the bell nothing happened. Then a small wooden Judas window opened, and an eye and part of a whiskered face became visible. I explained my business and produced a visiting-card. The gates slowly creaked open. Inside on guard stood two *chowkidars*, carrying stout staves. One led me to the house while the other carefully closed and barred the gates.

A white-clad bearer took me across a gaunt entrance hall, with a marble floor that could have done with a good scrub, to a room with windows looking on to the garden. The furniture was massive, gloomy, and smelled of cheap furniture polish. Except for large faded photographs of whiskered Hindus on the walls, it could have been the sitting-room of a nineteenth-century English ironmaster.

Suddenly from upstairs there came the shrill voices of several scolding women. The voices rose accusingly and seemed to pursue the object of their wrath. Then a door banged, there were footsteps on the stairs, and presently a small wrinkled man entered the room where I sat. He was looking vexed and was mopping his brow with a handkerchief. I remembered the six wives.

The conversation did not go well. His English was fluent enough, but I wanted to talk about his mill-workers and he wanted to talk about cows. It presently emerged that he had thought I wanted to write an article about his *goshalas*, the homes he had built for the cows. When we got on to the subject of his workers' wages and living conditions, he scowled at me suspiciously.

"They spend all their time listening to the Communists," he squeaked. "The Communists hire *goondas* to destroy my property." In India hoodlums are called *goondas*. "They are always striking, rioting, threatening to kill me." I remembered the two *chowkidars* at the gate.

"No, I do not think much of the present government, though

CALCUTTA:

I have given generously to the Congress Party funds. They are always passing laws against property, those Congress wallahs. Why should they tell me how to run my factories? They are mine, isn't it?"

Calcutta was a wicked city, he said, full of thieves and vagabonds. India was passing through bad times, and he did not think things would get any better. He now regretted the passing of the British Raj.

"It is all written down in our holy books," he said solemnly. "It is the Age of Kali."

He produced a tattered book.

"This is the *Vishnu Purana,* which tells of the Age of Kali. Now, see what it says."

He read the book.

" 'Women will become shameless: eating too much and talking too much.' " I thought of the angry voices upstairs. " 'Wars will depopulate the earth. The kings of the earth will be violent of temper and ever addicted to falsehood and wickedness. They will seize the property of subjects.' "

He banged a hand against the open page. "You see, you see? *They will seize the property of subjects.'* Confiscation! Communism! Precisely what is happening today!"

He had put on a pair of spectacles, and now he peered down at the book again. Then he nodded energetically and with no little satisfaction.

"Ah, see what it says next! 'They'—that means the wicked rulers—'they will rapidly rise and fall, their lives will be short.' It is so, isn't it? And the book also says: 'They will inflict death on women, children, *and cows.'* So, it is truly the age of the atom bomb and of cow slaughter that we are living in! We are indeed in the Age of Kali!"

I said I wasn't quite sure what the Age of Kali was.

"Ah, you are not a Hindu. I will explain. The Day of Brahma is 4,320,000 years, exact. It is divided into four ages. There is a golden age, 1,728,000 years, exact: now over. Two ages follow,

252

when virtue declines. Finally, the Age of Kali, in which the world comes to an end."

It justified for him, I suddenly realized, his treatment of his workers: the miserable wages, the *bustees*, the lack of latrines, and the deaths of children. A nineteenth-century ironmaster would have called it the iron laws of economics: more poetical, he preferred to call it the Age of Kali. And meanwhile there were always the cows to be succored, to prove he was on Brahma's side. The Victorians, also, had been deeply moved by the plight of the pit ponies.

India has great possibilities. KHRUSHCHEV IN CALCUTTA

A PRETTY Bengali girl introduced me to a group of Calcutta university students. They were very angry young men who regarded me with rancor and suspicion.

"India has ten thousand years of culture behind her," one of them insisted. "We are a wholesome and balanced people. We do not lie on psychiatrists' couches like the money-mad Americans."

He was, he said, training to be an architect. "India today has 450 architects. We are not going to allow ourselves to be used by those who think only of profits. We will not be producing sensational gadgets and silly skyscrapers. We do not want your so-called 'industrial wizardry.'"

"When Khrushchev was here," said another student complacently, "he remarked that in the Hydrogen Age it was foolish to build anything over four stories."

"America is a country of peak wealth accumulation," said the architect. "It is blinded by the thought of its 'progress' to its terrible human failure."

253

"Americans are always saying we are impracticable, they are practical," said a third student. "What could be more impracticable than the extinction of the human race?"

I thought it might prove only too practicable, but forebore to say so.

A young man with long black hair and a lantern jaw come up. He approached me with a friendly smile and held out his hand to be shaken. When I shook it, it felt boneless. But he looked expectantly at me, as if I ought to recognize him.

"Your face seems familiar," I said cautiously, "but I can't quite recall—"

"We have never met," he said, laughing heartily, "so how could you know my face?"

"Oh! Stupid of me."

"Ah, Westerners are always stupid about Indian faces. I wish to talk to you, because I have been in America. I studied economics and journalism. But it is very difficult to be a student of those subjects in America. You do not believe this because you close your eyes to everything in America that is bad, and you criticize and belittle everything you see in India that is good. The truth is that in America nobody is free and nobody dares speak out. But an Indian cannot be silenced. That is why I had to leave America."

"What did you speak out about?"

"About American Fascism. About how America is trying to dictate to all countries that need its aids. I wrote letters to the newspapers. The newspapers cannot help sometimes printing a few lines from letters that criticize America. This is to preserve the illusion of a free press.

"I wrote many letters. I wrote that SEATO is a great conspiracy by America against the peoples of Asia. They published that. I wrote that Mr. Dulles was a thorough reactionary. They published that, also."

"Then, what happened?"

"I am coming to it," he said crossly. "Do not interrupt. After

254

I had written the letters, I did not register for the fall seminar. They sent two immigration officers after me. They asked me why I was not at school. I said it was the blunder of the university authorities, who were very stupid.

"They went with me to my room. They searched my books. I had submitted a master's thesis on Lenin and Rosa Luxembourg and had many Marxist books. I was asked all sorts of questions, why wasn't I at school, how did I earn my living. So, in the end, I left America. I was lucky to be allowed to leave. Do you know that for American students who dare to speak up, there are concentration camps?"

Not all the Calcutta university students were Communists. But a good many of them were. And they were all bitterly critical of the West.

One of them asked me angrily: "Why is the United States preparing for a war of aggression?"

Another said: "If there is a war between the United States and Russia, I do not think India should fight, I think she should stay neutral. But if India did take sides, I hope it would be with Russia."

India's five greatest problems are land, water, cows, capital and babies. NEHRU

I WAS invited to a Bengal wedding. The bride's father was a glass manufacturer. Along the avenue leading to his home he had erected pillars of flashing glass, and the house itself blazed with colored lights. The total effect was dazzling.

The two families had spent anxious weeks consulting horoscopes and genealogies: for the couple's stars had to match, and marriages between even seventh cousins were forbidden.

CALCUTTA:

The bride's forehead had been smeared with sandal paste and her body with mustard oil, and she had been presented with 20 cowrie shells, 21 betel nuts, and a mango branch with 5 leaves.

The wedding was held after sunset, as tradition demanded. Over the main entrance of the house, a balcony had been specially built for the orchestra of pipers and drummers. Several family widows, dressed in white and with their heads shaved, were permitted to view the proceedings from behind a screen. On arrival the bridegroom, who wore a silk costume, was placed on a wooden platform. The bride, veiled, jeweled, and wearing a red sari, was placed on another platform. Then the bride on her platform was ceremoniously carried round the bridegroom seven times.

An elderly man, the bride's uncle, viewed those proceedings without enthusiasm.

"They pretend to keep up the old ways," he grumbled, "but, in fact, everything is changed. Formerly, it was compulsory for girls to be wed before puberty. My niece—imagine it!—is nineteen. Formerly even child widows were compelled to shave their heads and were forbidden to remarry. Now the parents think nothing of marrying them off again as soon as possible. In my day a wife treated her husband as a god. When he had done eating, she ate off his leaf: but first she purified the spot where it had rested with a solution of cow-dung. Wives prayed for long lives for their husbands, and hoped to die first. If a husband died first, everyone knew it was because the wife must have sinned. Now wives sit down boldly with husbands to meals; and they do not seem to care a fig if a husband dies."

A small man with a large head said he was sorely troubled by the whole subject of marriage. He was a professor of moral philosophy at a leading Bengal university.

"I believe child marriages are bad," he said. "But all the same, one cannot help being perplexed by the fact that the *Shastras* insist on them." The *Shastras* are an important part of the Hindus' religious literature. "The *Shastras* seem clearly to say that a girl can expect to reach puberty after the age of ten. And the *Shastras* say that if a man has not married off his daughter by the time she is twelve, 'his ancestors will be cursed to drink her menstrual flow month after month.'

"What I have therefore concluded," said the professor of moral philosophy, "is that the ancients had a different method of reckoning years, and that when they said 'puberty,' they really meant 'maturity.' Now a girl may not reach maturity until she is eighteen, nineteen, or even older; and the *Shastras* say that marriage should not occur until after that."

He shook his head mournfully. "All the same, it is very worrying; for one cannot be *sure* . . . "

XVI

EAST PAKISTAN: MOSLEMS DIVIDED

East Pakistan is a miserable overcrowded rural slum.

O. H. K. SPATE

THE CALCUTTA railroad station was crowded with Hindu refugees from East Pakistan. Ten years after the partition of India, they were still entering Bengal at the rate of 25,000 a month. They were herded into iron pens for health examination and crouched there in their rags, more like animals than people.

Partition was a typical piece of twentieth-century politico-surgery. The Punjab is at one side of India, and Bengal is right at the other side. Both those extremities, one in the west and the other in the east, were chopped up between Moslems and Hindus amid fire and pillage, massacre and rape. The operation involved the uprooting of a total of 17,000,000 people.

The Moslems found themselves in possession of a country, Pakistan, which instead of being a geographical unity, like all other countries, consists of two unequal pieces of real estate, with the whole breadth of Hindu India wedged between them. Divided by distance, the Moslem Punjabis and the Moslem Bengalis are also divided by customs and language. The Punjabis ruled the roost, for Karachi in West Pakistan was chosen as the capital, and West Pakistan included the great empty spaces of Baluchistan and Sind and the famous North-West Frontier Province, as well as part of the Punjab. The Moslem Bengalis separated from Karachi by 1,200 miles of India were also cut off from Calcutta and crammed into a flooded corner of the Ganges delta.

West Pakistan is bigger than Texas, and East Pakistan is smaller than Wisconsin. East Pakistan is woefully overcrowded, with 42,000,000 people to West Pakistan's 34,000,000. The Hindu minority who were stranded in East Pakistan after the partition continue striving to get to Bengal.

East Pakistan has other troubles. The Moslem peasants believed partition would rid them of their Hindu landlords. They did not foresee it would bring them under the political domination of faraway Punjabis. All the high posts in Pakistan were held by members of the Moslem League, which ruled Pakistan as the Congress Party ruled India; and the Moslem League was dominated by Punjabis, with whom the Bengali-speaking people of East Pakistan had nothing in common save religion. When East Pakistan rejected the Moslem League in the elections of 1954, an army general was sent from West Pakistan to "restore order" and rule by decree.

I flew to Dacca, the capital of East Pakistan, over a flooded countryside. All the rivers of Bengal and Bihar seemed to have burst their banks, and we might have been flying over an inland sea. We landed at Dacca with difficulty, for the city was mostly under water. It was a dismal introduction. On the way in from the airport we passed a building with queues of people wound round it. Men, women, and children stood patiently in the damp heat, their bare feet squelching in black mud. They clutched a few belongings that seemed to have been hastily bundled together. I asked what the building was.

"It is the Indian Visa Office," I was told. "These people are Hindus, who want to go to Bengal."

Ahead of them, if they got their visas, lay a slow, 380-mile journey by rail. At the end of it they would find themselves in the iron cages at the Calcutta railroad station.

In the last floods that had overwhelmed East Pakistan, American Globemasters had flown all the way from Tokyo with

food and drugs to fight famine and epidemics. Now the floods
had come again. No epidemic was threatened this time—not
yet—but it seemed to me that famine might not be far off.
The countryside around Dacca was hideously overcrowded,
and there appeared to be little food. The people lived in reed
huts built above the flood on mud platforms. In the humid
heat they sprawled listless and half-naked on their mud veran-
das, looking apathetically over the waters that had risen to
drown their rice.

I had introductions to a Moslem who worked in a foreign
embassy, and to a foreign missionary who had opened a library.
I called on the Moslem first.

He was a thin young man with a persecuted look, and he
spoke in a whisper that I could hardly hear. It soon became evident that my coming had thrown him into a panic. Once or
twice he got up, tiptoed to the door, and peered apprehensively
out into the stone corridor.

"Things are very bad," he said. "But it is better not to write
about it," he added.

I suggested that if he wanted privacy, we should close the
door.

"No: that might suggest I was telling you political secrets.
Did So-and-so get my last letter?" he asked, referring to our
mutual friend.

"He said he hadn't heard from you for about six weeks."

"Then he did not get my last letter. It must have been
opened. Oh dear, I wish I could remember *exactly* what I wrote
in it. I never keep copies, it is not advisable."

"Why should anyone object to what you wrote? Do they have
a political censorship in East Pakistan?"

"No, no, not a censorship, entirely. Sometimes though they
open one's letters. I have already been warned not to be sarcastic about our politicians. Sometimes," he added dolefully,
"it is very difficult not to be sarcastic."

"What is the political situation?" I asked.

"It is very complicated," he said vaguely. "The Moslem League is finished, but the United Front that ousted it has fallen to pieces. Now the Awami League is in power, but no one knows how long it will last, for they are all quarreling among themselves."

"Why is the Moslem League finished?"

He grinned. "Because their rapacity was intolerable even by Pakistan standards." Then he put his hand over his mouth. "Oh dear, I am being sarcastic again."

I went to visit the missionary. The library was not much, by Pakistan or any other standards. It was housed in a small, half-submerged building in a flooded back alley, near a swollen creek. There were several shelves of books, and a reading-room with nobody in it.

The missionary, who must have been a cheerful soul before he came to Dacca but who now looked harried, led me into what he called his den, behind the empty reading-room. He, too, lowered his voice when he talked, but he had sufficient spirit left to close his own door and let the suspicious-minded draw whatever conclusions they chose.

"They are a difficult people," he confessed. When he first opened the library the reading-room had been thronged with eager young students. One young man in particular, who seemed to be a student leader, had pored over the library books and taken copious notes. Then one day the students abruptly ceased coming.

"The next thing that happened," said the missionary, a little bitterly, "was a threat to have the library closed down." The diligent student had discovered a volume that contained a portrait of Mohammed—the Koranic law forbids portrayal of the Prophet—and had reported the matter to the police.

"When the floods came, we tried to organize some of the young men into help squads to build dykes. They agreed to come along, but when they discovered they were expected to dig, they all went away again. One of them explained: 'We thought you wished us to survey the situation and write a report for government. We are men of education, not ditch-fillers.' "

"What is the economic position of East Pakistan?" I asked.

"East Pakistan was never more than an agricultural backwater of Calcutta. Now it is divorced from Calcutta's industries and thrown enirely on its own resources, except for what it can beg from West Pakistan. The population is rising and the value of money is falling. There are almost no trained administrators, for most of the trained people of the area were Hindus. At Partition Dacca University lost 80 per cent of its lecturers; they were all Hindus. But congestion of population is the worst problem. In the Dacca district there are over 18,000,000 people: twice as many as in the whole of Belgium."

I had arranged to dine with my Moslem friend and then go on to a political meeting, followed by an appointment with a mullah. I got in a taxi and splashed my way to the new apartment house where the Moslem lived. It was a gray and undistinguished building, and its foundations had already started to sag. I climbed several flights of stone stairs and knocked on his unpainted door: paint was as scarce in Dacca as everything else. The front door opened directly on to a scullery and beyond the scullery was squeezed a tiny living-room that also served as a dining-room. My Moslem friend lived here with his wife, his four children, and his mother-in-law.

The other guest was a lecturer at the university. He was an excitable man, and he was bursting with grievances. We took off our coats and ties because of the humid heat, and sat in our shirtsleeves, drinking warm beer and smoking cigarettes. The lecturer began to address me at the top of his voice.

"The University of Dacca was once the pride of Bengal, but that was before the Moslem League vultures from the Punjab descended upon us. When those Punjabi imperialists arrived from Karachi, they seized everything for their own use. Most of our buildings were turned into bureaucrats' offices. The Arts Faculty was expelled in its entirety to what had formerly been the servants' quarters. When the university authorities requested building materials, the request was refused. They were told that all building materials had been requisitioned to build private mansions for top Punjabi officials."

"Hush!" said our host, alarmed. "Someone may hear you. Please to remember you are in my apartment."

"I do not care who hears me," shouted the lecturer. "Let them come. Let them arrest me. I am not afraid."

"But I shall lose my apartment. I managed to get it only because of my connection with the embassy. Also, I do not want to lose my job."

"They cannot touch you. They need money from that government you work for."

"It is because I work for an embassy that they suspect me," said our host gloomily. He brightened up as his wife and mother-in-law entered with plates. "Ah, here is our food."

We squeezed round the table. The wife and the mother-in-law served us, but nobody paid the slightest attention to them. The food was no sooner on the plates than our host began to eat rapidly. The reason for his haste soon became apparent. With the food came an enormous swarm of flies. They buzzed round our heads in a thick cloud. Our host warded them off with one hand, and quickly forked up his food with the other. Some of the flies fell on the table and crawled feebly about. They were green and bloated. I found I had little appetite.

The university lecturer ignored the flies. His attention was concentrated on politics.

"The Punjabis have treated us Bengalis as if we were only a colony of theirs," he shouted across the table at me. "They came from Karachi and put up large official buildings. Every Punjabi was a Minister, and every Minister had a Ministerial secretary. But in no government office was the face of a Bengali to be seen. All were fat smiling Punjabis. Not even in old Bengal, under the Hindus, was there ever such corruption."

"That is why the Moslem League was overthrown," our host

263

explained to me, speaking through a busy mouthful of fried chicken.

"The Moslem League was thrown out of office by the students of the University," said the lecturer. "It was they who led the fight. In the 1954 elections it was a student who defeated the Moslem League Chief Minister. The new Government led by Fazlul Huq sacked the Punjabi officials and replaced them all with good Bengalis."

"All the same, the Bengalis should not have killed the papermill manager," our host objected.

"It was the just vengeance of the people," said the lecturer. "This paper-mill manager was a Punjabi, was he not?"

"They should not have killed so many Punjabis," insisted our host.

"It was the Punjabis who opened fire on the people first. At the jute mills at least a thousand innocent Bengalis were shot down by Punjabi soldiers sent here by Karachi."

"If there had not been strikes and killings in the streets, Karachi would not have got its excuse to interfere in East Pakistan's affairs."

"Those Punjabi imperialists would have intervened in any case," said the lecturer. "They could not afford to lose East Pakistan, which their army was holding down so that their officials could rob it."

"A state of emergency was declared," our host explained to me, "and East Pakistan was placed under the rule of General Iskander Mirza, who was sent from Karachi. Mirza sacked all the Bengali politicians."

"What happened to them?" I asked.

"They all became traitors," shouted the lecturer. "When General Mirza arrived at the airport, they fought one another for the privilege of being the first to greet him. Some wept and begged his forgiveness; others hung garlands round his neck."

"They could not bear to be out of office once they had managed to get into it," said our host. "They implored Mirza to reinstate them. They needed the money."

"When General Mirza said he would consider giving them back their jobs, one of them kissed his feet and cried: 'Good days are in sight again!' " said the lecturer angrily.

"And what happened then?"

"General Mirza became President of Pakistan. He appointed one of the deposed politicians Governor of East Pakistan, and he allowed another to become Chief Minister."

"But these two men are bitter rivals. The Governor has secretly sworn to undo the Chief Minister, and the Chief Minister secretly calls the Governor a traitor."

"Also, both really hate Mirza in their hearts. They would very much like him to come to a bad finish."

"Many of Pakistan's leaders have come to a bad finish," said our host: under the influence of several bottles of warm beer, he was losing his caution and waxing sarcastic again. "One was assassinated, one was imprisoned for treason, and one went mad."

"Two went mad," corrected the lecturer loudly.

"In any case, most have been dismissed from office for corruption at one time or another."

"Unfortunately they are usually reinstated at the next turn of fortune's wheel," the lecturer said.

"Pakistan's first ten years have been very tumultuous," said our host.

After dinner we left the wife and the mother-in-law to wash the dishes, and went to the political meeting. It was being held in a small hall that during the day served as a schoolhouse, and it was in full swing. There was not one speaker, but two. Both had mounted chairs, and were talking at once. Each tried to shout the other down, and sections of the crowd were simultaneously cheering the one and booing the other. The roof leaked, and water had also seeped in under the door.

The lecturer shouted an explanation in my ear. "Both claim

265

to have been elected; each says the other tampered with the votes. Both are leaders of the Awami League."

I recalled that the Chief Minister of East Pakistan, who was also the chief leader of the Awami League, had recently declared in a public speech that East Pakistan was "a sinking ship." It seemed to me he might not be far wrong.

At this point all the lights went out. Considerable uproar ensued. The two rival groups in the hall shouted that their opponents had tampered with the lights as well as with the votes. The door burst open and there was a sound of trampling boots and also howls of anguish from those in the crowd who were barefooted. The lights went on again to reveal that the hall was now filled with helmeted policemen. One of the speakers protested; the other looked rather smug. But the meeting was clearly over. We left as unobtrusively as possible.

I got in another taxi and again splashed my way downtown, to keep my appointment with the mullah. A mullah is a Moslem religious teacher, and in Pakistan the mullahs are politically powerful. This one was particularly holy but was currently in political disfavor. He had played a large role in the ousting of the Moslem League and had consequently been accused by the ruling clique in Karachi of being in the pay of both the Communists and the Hindus. Compelled to flee, he had lent color to those accusations by turning up in Delhi at the Communist-staged peace conference, and also by attending a similar affair in East Berlin. But now he was back in Pakistan, as large as life, and apparently indestructible.

Most of Dacca's population seemed to live in back alleys that were under water, and the mullah was no exception. I waded along the alley and passed through a dark doorway. At the top of some waterlogged wooden steps I was challenged by two guards. They explained that the mullah was engaged in prayer and asked me to wait. Presently they got bored and went down the stairs and out of sight. I waited some time and nothing happened. Getting bored myself, I approached the door behind

266

which the mullah was supposed to be praying and took a quick look through the keyhole. An old man with a gray beard, wearing a skullcap and a *lungi*, which is a short white skirt resembling the Indian dhoti, was seated cross-legged on a bed. Drawn up before him was a table covered with dishes, and he was eating heartily.

I knocked on the door and walked in. The mullah looked up with no particular emotion and pushed aside the table, belching slightly as he did so. He removed his skullcap, revealing a bald head, and motioned me to a chair.

I asked him if it were true, as his critics claimed, that he was in sympathy with the Communists. The mullah smiled.

"I am close to the masses. That is why the politicians dislike me. Many politicians have sought my help: all have turned against me in the end. But the masses never have. They know I am on their side.

"First I am a Moslem. But second I am a Bengali. I spent nineteen years in British jails. I may die in a Punjabi one. I look to the masses to protect me."

"I don't understand this bitterness between Bengalis and Punjabis in Pakistan," I said. "If you are all Moslems—"

"It has a long history. Under the Raj, most of the Moslem politicians were Bengalis. But Jinnah, the founder of Pakistan, was a Punjabi. He centered political power in Karachi, and the Punjabis treated Bengalis like dogs. But West Pakistan will never be united. The Sindhis will fight the Pathans, both will fight the Punjabis, and the Punjabi politicians will fight one another. In the end, political control of Pakistan will fall to the Bengalis. We are more numerous, and more intelligent. East Pakistan is overcrowded, but West Pakistan is empty. It is the Bengalis who will rule Pakistan."

A young man with a hooked nose came quickly into the room and insisted on shaking hands with me.

"The mullah speaks no English," he said gravely. "I will interpret."

He spoke to the mullah in Bengali, then he turned to me. "The mullah says that the present Pakistan politicians in both the east and west are agents of American imperialism. The downtrodden masses of Pakistan want only peace, and friendship with the Soviet Union and Red China. They do not want to be the pawns of the American imperialist game, which the mullah has always fearlessly exposed and will continue to expose."

There was more in the same vein, but I was not listening. I was watching the mullah, who was gravely stroking his beard, and had a faraway look in his eyes. It was not entirely clear to me whether the Communists were using the mullah, or the mullah was using the Communists; but I thought I could make a very good guess.

XVII
WEST PAKISTAN: MOSLEMS UNITED?

In the Constitution of the Islamic Republic of Pakistan, women have been guaranteed equal rights with other citizens of the State. PAKISTAN GOVERNMENT OFFICIAL

I FLEW from Dacca in East Pakistan to Karachi in West Pakistan, across 1,200 miles of Indian territory. The green rice-paddies of Bengal were replaced by the stony hills of Bihar, the plains of Uttar Pradesh, and the mountains of Rajasthan. Finally we flew over the desolate deserts of Sind, in a violent duststorm.

We landed at two o'clock in the morning, at which hour any international airport looks unfriendly. A hot wet wind, bitter with salt, blew in over the sand dunes. The airport was being extended, and we walked from the plane across an oil-spattered concrete apron, where other machines were being serviced under the glare of Cyclopean arc lights. Nobody wanted to have much to do with us; everyone was tired and wished to go home.

I hired a taxi to take me into town, which proved to be a mistake. The taxi had once been painted maroon, but the paint had long since flaked off: it was the rustiest taxi I ever saw, and it sounded rusty, too. The driver had a cloth wrapped round his head in place of a cap, and I guessed his age to be about seventeen. He stowed my bags in his rusty trunk, and we set off.

Along the moonlit road from the airport new flat-roofed buildings were going up: they looked like pallid submarine turrets sprouting from the sand. They had not been there the last time I was in Karachi, so that was a sign of progress. But I had just come from East Pakistan, where another famine threatened; and I knew that Pakistan was spending about 60 per cent of its budget on arms, which the United States seemed fondly to imagine were to defend the country against Russia, whereas every Pakistani I ever talked to made no bones of his belief that they were urgently needed for possible use against India. Meanwhile, however. Karachi was undoubtedly growing. In a comparatively few years it had transformed itself from a fishing village into the capital of a brand-new country. It had a population of about 2,000,000. Most of them unfortunately still had nowhere to live.

These reflections were interrupted by the taxi jarring to an abrupt halt, after a wild swerve that left it stranded in the middle of the road. The young taxi-driver said apologetically: "Please wait," and jumped out. He opened the hood and began to poke experimentally into the car's silent innards. Then he came round to my side, said "wait" again, held up two fingers, and abruptly vanished into the night.

The two fingers presumably meant two minutes, and I assumed he had gone to get help. Either the mechanical problem was beyond him, or else he had simply run out of gas, which in Karachi happens frequently. I climbed out of the car to smoke a cigarette. Standing there, it occurred to me that a taxi apparently abandoned in the very center of the roadway was a natural target for Karachi's numerous hit-and-run drivers. I twisted the steering-wheel and maneuvered the vehicle out of the danger zone. Just in time. A truck, with one headlamp not working and the other blinking like a feeble semaphore, hurtled past with inches to spare.

The minutes ticked on. The taxi-driver did not return. Presently the air bus that I had been too impatient to wait for came lumbering along. I hailed it, removed my bags from the taxi's trunk, and climbed aboard.

The hotel, like the airport, was being extended. It had been built on the lines of a lamasery, with the simple object of holding as many people as possible. The numerous cell-like rooms were ranged round a central courtyard, rising tier upon tier and connected by long stone corridors. A lanky bellboy wearing the ragged remnants of a uniform led me along corridor after corridor: I began to feel like a Chinese Communist on the Long March. Finally he creaked open a damp-swollen door, after turning a rusty lock with a key attached by a piece of string to an enormous slab of wood with the room's number crudely painted on it, and ushered me into my cell.

"How long are you staying?" he inquired.

"Probably until Friday."

"Friday is my day off so I will take my baksheesh now, please."

I awoke to find Karachi paralyzed by a general strike. The Lucknow incident of the dog Mahmud had continued to smolder in Moslem hearts. Fresh flame had been struck from it by the publication in India of a book (written, as it turned out, by two Americans) which, the Moslems claimed, insulted the Prophet. The Karachi strikers were being led round the city by groups of university students, shouting "Death to Nehru." Delighted to reopen the dog incident, one of the city's leading newspapers celebrated the occasion with an editorial, in which it pointed out that, if Nehru were really sincere in his frequent denials of hatred for Pakistan, he would have seen to it that the owner of the lost dog was sentenced to death—the only possible penalty for belittlers of the Prophet—instead of letting the Hindu miscreant escape back to Nepal.

Apart from the demonstrators, the streets were almost deserted, except for women and some dung carts drawn by disdainful camels. On top of one dung cart the driver lay peacefully asleep, with a cloth, tastefully embroidered with flowers, drawn over his face. The women's faces were concealed, also, for they all wore *burqas*. The *burqa* is a tentlike garment made

271

of coarse white cotton which drapes its unfortunate wearer from head to foot. It lacks even eye-slits, having instead two tiny, square, pin-size holes, which at first glance look merely like a decorative flourish. Karachi's climate is both intensely hot and intensely humid. The women who wear *burqas* must find it almost impossible to breathe, and it is a fact that many such women contract tuberculosis, chiefly from having to put on this insanitary garment. Yet most of the women of Pakistan do not dare appear in public in anything else, and the men shrug their indifference, or hotly defend the custom.

I lunched with a pretty Pakistani girl who was fighting a spirited war against the *burqa* and against other women's disabilities. She was a small and fragile-seeming person with the breathless good looks of a Persian miniature. But she was about as gentle as a whip. She could not afford to be anything else. She successfully ran a women's magazine, had two healthy children, and kept her husband puzzled but devoted. Instead of a *burqa* she wore make-up and a dress that would have caused heads to turn in Paris, so snugly did it fit her small ripe figure. But she had very few friends, either men or women.

"It's an uphill job," she said, accepting a cigarette and allowing me to light it for her. "We shall win, of course, but—'the price of liberty is eternal vigilance.' We have the vote—but Pakistan has not had proper elections since the state was founded ten years ago. Elections have been promised for 1958; but that promise has been made before, and anyhow, we don't know how the women will use their vote, if at all. The country is run exclusively by men, and most of them are fanatical believers in the *burqa* and all it symbolizes. Begum Liaqat Ali Khan, the widow of our first Prime Minister—who was assassinated—is Pakistan's Ambassador to the Netherlands: but that is only window-dressing, to please the West and, particularly, the Americans.

"At present, we're fighting polygamy. More and more of the leading politicians, including the most Westernized ones, are taking second wives." She laughed gaily. "We go to their meetings and ask them embarrassing questions. They get furious. Some of them have been shamed into divorcing their first wives, but that's no improvement, of course. The wives have no proper protection and are just cast off. We're not going to let them get away with that."

Though a mere man, I wished her well in her struggle.

Later I called on a Moslem friend. I had known him a long time, and I also had met his wife. His name was Ahmad, and he had been educated in Europe. He was deeply interested in politics, and had written a couple of books. His wife did not wear a *burqa*; but she never accompanied her husband to parties, and, even in their home, she usually kept strict purdah.

We discussed politics for a while, then I mentioned my visit to the lady magazine-editor. He stiffened at the mention of her name, and frowned.

"But surely you of all people don't object to what she is doing!" I protested; I knew that his politics were if anything left wing.

"It is not a subject that I as a Moslem can discuss with a foreigner," he said gravely.

"Come, Ahmad!" I laughed. "We've known each other too long for you to try that one on me." A humorous thought struck me. "All this jealous seclusion of women—do you seriously believe that if Mrs. Ahmad and I were to be left alone together in the same room, sexual intercourse would take place?"

He looked me steadily in the eye. "Yes," he said, unsmiling.

There was nothing more to say. We went back to talking politics. I never saw Mrs. Ahmad again.

Pakistan should never have been created. NEHRU

KARACHI'S ANTI-NEHRU strike ended. The students returned to their classes. The hotel's long stone corridors rang noisily with

273

hammering, sawing, and chiseling. Concrete-mixers busily churned, and on the way to the dining-hall one picked one's way past giant stone slabs and piles of timber. The lamasery would soon be twice its present size.

I stepped out into the broiling street to find a maroon-colored taxi waiting for me. The youthful driver greeted me with enthusiasm. "Got plenty of gas now," he said. "No more trouble." He had patiently tracked me down and composed himself to lurk outside the hotel until I should emerge.

We drove to Jinnah's tomb. The streets were filled with light vehicles, furiously driven. Men pedaling cycle-rickshaws were triumphantly overtaken by men on motorcycle-rickshaws. The ambition of every owner of a pedalcycle-rickshaw is to save up enough money to acquire a motorcycle-rickshaw; and every driver of a motorcycle-rickshaw dreams of one day owning a taxi, even a rusty one. In the backs of the rickshaws the passengers sat under flapping canvas canopies, enjoying the breeze created by their own swift progress. This is the only way to keep cool in Karachi.

On every side new buildings were going up, encased in long twisted bamboo poles for scaffolding. The sidewalks were crowded with men in pajamas and women in *burqas*. Most of the shops looked dilapidated, and there was a great frequency of clinics, displaying giant signs which proclaimed: "Urine and Stools Examined Here." People milled outside the Cotton Exchange, Karachi's largest building.

Mohammad Ali Jinnah, the creator of Pakistan, was a frail man with a consumptive's face and demoniac energy. He made a large fortune at the Bombay Bar, and he wore a monocle on a black silk cord. He was born in Karachi in very humble circumstances, and he did not return to his birthplace until it had become the capital of the new state. He died in Karachi of lung disease not long after. His tomb in the center of the city is a grandiose affair of marble. Near by is the tomb of Liaqat Ali Khan, Pakistan's first Prime Minister. Liaqat Ali Khan, like

Gandhi, was assassinated. His assassin shot him dead at a political meeting; and a policeman who was supposed to be guarding the Prime Minister then shot the assassin. There were many rumors that the assassination had been planned by political rivals within the Moslem League. Years after her husband's death Begum Liaqat Ali Khan was still so dissatisfied with the investigation of the crime that she hired a Scotland Yard detective to reopen the inquiry. His findings were inconclusive, and the affair still remains a mystery. Pakistan has been in a state of political turmoil ever since.

Jinnah never expected to see Pakistan created in his own lifetime. Only a few years before the historic decision to partition India the majority of Moslems were still supporting the Congress Party, not Jinnah's Moslem League. Jinnah never attracted the masses as Gandhi and Nehru did: his black-rimmed monocle, his long black cigarette-holder, and his aristocratic manners were powerful barriers between him and them. The brand-new state had to be built up hurriedly on very shaky foundations. I took off my shoes and paid my respects to the cold marble, then looked around. The tombs of Jinnah and Liaqat Ali Khan were ornate oases in a human desert of thousands of refugee squatters' shacks.

I drove to the office of a government official. He was a Christian, but he had been in government service a long time, and his ability had kept him his job, for Pakistan woefully lacked trained administrators. He was a big, burly man, and he greeted me cheerfully and called for coffee.

"At last we have a Constitution," he said. "It took eight years to write it. Of course, it's an Islamic one. It makes me a second-class citizen of a third-class state." He laughed heartily at his own wry joke.

The birth of the Constitution had been a Caesarian affair. After the deaths of Jinnah and Liaqat Ali Khan, power in Pakistan passed into the capable hands of Ghulam Mohammad, the Governor-General. But Ghulam Mohammad was a Punjabi and the Prime Minister Mohammad Ali was a Bengali. The old dispute between Punjabis and Bengalis flared up and was complicated by disputes between Punjabis and Sindhis. After a tortuous period of in-fighting, all within the Moslem League, the Constituent Assembly tried to clip the Governor-General's wings by passing laws without his assent. Ghulam, who was upheld by the courts and backed by the army and General Iskander Mirza, thereupon declared a state of emergency and dissolved the Constituent Assembly.

Ghulam's triumph was shortlived, for he was stricken by paralysis and sank into a coma. But before he died, he appointed General Mirza in his place. Mirza, who had ruled East Pakistan with a firm hand after government broke down there, proceeded to put an end to faction fighting in West Pakistan by merging the Punjab, Sind, Baluchistan, the North-West Frontier, and a number of other areas into a single province. He also had himself proclaimed President, and the Moslem League changed its name to the Republican Party. Mirza had to find a new Prime Minister, and he chose another Bengali, Hussein Shaheed Suhrawardy.

"And now what will happen?" I asked.

My friend the official shrugged.

"We can only hope. We are creating industries as fast as we can, but our industrialists expect to get their capital back in five years. Profits are enormous, and wages are very low. We should be trading more with India, but the quarrel over Kashmir stands in the way. We have imported sugar from Brazil, coal from South Africa, and cotton cloth from Shanghai, though we could have got all those from India, much cheaper. Eighty per cent of our income still comes from cotton. The main issue is land reform, but our politicians will not face up to it, for they themselves are big landlords. We are adding 1,000,000 a year to our population by natural increase, but food shortages are becoming what Suhrawardy calls 'recurring features.' Experts have warned us that at the rate we are using up the soil, the valley of the Indus will be a desert in less than 50 years. But we need more water, and we are still mired in a dispute with India over the use of the canals that the British built."

"Yet you don't seem to despair," I smiled.

He threw out a big hand to indicate his office. It was a bare enough room, containing only two desks, a couple of telephones and typewriters, and some straight-backed wooden chairs.

"After Partition there were no desks, no telephones, no typewriters; there were not even chairs. We started absolutely from scratch and had to build up from nothing at all. We are not doing so badly."

I told the taxi-driver to take me to the Assembly building, but on the way I stopped at the Central Telegraph Office. I wrote my telegram standing up at a tall counter, for there were no chairs or benches; underneath the counter, a goat grazed peaceably on wastepaper from a black-painted iron trashcan. From the bare and peeling yellow wall a very bad portrait of Jinnah glared down at me: he was wearing a black fur hat and his thin lips seemed to curl with contempt. The founder of Pakistan had been a very arrogant man; probably he had needed to be.

The Assembly building was a domed white structure set uncompromisingly in the middle of a glaring stone quadrangle. Buzzards circled slowly in the blue sky above it, and a green flag with a white crescent hung limply from a flagpole. A procession carrying banners inscribed "Liberate Kashmir" straggled round the building, and the entrance was guarded by soldiers carrying rifles, and also by plain-clothes men, wearing astrakhan hats.

After all this the legislative chamber seemed disappointingly small and ordinary. The politicians sat on benches, under rapidly whirling ceiling-fans; when one of them rose to speak, he obligingly waited, smirking, until the newspaper photographers had got their floodlights trained on him before launching into

277

oratory. I amused myself by counting those who had been sitting there off and on through one constitutional crisis after another, compelled to vacate their places from time to time to face charges of corruption and abuse of office, but always somehow managing to bob into prominence again: it came to a goodly total.

But a comparatively new face in that chamber was Hussein Shaheed Suhrawardy, the Prime Minister. He was a small plump man who looked as if he had been carved out of dark butter. He had had a remarkable career. Before Partition he was Prime Minister of Bengal, and contrived to be both secretary of the Moslem League and a close friend of Mahatma Gandhi. When India was politically divided into two separate countries, he found himself in the astonishing position of being both a citizen of independent India and a duly elected member of the Pakistan Constituent Assembly. He had had plenty of ups and downs since then.

Suhrawardy, like Jinnah, was a lawyer, but, unlike Jinnah, he had rich parents. His father was a wealthy Calcutta mill-owner who sent him to study at Oxford University. In spite of this background, Suhrawardy proceeded after Partition to turn himself into a champion of the East Pakistan masses, and harangued crowds in the ricepaddies, going about unshaven and wearing a *lungi*. He helped oust the Moslem League from power in East Pakistan, but was involved in the debacle that followed, and prudently retired for a time to Switzerland.

The last time I had seen him had been at his big gloomy house in Clifton, a Karachi suburb where only the very rich live. The house was a jumble of junk and genuine art treasures, and I got the impression that Suhrawardy was a man with a split personality. He was steeped in politics, and yet at the same time he loved to climb into a dress suit and go the round of Karachi's nightclubs, for he boasted that at sixty-four he could still rumba until dawn.

I was ushered into a vast cluttered bedroom which among

numerous other objects contained two beds. Only one of them was used as a bed, for Suhrawardy was a widower. The other bed he used as a sort of impromptu desk, heaping it with books, papers, writing-pads, parliamentary reports, and two telephones, both of which constantly rang. Mr. Suhrawardy was still in his nightshirt, and was in the middle of shaving. But he evidently regarded this as of no importance, and it was not for me to demur. He immediately launched into a long denunciation of other Pakistan politicians, delivered in a deep, impressive voice, and with gestures recalling Charles Laughton in the role of Captain Bligh. His especial bête noire was General Iskander Mirza, whose ancestry he described in picturesque detail. He became so heated that he sliced his finger with the razor he was still wielding.

A servant sprang to his side, but Suhrawardy waved him off. Half his dark face still covered with white lather, he marched up and down the room, declaiming.

"Mirza is an unscrupulous schemer!" he cried. He wheeled round and shook his bleeding finger at me, and drops of blood spattered all over me, and over the bed that held the piles of books and papers and the two ringing telephones.

From that interview I went to call on General Mirza. He received me jovially in his large house in the center of Karachi. We sat on a cool *stoop* overlooking dewy green lawns, and the general offered me a Turkish cigarette from a large silver box, and mixed me a scotch and soda. He mixed one for himself, also, and lit himself a big cigar. Moslems are not supposed to drink hard liquor, but Mirza was no ordinary Moslem.

He was a very broad-shouldered man, with a wide brown face, black eyebrows, and the brooding eyes of a perplexed but good-humored bloodhound. He had had a distinguished career as a soldier, fighting for the British on the Khyber Pass, and had received the O.B.E. for keeping order among the warring tribesmen. He understood soldiering and he had no quarrel with the tribesmen, whom he regarded with British-inculcated good-natured contempt as natives: what puzzled him were the Pakistan politicians.

"I have no time for politicians and mullahs," he said frankly. "The politicians are corrupt intriguers and the mullahs are all mad. My job is to keep order . . . People talk to me about democracy. What do the peasants know about government? They would give all power to the politicians, who are rascals doing their best to ruin the country. Only the army and I stand between the masses and the politicians who would destroy them as wolves destroy sheep. I call this 'controlled democracy.' "

I said there were rumors that Suhrawardy hoped to become Prime Minister.

"He will become Prime Minister only over my dead body!" roared the general.

Only a few months later, however, General Mirza became the President of Pakistan, and accepted Suhrawardy as his Prime Minister, garlanding him with roses and jasmine. As I did not believe the general was an unscrupulous schemer, but thought of him as an able soldier in a political fix, I concluded that the choice had been forced upon him, and that no love was lost between President and Prime Minister despite the roses and jasmine. Politics in Pakistan were merely pursuing their normal course.

By summarily merging the different areas of West Pakistan into one united province, Mirza had at least halted the local rivalries that were threatening to ruin the country. But he had not solved Pakistan's two major political problems: the bitterness between West Pakistan and East Pakistan, and Pakistan's quarrel with India over Kashmir. The Bengalis of East Pakistan believed that they were being treated as a colony of the faraway Punjab. The truth was that there were simply not enough funds available for the proper development of either West or East, and that in both areas the peasants groaned under a tyrannical landlord system. But, simply by moving to Karachi as Prime Minister of all Pakistan, Suhrawardy had largely lost the confidence of the Bengali peasants, who believed he had sold himself to the Punjabis.

Mirza had told me he would like to finish the dispute over Kashmir and become friends with India. Suhrawardy said much the same thing. I believed them both. A poor and divided country is unlikely to plan to go to war with a neighbor that has five times its population, especially when its two unequal halves are separated from each other by that neighbor's vast bulk. Nevertheless, Pakistan was spending 57 per cent of its budget on arms, and India was spending 40 per cent of its budget for the same purpose; and fear of each other was the primary motive in both cases. There was only one practicable solution of the Kashmir problem, and that was to accept the cease-fire line as a borderline between India and Pakistan. But no Pakistani leader, not even Mirza and certainly not Suhrawardy, was likely to risk assassination by publicly discussing such a solution. The Moslem fanaticism that had created Pakistan in the first place, and of which Jinnah had been the fiery-eyed, chilly-faced embodiment, was rooted in a hatred of Hindus; and that hatred had become concentrated on the Kashmir issue.

I found out how strong this feeling was when I climbed into my maroon taxi and drove from the Assembly, with its white-crescented green flag, to the home of a Moslem religious leader. He was the man who had inspired the absurd editorial demanding the death sentence for the Nepalese dog-owner, and who had organized the students that had led the mobs crying "Death to Nehru." And he was a very different kettle of fish from the mullah in Dacca who flirted with Communists and wanted to free the peasants.

The house was silent and tightly shuttered. A soft-footed servant led me into a darkened room, and presently brought me a very small cup of exquisite coffee. From the outside the house had looked forbidding, but the interior was austerely but tastefully furnished with soft low couches and very fine carpets. The man who came in saluted me gravely. He had a long thin beard and a pair of very intense dark eyes. We sipped our coffee and regarded each other in thoughtful silence.

I began to ask him some political questions, but he put them aside with a motion of one fine hand.

"Politics and politicians! My concern is with higher matters. The people do not read the Koran and think only of their bellies. First they must regain their souls. Pakistan was created to be an instrument of the divine will. It must be tempered and become a sword. Among unbelievers our deadliest enemy is the Hindu, who tirelessly seeks our destruction. Our fathers knew this well: they knew how to treat Hindus. Sooner or later there must be a *jehad*—a holy war against the Hindus who slaughtered our men and debauched our women. If the people of the plains fail us, we shall turn to the people of the hills, as we did nine years ago in the war for Kashmir. It is from the hills that our salvation has always come, for there the fire of Islam still burns."

I looked into his glowing eyes and realized he was utterly sincere. Pandit Appasamy in Benares had been sincere, too, after his fashion. There was no arguing with such views, and I did not attempt it. Both Pakistan and India were queer compounds of fanatical religious zeal and political corruption, ecstatic bloody-mindedness and outrageous self-seeking. Whether they could coexist for long on the same continent was anybody's guess.

A *very advantageous, useful, humane piece of rascality.* SIR CHARLES NAPIER ON THE CONQUEST OF SIND

THREE COLORADOS could be squeezed into West Pakistan; but over a third of the area consists of the mountainous wastes of Baluchistan, which is the size of Montana and where only about a million or so of West Pakistan's 34,000,000 people live. Two thirds of the population are in the Pakistan Punjab, and most of the remainder are sparsely scattered throughout Sind and the North-West Frontier. The political life of the federal capital of Karachi is dominated by Punjabis, though Karachi is really a part of Sind.

I traveled by rail from Karachi to Hyderabad, the capital of Sind. Hyderabad in Sind is where they make the embroidered saddles for the riding camels, and is not to be confused with Hyderabad in India. My traveling companion was a professor of English literature, a gentle-eyed man with a lost look, and from him conversation flowed as from a tap. He put down his book when I entered the compartment and plunged eagerly into a literary discussion that lasted us the entire journey.

"Kipling says fact is fact and fiction is fiction, and never the twain shall meet. But I ask myself if this is really so. Does not every author mix the two? Take Somerset Maugham!"

He held up the book he was reading: it was an early novel, *Liza of Lambeth*—no doubt an admirable if startling antidote to the tedium of train travel in a desert not many miles from the borders of Persia and Afghanistan.

"Somerset Maugham says: 'Fact and fiction are so intermingled in my work I can now hardly distinguish the one from the other when I look back.' And it is so. In this story, for instance, he confesses he uses material that he gathered from attending to sixty-three confinement cases in three weeks at St. Thomas Hospital, London!"

The professor laughed gently: he was thoroughly enjoying himself.

"And this mixing of fact and fiction—that is also what lunatics do." He rolled his eyes comically. "Hence, Shakespeare put poets and lunatics in the same category.

"But now, what does Huxley say? Huxley was, after all, a scientist. Huxley says: 'Logical consequences are the scarecrows of fools and the beacons of wise men.' And then there is Hum-

283

boldt. Humboldt has written: 'Every understanding is a mis-understanding.' "

He beamed at me. "Are mental processes factual? Do they travel in the same direction as facts? On those questions, science is silent. But Montesquieu is not. For Montesquieu says: 'Observations are the facts of science, and theories are its fairy tales.'

"Now let us turn to modern psychology. No more fairy tales, please! cries the modern psychologist. Only facts! But then psychology begins itself to use fictions as facts. Dreams! Nightmares! A gorgeous palace built only on fanciful fictions!

"Let us see then what Aristotle says. This brainy chap dubs science: 'outcome of minimum of experience satisfied for maximum of inference.' It is so. 'Orderly universe' is a concept that no serious intellectual now subscribes to. Ptolemy believed that the sun revolved around the earth. Fact then: fiction now! Our conclusion is, society takes pride of place in its own fickleness."

I confess that, after the politicians, I found the professor refreshing. Following my conversation with the Moslem zealot, I needed reassuring that India had only recently been torn in two and that despite this political change Indians and Pakistanis were fundamentally the same sort of people who had long lived under the same government, even though it was an alien one that both resented. The professor furnished me with just the reassurance I needed. He and Mr. Kaviraj Lal might have been brothers.

But in Hyderabad, a hot little town without beauty, I was back in politics once more.

Everyone was still talking about the martyrdom of Mir Ghulam Ali Talpur, an aged aristocrat who had been Speaker of the Sind Assembly. The Mir had been bold enough to challenge the power of the political boss of Sind, Khan Bahadur Mohammad Ayub Khuhro, and retribution had swiftly followed.

In an attempt (which inevitably failed) to deal with local political bosses, the Karachi Government had passed a whopping piece of legislation called the Public and Representative Offices Disqualification Act, or PRODA for short. The measure threatened to deprive Mr. Khuhro of his power, and emboldened the Mir to organize a parliamentary revolt against the Khuhro regime. Mr. Khuhro was due to be removed from office anyway, but the Mir was in a hurry, and with good reason. The landowners of Sind, of whom the Mir was a leading representative, were $12,000,000 in arrears with their tax payments—the total revenue of Sind was $18,000,000—and Mr. Khuhro had suddenly announced that if they did not pay up, he would have them all arrested.

An obvious countermove might have been for the rebels to ask Mr. Khuhro pointedly if he had paid his own taxes: he owned 25,000 acres of land. But the landowners preferred not to draw too much attention to the tax issue. Instead, they planned to get up in the Assembly during the budget debate, refuse to vote the budget, and so hasten Mr. Khuhro's departure from office.

It did not quite work out that way, for when the members of the Assembly who were privy to the plot turned up on budget day, they found the legislative chamber surrounded by Mr. Khuhro's policemen. Mr. Khuhro opened the proceedings by announcing that the chief plotters, including the Mir, had all been arrested the previous night on a charge of planning to assassinate him and his entire Cabinet. Mr. Khuhro then blandly called on the members of the Assembly not yet under arrest to demonstrate their loyalty to Pakistan and to himself, first by voting for a new Speaker to replace the fallen Mir, and second by passing the budget. The legislators did both, without a murmur.

The Mir turned up a few days later, safe and sound, for Mr. Khuhro was not a vindictive man. He had a hair-raising story to tell, which he gasped out to hastily summoned newspaper reporters between long rests ordered by his doctors.

According to the Mir, he had been seized the night before the budget debate and hustled off to a mosquito-infested bun-

285

galow. "I was refused medicines," quavered the Mir pathetically, "and policemen went with me when I wished to perform even the necessities of life."

Next, he was driven through the desert in a jolting jeep to another and more remote place of confinement. "I was given no water to wash with, and had no food," cried the Mir, but rather spoilt it by adding, peevishly, that the food was "full of sand." When the budget debate was safely over, the Mir was brought back to Hyderabad, and released. Nothing more was heard of the great murder plot. When I asked Mr. Khuhro about it in Karachi, he blandly waved the question aside.

The Indus river saves Sind from being entirely desert. The British began the building of the famous Sukkur Barrage, which when finally completed will irrigate 5,500,000 acres— more than the present cultivated area of Egypt. Sind was conquered by the British in 1842 by Sir Charles Napier. Until then it had been ruled by three Moslem robber barons, who levied piratical toll on the Indus river traffic and called themselves the Mirs of Sind.

Napier was a British eccentric. He was sixty years old when he marched his Bombay army into Sind. Dickens's *Oliver Twist* had just been published, and Napier's soldiers called him Old Fagin. He wore a huge helmet of his own design, a large pair of spectacles decorated his huge nose, and he grew his whiskers down to his waist. Hindus as well as Moslems protested against Napier's military action, for he proposed to prohibit some of their most cherished customs. Napier cheerfully told the protesting Brahmins: "You say suttee is your custom. Well, we too have a custom, which is to hang men who burn women alive. Build your funeral pyre, and I will build a gallows beside it, and let each act according to his own custom."

The British had no shadow of justification for annexing Sind, which gave them the port of Karachi and control of the Indus. But Napier's comment was characteristic. "We have done what is best for the good government of the population," he said. "We refused to sacrifice that in an endeavor—hopeless,

I might add—to give those drunken, debauched, tyrannical, cheating, intriguing, contemptible Mirs a due portion of the plunder they had amassed from the ruined people. There was bound to be hardship on someone. It has fallen on the Mirs. And it could hardly alight on a crew more deserving to bear it."

Which would have been fine, a Hyderabad friend said sharply, if the British had really followed through. "But they didn't. They left the land system exactly as it had been before. Now in addition to Mirs we have political bosses who have no lineage but own most land. In Sind we grow cotton, rice, and wheat, but the land is held by a few wealthy men with enormous estates, and the masses of the people are mere sharecroppers."

We were passing a building whose entrance bore the sign: "Health Inspector." Outside it an old man wearing a black fur cap and a tattered khaki tunic sat in the dust, picking dirt from between his toes.

"There you have a typical Pakistani," said my friend. "He is dirty, he is ignorant, he is diseased. Most Westerners see only Karachi, with its big international airport and its busy streets. The Americans are impressed by our rate of industrial growth. 'A 154 per cent increase in only four years!' they exclaim. 'Pakistan is doing better than India.' But India has made at least a start with land reform. We have done nothing, and our great industrialization program will only replace what was lost through the Partition. We are building cement factories; but can the peasants eat cement?"

The Punjab is the heart of Pakistan. JINNAH

I FLEW to the ancient city of Lahore, with its thirteen gates, in a Pakistani plane that was modern enough for the passengers

to be permitted to smoke. On the plane I met a Punjabi, and
began to understand why the Punjabis dominated West Pakistan and why the Bengalis of East Pakistan disliked them so
much.

He was a powerfully built man, with arrogant nostrils and
heavy-lidded eyes. He lit a cigarette, and examined me curiously.

"You are traveling in our country? You have been to many
places?"

I said I had come from Karachi, and before that had been in
Dacca.

"Ah, those Bengalis of East Pakistan!" he said, with contempt. "They are not people one should bother oneself with.
They call themselves Moslems, but it is only skin-deep. Actually
most of them are low-caste Hindus who embraced Islam at the
point of the sword. Now they would like to go back to India
and Hinduism, if they could. They can talk about nothing but
'Calcutta, Calcutta, Calcutta.' They are born twisters and intriguers, every one of them. If it were not for its jute, we would
be well rid of East Pakistan, I tell you."

He laughed. "Losing the jute would be a small price to pay
to free ourselves of the Bengalis, with their limp handshakes
and false smiles. Punjabis and Bengalis have nothing in common. We eat wheat, they eat rice; we speak Urdu, they speak
Bengali."

East Pakistan had been a mistake, he thought. "The Moslems should have demanded the whole of the Punjab, including
the five rivers. To get it, we could have made common cause
with all the hill people, who have always been true Moslems.
India would have been dependent on us for its water, and
would not have dared to seize Kashmir. Instead of this, we
have East Pakistan, which we have to subsidize and which is
full of Hindus; and Nehru is left in control of the canals system
and can blackmail us by threatening to dry up our fields."

He hated the Sikhs and the Hindus. "The Sikhs are butchers.

When they ruled in Lahore, they persecuted the Moslems far more than they did the Hindus, though they claim that their religion is closer to ours. At the time of the Partition it was the Sikhs who turned the Moslems out of the Punjab, which is rightfully ours. There was a great killing of Moslems, and the Sikhs did the killing. The Hindus, who have no stomach for fighting, waited until the Sikhs had done their dirty work for them, then preyed on helpless Moslem women. Thousands of our women were abducted into India by Hindus. It is a wrong that has still to be righted, and in God's good time it will be," he said fiercely.

We parted when the plane came down at Lahore, but we were to meet again, in peculiar circumstances.

The undivided Punjab was the size of Nevada. At the Partition it was split between Pakistan and India, with Pakistan getting two thirds of it. The division may or may not have suited some politicians, but it created an enormous problem for the irrigation engineers of both countries. Until 1917 the whole of the Punjab suffered from alternate floods and droughts. A British official wrote: "Half the country is burned up by the sun, and the other half drowned by the rivers, while the whole is waterlogged with debt." But in 1905 the British had begun to harness the rivers by a vast and intricate system of canals, and when the system was completed, the Punjab became an immense food factory, the granary of British India. The political solution of partition cut right across the canals system. Unable to get enough water from the three western rivers, the Indus, Jhelum, and the Chenab, Pakistan had to draw from the three eastern rivers, the Sutlej, the Beas, and the Ravi. In the state of tension between the two countries, this led to perpetual disputes, with the Pakistanis claiming that India was deliberately restricting the flow of water in order to blackmail Pakistan into abandoning her claim to Kashmir.

I arrived in Lahore to find that this charge was now being hurtled at India in reverse. The Ravi had flooded the city, and the Pakistani radio was in full blast, accusing India of trying to drown out the capital of the Punjab and West Pakistan.

A smiling Ashiq met me at the airport. Mohammad Ashiq and I were old acquaintances. He was a Moslem who had been forced to leave Delhi at the time of the Partition, but since then he had been back several times. His Hindu friends always received him warmly, for Ashiq was a man who bore no grudges. If there had been more Ashiqs in both camps, India would not have had to be divided.

"Do you mind if we drive past the railroad station?" he asked anxiously. "I have to meet a man who is coming by rail from Delhi. He is a Hindu." Ashiq laughed. "He and I are in the same boat. He used to live here in Lahore, but he had to flee to Delhi during the trouble, and he has been there ever since."

"I thought the Pakistan Government objected to Hindus visiting Pakistan: especially Hindus who once had their homes here."

"Ah, but these Hindus are coming to watch the cricket," said Ashiq seriously. "For that reason they have been given special permits. My friend seized the opportunity, though he is not a cricket fan."

We drove to the railroad station. It did not seem to me that there was much likelihood of cricket. The floodwaters had receded, but had left much damage in their wake. Lahore looked muddy and battered. "There were many drownings," said Ashiq, shaking his head. "I'm afraid the people are very mad with India." He brightened up. "But the Hindus who have come all the way to watch the cricket will be all right. Cricket is different."

A large crowd had gathered at the station. They were obviously on hand to meet the trainload of Hindus from Delhi, and despite Ashiq's assurance I felt rather apprehensive. I had no wish to see a massacre of Hindus by Moslem victims of the recent flood. I need not have worried. When the train pulled in and the passengers began to alight, the crowd surged forward,

but only in order to shake hands. "They are all cricket fans,"
said Ashiq. "Even during the trouble, cricket continued. The
Indian cricket team is very popular in Pakistan."

"Ah!" he cried, "there is my friend," and started shaking
hands with a small, middle-aged bearded man. Ashiq's friend
Dr. Gopal wore a blue-and-white striped blazer and white trousers, like all the other cricketing tourists. But in his case this was
purely for camouflage. As soon as we could, we slipped unobtrusively away from those who had come to Pakistan to
watch and play cricket, and got into Ashiq's car.

As we drove through flood-damaged Lahore, Dr. Gopal
looked about him with much interest. "I have not been here
for over nine years," he told me. "I was born and brought up
here." He shook his head regretfully. "It has changed a great
deal—a very great deal." He turned to Ashiq. "My dear fellow,
the city has not improved. It looks very run-down. Lahore was
formerly the pearl of the Punjab. What has happened to it?"

"But it is the flood," Ashiq cried. "Have you in Delhi not
heard about the flood? The Ravi came down in force, sweeping everything before it. There was no time to take precautions,
for we received no warning. The Indian side could have told us
to be prepared, but they did not bother. Many people were
drowned. I think the Indian side was very mean about the
whole affair."

"That is not the story we heard when we passed through
Amritsar," said Dr. Gopal. "There they told us that repeated
warnings were given, but that your authorities refused to heed
them. Your people thought it was just an Indian trick to fool
them, so they did nothing."

"Ah, then we shall never know the truth of the matter,"
said Ashiq. "Probably both sides blundered."

Ashiq lived near the Mori Gate on the top floor of a tall,
narrow-chested building crammed with tenants and surrounded
by open-air booths selling everything from new bicycles to
second-hand clothes. We climbed a steep narrow wooden stair-

case, pausing for breath on each landing. Ashiq's wife served us coffee and told us briskly that lunch would soon be ready. She was a pleasant-faced young woman and I was glad to see that she did not wear a *burqa*. Ashiq petted his two pretty daughters —one was six and the other eight—while we drank our coffee. All the windows were open, and from the crowded quarter below there came the constant thunder of passing trucks and the hooting of bicycle-rickshaws. "One gets used to it," said Ashiq philosophically.

Dr. Gopal excused himself to wash his hands. "Through that door and to the right," said Ashiq carelessly. The doctor walked through the doorway, and a few seconds later there was a piercing female scream. Mrs. Ashiq dashed out of the kitchen; Dr. Gopal came dashing back into the room. He looked shaken.

"I am sorry," he said. "I must have taken the wrong turning. There was a woman seated with her back to me, and when she saw me in a mirror she started screaming."

"It is my fault," said Ashiq remorsefully. "I should have warned you. It is my aunt. She is in strict purdah."

Presently we sat down to lunch, without the aunt.

Dr. Gopal told us how he and his wife had fled from Lahore when the Partition killings began.

"I could not believe that anything would happen to us," he said. "Everyone knew us. We had scores of friends. Half our neighbors were Moslems, the others were Hindus. We all got on well together. I had lived in the same part of town for many years, and most of the people around us, both Moslems and Hindus, were patients of mine. Hardly any of us bothered much about politics."

When tensions began to rise, Mrs. Gopal proposed that they should leave the Punjab, as other Hindus were doing. The doctor scoffed at the notion. Mrs. Gopal insisted on sending their three children to relatives in Delhi. "Such nonsense!" the doctor had snorted, but he had grudgingly consented.

Some Moslem friends came in secret and urged the couple to quit Lahore. Dr. Gopal was shaken, but this only made him more stubborn. "Let them come and kill me, then," he said. "You are a fool," said his more practical wife. "At least let us draw our money from the bank and keep it in the house, in case we do have to leave suddenly," she added. Dr. Gopal brusquely rejected this advice.

Then the killing started. There were wild rumors of people being shot and stabbed in the streets, and of houses being burned down with people still in them. They could hear shooting, at first faint and sporadic, then drawing gradually nearer. Mobs were going through the district, systematically breaking into houses and killing all Hindus and Sikhs. It was impossible to go out except after dark, and even then it was extremely risky.

"I wanted to die," said Dr. Gopal simply. "Life had become too horrible. The people who were being killed were my friends, and those who were killing them had also been my friends. I decided that, if they really wished me dead, I was ready."

But Mrs. Gopal was made of sterner stuff. What would become of their children, she asked, if they allowed themselves to be slaughtered? There was still time to escape, she urged, if they abandoned everything and left immediately. It might be only one chance in a thousand, but it was worth taking.

Dr. Gopal smiled reminiscently, and stroked his beard. There was a twinkle in his eye.

"I said it was too late, for we had no money. I admitted it was my fault, for if I had taken her advice earlier and drawn out all our money from the bank, we might have got away. But now all the banks were closed down.

" 'Fool!' she said. 'Do you think I sat with folded hands while you kept on saying there was nothing to fear? No. I drew the money from the bank.' And from under our bed she pulled out a tin box that was crammed with rupees. 'I also have my jewelry,' she said. 'What we cannot take, we shall hide. But the jewels may help us buy our way across the frontier.'

"And that is just what we did," said Dr. Gopal. "We left at once in my car. We did not get very far in the car, of course: the mobs were stopping all cars, looking for Hindus or Sikhs. But we abandoned the car, and continued on foot. It took us three days and nights to get out of Lahore. After that, it was less difficult. We simply walked and, when we saw people, we hid. But they were not all murderers. Most of the people we saw, Moslem or Sikh or Hindu, were refugees like ourselves, and utterly bewildered by what was happening. People were helping as well as killing one another. I began to feel a little better about human beings. And so, after a long and troublesome journey, we reached Delhi and were reunited with our children."

"Meanwhile," said Ashiq, dryly, "I had been compelled to flee from Delhi, and come to Lahore."

Dr. Gopal was not revisiting Lahore merely out of curiosity or nostalgia. He had come on a definite and rather daring mission. Before fleeing from his home he had concealed such of his wife's jewels as they could not carry with them. He hoped they might still be there, and he proposed to try to retrieve them.

"I was told the house is now standing empty," he said. "It was not burned down, like so many others were, and it is just possible the jewels were never found. I hid them well. If they are still there, I would like to have them. After all," he added, rather defiantly, "they do belong to me, or at least to my wife."

Ashiq nodded. "It is true that nobody is living in that house at the moment," he said. "I made inquiries."

I didn't know what the law was on the subject, and neither did Ashiq; but it seemed to me the doctor had a strong claim. "We shall all go together," said Ashiq happily, rubbing his hands. "I shall say I want to look over the house. Dr. Gopal will hunt for his jewels. It should not be difficult."

Dr. Gopal had lived on the road to Shahdara. We drove in Ashiq's car. Evidence of flood damage increased as we went along, for we were approaching the Ravi riverbank. Parts of the road were still under water, and we had to go slowly. We passed a grim procession of carts which were coming back from the river carrying bodies. And then we came to where the flooded river had taken a vast bite out of the land. The road went no farther. There were piles of debris, sunken carts and automobiles, twisted girders, the rubble of houses that had tumbled down, and a vast hole filled with water in which scores of drowned animals floated.

Dr. Gopal pointed to the hole. "That is where my house was," he said.

"Ah!" Ashiq exclaimed sorrowfully. "If only you had come a few days earlier—"

The doctor shrugged. He had already recovered his habitual good humor. "I never really hoped to find anything," he admitted. "At least let us be thankful that the house was empty when it happened."

For the North
Guns always—quietly—but always guns. KIPLING

PESHAWAR MEANS "frontier town," and has twenty gates, seven more than Lahore. The town was full of Pathans, wearing bright-colored scarves and carrying fierce-looking knives. Picturesque tribesmen are usually frauds, but there was nothing phony about the Pathans.

"Some of these men are undoubtedly spies of the Fakir of

Ipi, who is in Afghan pay," said the Pakistani official who trudged with me through the dusty, brassily bright bazaar. "Unfortunately we do not know which ones, and there is not much we can do about it. Many of the others support the Red Shirt leader, Abdul Ghaffer Khan."

Peshawar looks out toward the sharp-edged mountains that flank the Khyber Pass on the way into Afghanistan. The British, whose famous Khyber Rifles held the Pass against the tribesmen, were pretty well content to leave the tribesmen alone so long as they did not close the Pass or attack Peshawar. Not so the Pakistan Government, which in this North-West Frontier has become Britain's heir. Pakistan, which regards the tribesmen as Moslem brothers, is determined to turn them into sound citizens. A lot of money is being spent on farming schemes, and schools are being built.

This policy gets its inspiration from General Mirza, who as a young soldier in his twenties—he is now in his late fifties—fought little wars against the tribesmen, with such British units as the Cameronians and the Poona Horse. Afterwards he was appointed Britain's "political agent" at the Khyber Pass, and subsequently was Deputy Commissioner of Peshawar. Being "political agent" meant that Mirza had to know what was going on in the tribesmen's heads. Sometimes the only way to find out was to be your own spy, mixing with the tribesmen as one of themselves. This was a risky business, and many a political agent failed to report back. From his experiences with the tribesmen, Mirza concluded that they were good fellows who liked a bit of excitement but who were eminently civilizable, being on the whole brave, loyal, truthful, upright, sincere, and not afraid of hard work—in other words quite unlike politicians.

While acting as an agent for the British, Mirza frequently crossed swords with the Red Shirts led by Abdul Ghaffer Khan. The Red Shirts' simple aim was to throw the British out. When the British quit India, it was generally assumed that the Red

Shirts, being Moslems, would willingly throw in their lot with Pakistan. The Pakistani politicians were astounded and aggrieved when, instead of doing this, Abdul Ghaffer Khan declared that he had been fighting for Pathan independence and meant to go on doing so. Abdul Ghaffer 'Khan was a giant of a man, grizzled but still formidable, and since 1947 he had been entering Pakistan jails with the same regularity as he used to enter British jails. The Red Shirt movement was still very much alive.

Another dissident was the Fakir of Ipi. He first appeared on the Frontier scene in 1911, and he fought the British for thirty-six years. He was as critical of the new Pakistan Government as Abdul Ghaffer Khan was, and for the same reason, but unlike the Red Shirts his men played no part in politics, preferring to remain in their remote caves and fight with rifles in their hands. The Fakir was a tough-minded old man who suffered severely from lumbago; but he was even more of a problem to Pakistan than Abdul Ghaffer Khan, for his guerilla activities had been getting the backing of the Afghan Government of Daud Khan.

Though Afghanistan has a King, Daud Khan as Prime Minister was virtually dictator, and not less powerful from being the King's cousin and also his brother-in-law, for Daud married the King's sister. Daud, who was in his late forties, was a martinet with a close-shaved bullet-shaped head and very rough manners. He had been known to whip his own chauffeur in public, and his personal bodyguard wore uniforms that recalled Hitler's SS-men. His boast was: "An Afghan can outwit any man," and after the death of Stalin (whose funeral he attended), Daud proceeded to get military aid from Russia and Czechoslovakia, while simultaneously wangling American credits for big irrigation schemes. Daud called this "milking two cows."

But one of his primary ambitions was to take the Pathans and as much of their country as possible away from Pakistan. Afghanistan is about the size of Texas, and a third of its 12,-000,000 people are Pathans. To the Pathans of the North-West

Frontier of Pakistan, Daud held out the bait of an independent "Paktoonistan," to be carved from Pakistan's northwest flank. "Paktoonistan," if realized, would include Peshawar and as much of Pakistan east of the Indus river as Daud could contrive to tear away.

The Sikhs under Ranjit Singh captured Peshawar in 1834: before that it was under Afghan rule. The Afghan ruler Dost Mohammad sought British help to oust Ranjit Singh and retake Peshawar; but the British wanted Peshawar for themselves. Dost Mohammad turned to Russia; the British invaded Afghanistan to forestall the Russians. They unseated Dost Mohammad, but their retiring forces were massacred, only one man surviving to reach Jalalabad. Forty years later essentially the same story was repeated. The British compelled the Afghan ruler Yakub Khan, who had been listening to the Russians, to accept a British adviser. The adviser Sir Louis Cavagnan was murdered, with his entire mission, six weeks after reaching the Afghan capital, Kabul. General Roberts marched to Kabul and installed a new and more compliant Afghan ruler. In 1929, for the third time, an Afghan ruler who was becoming too friendly with the Russians was unseated and replaced by a more pro-British King.

In the Khyber country, only the names change. Pakistan, Britain's heir on the North-West Frontier, was confronted by a hostile Afghanistan whose policy had the approval of Moscow.

I traveled over the Khyber Pass as far as the Afghan border. The road, bright with yellow dust, twists over the mountains like a coil of hose. Over it there used to come camel caravans laden with Karakul pelts and fruit. The caravans were escorted by armed soldiers, and veiled women piled children and baskets of protesting hens on the backs of pack mules, while the men of the caravan rode alongside with rifles slung on their backs, and rolled-up blankets.

Nowadays the caravans consist of convoys of trucks. But the

traffic had been temporarily halted, by politics. A mob shouting "Paktoonistan!" had looted the Pakistan Embassy in Kabul, while Daud Khan's police looked idly on. The Pakistanis had therefore begun to place obstacles in the way of Afghanistan's export trade through the Khyber Pass.

At the frontier post several Afghan trucks were halted. Their drivers, smoking cigarettes and looking sullen, hung about with a disconsolate air. The Pakistani frontier guards kept a close unfriendly eye on them. The trucks, which were loaded with peaches, pomegranates, and white grapes carefully wrapped in cotton wool, had been there some days, and the fruit was palpably rotting. The Pakistanis explained with straight faces that the trucks' papers were "not in order," and that they could not let the trucks proceed over the Khyber Pass until they received instructions—from Karachi. "It may take some considerable time," one of them said, with satisfaction.

Along the winding road on which the trucks had come, beyond the sharp-edged mountains and black cliffs, lay Kabul in its circle of snow-capped hills. When I had visited Kabul some months before, the town had been full of comic-opera traffic policemen and burly Russians wearing white Panama hats. The policemen, in purple uniforms, stood on tall concrete pillars at the city's intersections, blowing whistles and making violent gestures. But the traffic they were supposed to be directing was almost nonexistent, for it consisted only of a few horse-drawn tongas and a handful of jeeps. The Russians were mostly engineers, for Russia had presented Daud with a hundred million dollars worth of projects, ranging from oil storage tanks to a new Kabul bakery. When not working, the Russians wandered through the crowded bazaar, near the Bagh-i-Ammun bridge, where they bought American cigarettes on the black market. The cigarettes had been plundered from the American Embassy's stores. The first secretary of the Russian Embassy was a dapper, heavily scented man called Bogachev. When a party of Russians were due to go home, a plane came from Moscow to fetch them, and they departed carrying smart new leather suitcases, with their women wearing smart bourgeois clothes and carrying bouquets of roses. They were the envy of the Afghan officials, none of whom earned more than twenty-five dollars a month. Meanwhile, Daud Khan's policemen kept a close watch on the American Embassy, and pointedly wrote down the names of all Afghans who dared to make use of the United States Information Agency's library.

I remembered that all the public buildings in Kabul had smelled strongly of mutton fat, and how the previous winter, when there had been deep snow, one of the gorgeously uniformed traffic policemen had been found lying at the foot of his concrete pillar, half eaten by a wolf.

The women of Kabul wore thick, unbecoming black *burqas*; but some of them also wore—underneath—Western dresses and silk stockings. I had flown from Kabul to Kandahar and one of the other plane passengers had been an Afghan princess: she wore her *burqa* when she entered the plane, but once we were in the air she threw it aside with a slim shrug of disgust, and lit an American cigarette. Kabul had four cinemas, and two of them were reserved exclusively for men. Only the men ever went to parties, and they never brought their wives. On the whole, the happiest women in Afghanistan were the gypsies who lived in the blackskin tents; nobody expected them to wear *burqas*.

"They are rough people, over there," said my Pakistani guide, as we turned back toward Peshawar. "Criminals are still executed in public by having their throats cut." And he told me a story he had heard from one of the truck-drivers.

"When Nadir Shah, the present King's father, was assassinated in 1933, many people were thrown in prison. One was a government official who never knew why he had been arrested. No charge was ever brought against him, but he was not set free.

"After Daud Khan became Prime Minister, the man one day

was taken from his cell. He was shaved, bathed, and given fresh clothes, but no one would tell him why. He had been in prison for many years, and he was terrified. He was sure he was going to his execution.

"Then he was marched into Daud Khan's presence, and to his bewilderment the Prime Minister shook him warmly by the hand.

" 'My dear fellow,' said Daud Khan, 'where have you been all this time? I cannot understand why you have not called on me.'

"The man began to stammer out the story of his imprisonment, but Daud Khan cut him short. 'We have no time now,' he said, 'for your plane is leaving in a very short time. I trust you have everything you need?'

" 'But where am I being sent?' the poor fellow inquired.

" 'What, haven't they told you?' Daud demanded. 'You're our new Ambassador to Indonesia!' "

I traveled from Peshawar to Sialkot. In the sixth century it was the capital of the Punjab, under the White Huns: but it was now a sadly diminished town. For years its four factories and its 70,000 cottage workers had been busily employed, making cricket bats. Both Moslems and Hindus took enthusiastically to cricket from the moment the British introduced the game to India, and it is now perhaps the one real bond between them. But this common bond had not done Sialkot any good, for the willows for making the bats had come from Kashmir, which was now closed to Pakistan.

There was one Englishman still living in Sialkot. He was needless to say a keen cricketer. He fumed against Nehru for having seized Kashmir, pointing out that the cutting off of the supply of willows had made bats so scarce that there was serious danger of the local batsmen losing all their skill.

I suggested that the Kashmir problem had even graver implications than that.

He looked at me, aggrieved. "Oh well, if you want to drag

in politics and are going to be flippant about cricket, I have
no more to say."

Nehru held the famous Vale of Kashmir, but Pakistan had
occupied some five thousand square miles of mostly hilly and
desolate country. The Pakistanis promptly named it "Azad,"
or "Free," Kashmir; and put it under military rule. It was pretty
evident that, whatever else "Free" Kashmir had gained, it did
not have freedom. The people were wretchedly poor, and very
little was being done for them. They had the sullen and secre-
tive look of people who were continually spied on, were liable
to summary arrest and inquisition, and knew it.

Sialkot is almost within loud-speaker distance of Jammu, and
it was necessary for me to pass through Jammu on my way to
Srinagar, the capital of the part of Kashmir that India held.
But it was impossible to go direct from Sialkot to Jammu. It
would have been like trying to cross the demilitarized zone between South and North Korea, or like proposing to go direct
from Formosa to Fukien. Instead, I had to return to Lahore, in
order to cross from there into India to Amritsar, before entering Kashmir.

On my last evening in Lahore Ashiq suggested I should see
some of the city's night life. I was surprised. I had not known
that Lahore had any night life.

"I meant the slave market," Ashiq said.

We visited one of a series of opulent houses, all under the
same management. They were gaudily furnished, and the pa-
trons obviously had money to burn. In a large hall, gay with
cushions, men sat cross-legged, puffing contentedly at hookahs,
and waiting for the evening's entertainment to begin. The
crimson curtains parted, and a girl came in. She wore a silk
veil, a pair of silk trousers, and very little else. An unseen orchestra struck up, and the girl performed an elegant belly-
dance. Then she mounted an ivory-and-gold pedestal, and the
men began to bid for her. She was finally knocked down to a
fat, whiskered man with a perspiring bald head, who eagerly

led her away. The curtains parted, and another girl came in. "Some of them are members of old courtesan families, who are trained to this sort of thing from childhood," Ashiq explained. "But many are from refugee families. They sell themselves in order to keep their fathers and mothers from starving. It is a great temptation, for they may even win a husband, or at least a wealthy protector who will not treat them badly."

A man was walking through the hall chatting with the customers. He had heavy-lidded eyes and a powerful hooked nose. His air was one of arrogance. I easily recognized him as the Punjabi I had met on the plane, the man who despised Bengalis and hated Hindus and Sikhs.

"It is the proprietor of the establishment," Ashiq whispered. "He is very rich."

I could not help wondering how he reconciled his profession with his horror and indignation at the thought of Hindus preying on helpless Moslem women.

XVIII
KASHMIR: MEN IN FUR HATS

Sheik Abdullah is a brave man and a great leader of his people. NEHRU

A period in prison is a very desirable part of one's education. NEHRU

At AMRITSAR I was joined by Singh, who had brought the Studebaker up from Delhi. Beyond Pathankot we were in the hill country. Dawn came with a quiet shake and shiver, revealing bright green parrots wheeling and squawking over wheatfields, against a towering background of ice-capped mountains. We were stopped at a checkpost, and our papers were examined by turbaned officials seated round a bare wooden table in the open. We were still in Hindu country as far as Jammu, and we drove past white temples and stones smeared with red ocher to represent *lingams*. But after Jammu the scene changed. Turbans became fur caps, and noses became more semitic. Strung out along the twisting mountain road were yellow buses whose wooden sides had flowers gaily painted on them. The drivers, all Moslems, wore flowers stuck rakishly behind their ears, and they sang plaintive love songs, most of them addressed to imaginary delectable boys. The most popular ditty had a refrain which began: "There's a boy across the river with a bottom like a peach."

At one place a white fox loped disdainfully across the road.

At another we stopped for tea, which was served in scalding brass cups from an open wayside booth.

Singh had driven my family from Delhi to Srinagar, where they were living on a houseboat and had been awaiting me for some weeks. They had had a bad journey, for the roads had been flooded. At Jammu they found a great number of bus and plane passengers stranded, and there was a shortage of beds. A polite Indian had surrendered his room to Jane, on condition that she shared it with his two wives. He visited his wives several times during the night.

We lunched at a village called Kud. The resthouse clung to the steep hillside; just below the level of the roadway were the roofs of villagers' cottages. Everything was canted at a sharp angle, and all the lines sloped up toward the tall mountains that still lay ahead. There were plenty of sharp-eyed police about, for Kud is where Sheik Abdullah is imprisoned. The Sheik, a handsome six-footer, was a Moslem member of Mr. Nehru's Congress Party. He headed the first Kashmir Government, after Indian troops marched into Kashmir. But when he began talking about an independent Kashmir, he was summarily arrested; he had lain in prison at Kud for four years, without ever being brought to trial.

We climbed to the Banihal Pass and drove through the famous tunnel into another world. Snowy peaks encircled us, looking close enough to touch. Nine thousand feet below us the Valley of Kashmir was spread out like a carpet, decorated with silver lakes and vivid-green ricepaddies. The road corkscrewed wildly downhill in a hair-raising sequence of hairpin bends.

We made the descent safely, more fortunate than the jeepload of Indian army officers whose fall was commemorated by a large white stone tablet. The terraces of the ricepaddies came up to meet us. Tall straight poplars lined the road into Srinagar, which Mr. Nehru's Brahmin forebears called the City of Knowledge. Singh parked the car beside the lakeside clubhouse, and hailed a *shikara*, a gondola-like affair with plump silk cushions and crimson carpets, to row us to the moored houseboat. Skimming past floating islands of plaited reeds on which melons and cucumbers grew, we were jubilantly trailed by other *shikaras*, whose owners offered to sell us newspapers, cigarettes, scarves, carpets, candy, fruit, silk, toy houseboats, trays, ashtrays, tables, tablecloths, and wooden animals. When we climbed on board the houseboat, the salesmen climbed on board, too. In a cloud of mosquitoes, which had also been attracted to the scene, they spread out their carpets, displayed their scarves, and held up their wooden animals. The owner of the houseboat, our temporary landlord, stood by with folded arms, his face beaming with delight. The eager salesmen were all cousins of his.

"This has been going on since we arrived," Jane said. "They usually come on board before breakfast and stay all day." She was looking strained.

We fled from the houseboat and the clamoring salesmen and went for a stroll along the Bund. The Bund was crowded with Indian soldiers and with Indian tourists from Bombay. It was also filled with Kashmiris selling pewter teapots, brass trays, hookahs, carpets, scarves, inlaid tables, toy houseboats, and wooden animals. One Kashmiri called his store "Suffering Moses' Emporium." Another described himself proudly as "Sethar the Worst."

When I asked the latter why, he grinned. "To protect the tourists the Kashmir Government published a list of stores that overcharged. I headed the list." He seemed inordinately pleased about it.

Three quarters of the population of Kashmir are Moslems. When India took over the state, Mr. Nehru promised that a plebiscite would be held to find out if the Moslem majority preferred to join their country to Pakistan. This promise was several times repeated, but no plebiscite was held. Most Indians with whom I talked about Kashmir reluctantly admitted that in a plebiscite most of the Moslems would vote for Pakistan.

We entered a store selling antiques, and Jane admired a golden topaz ring. The store was crowded with jostling Indian tourists. They were talking in loud voices, and the Kashmiri storekeeper watched them with a coldly hostile eye. He was a thin man with a black fur cap, and he looked rather like Mohammad Ali Jinnah.

When the tourists had swept out, exclaiming loudly at the outrageous prices, he angrily replaced on the shelves the articles they had been handling.

"You have many tourists this season," I said.

"Tourists?" He looked at me bleakly. "Only Indians. They buy nothing. They behave as if they owned Kashmir. They treat it as their colony. Let them take their soldiers away, and then we shall see what will happen!"

We went to have coffee at the Indian Coffee House on the Bund. The tourists from Bombay were seated at the next table. They were still talking loudly. A plump Hindu dominated the conversation.

". . . colonialism!" he was exclaiming. "Terrible! Disgusting! *Achya*, I tell you, the people are ground under an imperialist heel. They are kept down by bayonets. They would rebel if they could, but what can they do against so many soldiers? Their voice is not heard at all, yet the colonialists say: 'The people are happy with our rule.' What hypocrisy, isn't it? Ah, colonialism is a terrible thing."

But presently it became clear that he was talking about Goa.

That evening after our lamplit meal of boiled chicken—the chicken tasted of oil and the oil-lamp smelled mysteriously of chicken—we were visited on our houseboat by two cordial and smiling men from the Kashmir Government's Information Department.

They accepted whisky and cigarettes, and said how lucky we were to have found such a delightful houseboat.

"You will like Kashmir," one of them said enthusiastically. "There is so much to do, so much to see! Here you may relax."

"Go to Sonamarg," the other urged. "Visit Gulmarg. See the famous Shalimar garden where the Emperor Jehangir passed the summer months. Try our trout fishing."

"Almond flowers," murmured the first man rhapsodically, "almond flowers stretching for miles in the golden rapeseed fields."

"Snow-capped peaks gleaming under the azure blue sky."

"Rainbows in the Mogul fountains."

"Lovely lakes amid some of the world's most beautiful scenery."

"And, if there is anything we can do for you," said the first man earnestly, "please do not hesitate to call on us. We are entirely at your service."

"We are very honored to have you here in Kashmir," said the second man. "We *like* to have Western correspondents visit us and see all there is to be seen. We welcome them."

"Ah, he would not wish to be bothered here with business," the first man protested. "He is here purely on a holiday. He wishes to rest, to forget politics."

"Of course," the second man agreed. "He is not here to talk about politics."

"It would be a shame if anyone talked politics to him."

"Not only that," said the second man, avoiding my eye and looking thoughtfully at the ceiling of the houseboat. "Not only that: it would be impolite for one to come here as a tourist and then to proceed to make inquiries into politics."

"It would be very impolite," said the first man. "It would be tactless, and might lead to complications. But, of course, he would not dream of doing anything of the kind."

"Naturally not," said the second man.

Then they finished their whiskies, shook hands with us, and went off smiling back to Srinagar.

In whatever manner I look at the case, I do not see how Pakistan has any rights whatsoever. NEHRU ON KASHMIR

WE WENT for idle excursions on the lakes in cushioned *shikaras*, visited the Mogul gardens, explored the town, and took healthy hillside walks. Every morning at breakfast the salesmen would come on board and spread out their wares; each evening when we returned from our expeditions they would be waiting to greet us. They were as impossible to get rid of as the mosquitoes.

Srinagar had two bookstores, both kept by sad-eyed, black-bearded Sikhs, and we armed ourselves with thick histories of Kashmir which we never read and paperback detective novels which we devoured. We drove out into the countryside through villages ablaze with embroidered carpets, whose makers wound them round the trees to attract tourists; and we visited Gulmarg, the Meadow of Roses, to admire the snowy peak of Nanga Parbat, and Pahlgam, which was filled with wild horsemen and which had a notice that warned: Do not gallop through the main street.

But the young men from the Information Department rankled, and I decided to call on a Kashmiri Moslem politician who supported Sheik Abdullah but who had not yet been imprisoned.

He was a little man with a brown fur cap and a beaky nose, and he seemed very glad to see me. He sent for other politicians whom he wanted me to meet, and while we waited for them we sat drinking coffee.

"Kashmir is a police state," he told me. "The people live under a reign of terror. The traitors who betrayed the Sheik have made themselves dictators. They are plundering the people day and night. Scores have been shot, and hundreds arrested. Thousands of supporters of the Sheik are beaten and tortured. Kashmir is in the hands of Communists."

"You have not been arrested," I said.

"Ah, no: not yet. They are afraid of what the people would do." He sounded a little complacent. "Besides, they are still hoping to bend the Sheik to their will. They would like to persuade him to abandon his principles and lend them the support of his name. But he will never do so: he assured me of this only last week."

"He is permitted visitors?"

"Oh, yes, I see him from time to time. He also writes long letters. He has just written one to the United Nations, exposing Nehru."

"He is in good health?"

"He is in excellent health."

A number of men came in. They all wore fur caps, and were exceedingly voluble. All declared they were frequently beaten and tortured.

"But we continue to hold meetings and rouse the people," said my host. "We refuse to be intimidated. We defy the gangster police and the *goondas*."

He invited me to stay to lunch. I accepted. Everyone sat down at table in their fur hats. We ate mutton that had begun to go bad. To disguise the taste, it had been smothered in a bright yellow mustard sauce.

"The traitors' day of reckoning is near," said our host. "When it comes, they will be sorry. After our sufferings, we cannot be expected to show them much mercy. There will be a purge."

He ate the mutton with his fingers, letting the yellow sauce drip down between them. With his fur cap, beaky nose, small eyes, and busy mouth, he made a sinister sort of figure. I could well believe in the purge, if he ever got back into a position of power.

I was much less impressed than I had expected to be by Ka
mir's opposition politicians and their broad hints at a comi
Night of Long Knives. It seemed to me that, however bad tl
existing regime might be, the Kashmiris were not likely to gai.
from such an exchange. This impression was considerabl\
strengthened by what I was able to glean about the Sheik Abdullah government's doings.

Kashmir, about the size of Minnesota, has a population of
around 4,000,000. Last century the British casually sold it to a
Rajput maharaja for £1,000,000. He and his Hindu descendants
gave the majority a bad time. A Moslem who accidentally killed
a cow was liable to be hanged.

When India was being divided up between the Hindus and
Moslems, it was agreed that rulers of princely states must
choose between India and Pakistan. The Hindu maharaja of
Kashmir refused the difficult choice: when pressed, he took to
his bed with a diplomatic stomach-ache. The impatient Pakistanis then committed the major blunder of sending wild
tribesmen over the border to take Kashmir by force. The loot-
ing tribesmen proceeded to slaughter Hindus and Moslems
alike, as well as any Christians they came across. The frightened maharaja appealed to India for help, and Nehru rushed
in troops. Meanwhile Sheik Abdullah seized power, pushed the
maharaja into the background, and set up his own government.
Nobody elected Abdullah, and nobody got the chance to vote
for or against him. After the tribesmen were driven out Abdullah stayed in power, backed by the Indian Army. He set up a
one-party state and ruled like any other dictator. Anyone who
opposed Abdullah was promptly thrown in jail. Much money
was voted for public works, but somehow the works never got
started. The peasants were more heavily taxed than before, but
they received no benefits in return.

It was not this corruption that brought about Abdullah's
downfall, but his harping on the need to hold a plebiscite to
let the Kashmiris decide whether they wished to stay with India

or join Pakistan. Abdullah's own wish was that Kashmir should achieve some sort of independence of both. It turned out that he was, after all, a Kashmiri. Abdullah's chief lieutenant, Bakshi Ghulam Mohammad, turned against him and in a lightning coup had him arrested. Abdullah was removed from his home in the middle of the night, in his pajamas, and was sent to languish in prison at Kud. Bakshi took over. But Kashmir remained a one-party state—the Abdullah party was called the National Conference, and Bakshi retained the name—with merely a change of dictators. Those who opposed Bakshi were thrown in jail.

Jane and I were invited to a Mogul garden party at which Bakshi was to appear. He went round shaking everyone's hand, including ours. Bakshi was a stocky, broad-shouldered man buttoned into a tight-fitting, long brown coat and wearing the inevitable fur hat. He looked rather like a prosperous butcher. But he did not strut like a dictator, and he had an air of easy informality. He laughed frequently, in a full-bellied fashion, and he was not followed around by guards. Later on I ran into him in a village, and he was walking about with the same informality, chatting easily to the villagers. Again there were no guards in sight, and anyone who wanted to take a potshot at him would have found no difficulty. I had no doubt that Bakshi was a dictator, and that opposing politicians had a rough time; but it seemed to me that his reign of terror must be one of the mildest on record.

The Kashmiris, when not trying to sell doubtful *objets d'art* to tourists, were a hard-working and cheerful race. They diligently tended their floating vegetables gardens, sang rollicking songs, were constantly bathing in the river, into which they plunged literally from the doorsteps of their tall wooden houses, and were passionately addicted to gambling. On the lakes one would pass crowded houseboats filled with hookah-puffing gamblers intent on losing their shirts. The only thing that marred their cheerfulness was the swarm of Indian tourists,

whom they obviously loathed. The Indian soldiers they appeared to tolerate good-naturedly as an unavoidable evil: they disliked the loud-mouthed tourists, but I doubted if they wanted the murdering tribesmen back.

The Bakshi regime had instituted many reforms, and was busy introducing more. Land reform led the way. A maximum ceiling of 22¾ acres had been set on land holdings. Anything in excess of that was confiscated, without compensation, and handed over to the less-fortunate peasants. This had led to a considerable increase in land ownership. Peasants who were still tenants paid their rent in the form of crops, but a ceiling was placed on rents—one quarter of the crop—and the landlord, not the tenant, paid the land tax. Other taxation was negligible. Government spending on education was three times greater than before, and on health it had doubled. Public works were in full swing, and new power plants and irrigation works were being built. Food prices were low, because food was subsidized. The Indian Government made Kashmir a development grant that equaled half the grant paid to Bombay State, which had twelve times Kashmir's population.

I thought the suave gentlemen from the Information Department who had made a special trip to my houseboat to warn me not to pry into Kashmir's politics were fools. If I had been in their shoes I would have encouraged visits to unimpressive opposition politicians, and then invited attention to what the Bakshi regime was doing for the people.

"After Bakshi struck down Abdullah," a Kashmiri told me, "he behaved like a man who was terrified by what he had done. He scarcely dared appear in public, and he was always heavily guarded. But he has become increasingly self-confident and he now mixes freely with the people."

The Indian Government had encouraged the Bakshi reforms, and I suspected it had also put a brake on the corruption, and warned Bakshi that if he did not behave, he could easily go the same way as Abdullah. Bakshi was obviously leaning heavily on India for his success. He was more in Nehru's power than Abdullah had ever been.

Kashmir was a well-run colony, but it was still a colony. I asked an Indian how Nehru reconciled that with his frequent attacks on colonialism. How for that matter did Indians reconcile it?

"Pakistan would never spend as much on the development of Kashmir as we are doing," he replied. "Look at what is happening in 'Azad' Kashmir! The standard of living there is going down, not up. In a few years it will be impossible to reverse the present economic trend in Kashmir. All Kashmir's ties now are with India. The people are becoming too prosperous to want to change. To hold a plebiscite now would simply unsettle them. But we will hold one eventually, and when we do, the people will vote to stay with India."

It was perfectly clear that no plebiscite was going to be held until India was quite sure of that.

XIX
AMRITSAR: MEN IN BLUE TURBANS

A Sikh is as saintly in peace as he is victorious in war.

MASTER TARA SINGH

I ARRIVED in Amritsar to find the Golden Temple under siege and Sikhs dancing through the streets brandishing swords. Amritsar is a town of innumerable winding alleys; and in the middle of the maze stands the Golden Temple of the Sikhs, where blue water laps the marble sides of a huge square pool, and relays of bearded musicians play all round the clock, while priests indefatigably intone hymns.

I removed my shoes and socks and entered respectfully on the temple's 10,000 square yards of marble. A Sikh guide got hold of me and told me in tones of quivering horror that the enemies of his religion had bricked up the great guru Fateh Singh—alive. This happened in the seventeenth century, but he spoke of it as though it had occurred that day.

The Sikhs had a more immediate grievance. Having helped to root out the Moslems, they wanted a bigger say in the Indian Punjab which, they complained, was controlled by Hindus. They had launched a campaign for their rights and, they said, had been brutally attacked by the police. On display in the Golden Temple were large photographs of policemen chasing Sikhs, and also a mound of teargas shells which, the Sikhs claimed, the police had fired into the sacred precincts.

Sikhs of all ages, but mostly bearded and all wearing bright blue turbans and broad blue sashes, had gathered inside the temple to pray, to make political speeches, and to vow vengeance on the police. Meanwhile, in the vast stone kitchens behind the temple, women were cooking vast quantities of food to keep their menfolk's spirits up.

Outside the temple the police were waiting to arrest the Sikhs when they emerged. The constables patrolled the lanes, and the officers sat on adjacent flat roofs, looking on. Surprisingly, the police were all Sikhs. I climbed to one of the rooftops and asked a Sikh police officer what he proposed to do if the Sikhs refused to come out. He was a handsome man with a yellow turban and a silky black beard.

"Oh, they must come out some time."

"You don't intend to enter the temple to make arrests?"

"Certainly not, that would be sacrilege. Besides, we would have to take off our shoes."

Finally the defiant Sikhs came out, in small groups. The police drove patrol wagons as near the temple gate as religious scruples would allow, and the Sikhs obligingly entered them, singing hymns.

I went to talk to Master Tara Singh, the leader of the Sikhs.

Tara Singh sat cross-legged on a charpoy, under a small tree in a stone courtyard. He looked like Father Christmas. He had a spreading white beard and jovial eyes in a merry, wrinkled brown face. He wore a blue turban, and had on a pair of white pajama trousers, whose strings had come undone. Fortunately no ladies were present. He greeted me cheerfully and told me that the Sikhs were winning hands down.

Tara Singh was in his mid-sixties. His family had been Hindus, and he had not turned Sikh until he was seventeen. He became a schoolteacher and also plunged into politics. He challenged British rule of India and was arrested. He defended himself with imperturbable good humor against a charge of "conspiring to depose the King-Emperor," and by his untiring eloquence spun out his trial to three years. This made him famous and his followers nicknamed him "Patthar," or "the stone." He was soon in trouble again and was jailed for conspiring with the Red Shirt leader Ghaffer Khan. His contact with the Red Shirts made him think of an independent Sikh State. "If Pakistan," said Tara, "why not Sikhistan?" Gandhi remarked grimly: "Your sword is becoming long."

When Sikhs began slaughtering Moslems in the Partition riots, Master Tara Singh rescued a seven-year-old Moslem girl whose parents had disappeared. "I will bring her up not as a Sikh but as a Moslem," said Tara, "and then restore her to her parents if I can find them, pure as the white snow of the Himalayas." The girl lived for six years with his family—he and his wife have three daughters—and was the only Moslem in the district. Then Tara located the girl's father, who had fled to Pakistan, and restored her to him. "If I thank you 125,000 times, it will not be enough," said the grateful father.

In independent India Master Tara Singh continued to fight for Sikh rights. "Jinnah got Pakistan, the Hindus got India, the Sikhs got nothing," he cried. He quarreled fiercely with Nehru and was jailed for his pains. But the conditions of his imprisonment were unusual. When he expressed a wish to play badminton, the prison authorities obligingly prepared a badminton court for him.

When I visited him he had just emerged, haler and heartier than ever, from another spell of imprisonment.

"There are 6,000,000 Sikhs in the Indian Punjab," he said, "30 per cent of the state's population. But the state is ruled by Hindus, and the Sikhs are persecuted."

I took this contention with a grain of salt. The Sikhs held 34 per cent of the civil-service posts, and most of the police were Sikhs. There were three Sikhs in the Punjab Cabinet, and four Hindus. In India as a whole, the Sikhs formed only 1.7 per cent of the population, but 15 per cent of the army were Sikhs, and 21.7 per cent of the army officers.

"It will be all right," Master Tara Singh told me cheerfully. "Nehru is here in Amritsar and I am seeing him tonight. We shall fix things up between us." I was sure they would: the sagging Congress Party needed the support of the Sikhs.

Meanwhile the Sikhs of Amritsar with Master Tara Singh's benevolent approval continued to take out processions. They danced through the town's narrow lanes, beating sticks and drums and twirling faster and faster to the music of brass bands that played, incongruously, Scottish airs and "Way down upon the Swanee River." I stood at the Hell Gate bazaar and watched thousands of Sikhs parade past, all wearing blue turbans and brandishing curved swords. The bandsmen blew into enormous, curving brass trumpets shaped to resemble dragons' heads. And several elephants had been inspanned. All other Indians regard the Sikhs as slightly crazy, and treat them with careful respect. They are the Irishmen of India.

The Congress Party was also holding a rally in Amritsar, and was also recalling its martyrs. The Jallianwalla Bagh had got a new coat of red paint, and a signboard proclaimed: "Here nonviolent Hindus, Moslems, and Sikhs who were holding protest meetings in this garden were massacred by the British General Dyer." In 1919 General Dyer opened fire on a large crowd. The nonviolent mob had just set fire to a bank and killed five people. The Indians claimed that General Dyer killed 2,000, the British admit to 149. The 1919 bullet holes had been carefully covered over with glass to preserve them.

At the Congress Party rally Mr. Dhebar, the Congress Party president, was taken out in a procession, standing up in a jeep and escorted by 61 maidens, 61 motorcycles, 61 bullocks, and 361 horses and 361 camels. The numbers apparently had some mystical significance. Mr. Dhebar passed under 1,000 arches, erected at a cost to the taxpayers of $40,000. He was followed by a giant float in which hideous demons called "provincialism" and "lingualism" had arrows shot at them by virtuous persons representing "national unifying forces," which otherwise remained unspecified. When he arrived at the meeting Mr.

Dhebar was presented with a gold statuette of Mahatma Gandhi and some thousands of rupees' worth of roses and narcissuses. The slogan of the rally was "Toward a casteless society on a socialist basis."

Eighty Congress Party leaders attending a "construction workers' conference" at the town's Khalsa College left their shoes outside: when they came out four hours later, all 80 pairs of shoes were gone.

Amritsar received hundreds of badly needed telephone lines, so that the politicians could keep in touch with Delhi: a cynic remarked that they would normally have taken twenty years to install. "The Congress Party has a new plan to end corruption," the newspapers proclaimed.

Official cars carried stickers saying: "On Official Duty." An unscrupulous printer turned out some thousands of these and sold them to all and sundry. The official stickers were changed to: "VIP." The printer copied these, also. The official stickers were changed again to read: "VVIP." Only cars bearing the "VVIP" sticker were allowed to enter the meeting-ground.

I secured a "VVIP" sticker and drove to the rally. The reception committee had prepared vast quantities of literature. Mr. Chaudhury Ranbur Singh, M.P., was described as "a rigid Congress man accustomed to strict discipline without making even the slightest allowance for mental reservation: he wields great influence." Mr. Singh was the general secretary of the reception committee. The Chief Minister of the Punjab was described as "a brilliant orator, extraordinarily diligent, an enthusiastic reformer, a persistent crusader against corruption, a terror to publicmen of questionable integrity. Nobody can imagine that he holds a Master's degree in political science of an American university." It struck me as an odd sort of tribute.

The hucksters had turned out in force for the rally. One offered "a magic purgative (number of stools as desired)." Another displayed "a powder composed of pure pearls for all diseases of the eyes." A third high pressured customers with his "best specific for spermatorrhea."

Indira Gandhi made a speech scolding the United States. "The amount of foreign aid we get is not much compared with our own efforts," she grumbled. "Even to get that much, we give a sort of right to foreigners to slander our leaders and our country. Some of them take it into their heads that they have a right to interfere in our affairs. We cannot tolerate this." Indira was evidently still in favor of discipline, especially for foreigners.

Meanwhile former "criminal tribes" paraded outside, begging the Congress Party to give them ten acres of Punjab jungle land per family, which they humbly offered to clear with their own hands. "As sturdy tillers, we will add new luster to the prosperous lap of Mother India," their leaflet proclaimed.

Mr. Nehru, in a more sober mood than his daughter, warned that "continued violence will lead to civil war." But nobody paid much heed to that.

Do not sleep on the railroad tracks. SIGN AT BHAKRA NANGAL

THE PEASANTS of Patiala were afflicted by a plague of wild cows. Over a thousand of the beasts were on the rampage. The peasants had to sit up night after night to protect their fields: disgruntled by official inaction, they had launched a civil-disobedience campaign and were refusing to pay rent. "The cows are God's herds," said an official, shrugging. "What can we do?"

India has 140,000,000 cows, but most of them are useless beasts. They contribute 100,000,000 tons of cow-dung a year to the economy, for use as fuel and manure, but only a thin trickle of milk. The Hindu's religion forbids him to kill useless cows.

The cows of Patiala had gone dry and, therefore, had been turned loose in the jungles in the hope that they would die. Instead, the cows had turned savage and were raiding their former owners' fields.

Ludhiana was celebrating *Maghi,* the day Guru Govind Singh converted sinners. The celebrations took a novel form. At a public ceremony the Sikh superintendent of police had 17 repentant criminals paraded before him. Their names had been picked at random from the police dossier of local bad characters. The superintendent made a speech, addressing the criminals on the error of their ways. Would they please promise to try to reform? They would indeed. "In that case," said the superintendent magnificently, "you may go: from this day henceforth, you will no longer be known as bad characters." Then he went off to open a brand-new children's park.

We drove to Bhakra Nangal, where under American supervision 125,000 workers were digging 700 miles of canals and building a dam 680 feet high. It was Nehru's pet project, and was costing the Indian Government $320,000,000. The man in charge was Harvey Slocum, who built the Grand Coulee and had put up dams in Mexico and Cuba, the Argentine and Alaska.

The Indian Punjab, with a population of 16,000,000, is the size of Mississippi. By harnessing the Sutlej, the Bhakra Nangal project will turn the Punjab into the sort of granary the undivided Punjab was before Partition. The dam, which Nehru called "the biggest and toughest job being done anywhere in the world," should be ready by 1960. Meanwhile Mr. Slocum was having plenty of problems.

I spoke to some of the 40 American construction workers and their families who were living at the site. They were wryly amused by the fact that the Indian engineers privately referred to them as "mere workmen without education." The Sutlej is a sacred river: one of the Indian engineers had gained such prestige from his contact with it that he had abandoned engineering and retired to Agra, where he was currently worshipped as especially holy. The Communists, however, were busy telling the Punjab peasants that the water would not irrigate their fields, because the Americans were removing its electricity.

"It's a constant uphill battle against ignorance, overconfidence, and corruption," said one of the Americans. Most of the Indian workmen had not known one end of a tool from the other. They had never seen a locomotive and were in constant danger of being run over. Punjab officials were chagrined to discover that they would not be permitted to hand out sub-contracts to their relatives, and had acquired a deep loathing of the Americans in consequence. There was some mild sabotage, and there were constant pinpricks.

"The police are constantly arresting our domestic servants on imaginary charges," the American said. "Then it's hinted to us that we can have them released by paying their 'fine.' If we don't pay promptly, the servants get beaten up."

We came down out of the rocky canyons through which the Sutlej swiftly flows to Chandigarh, the new capital of the Indian Punjab. An area of 15 square miles had been handed over to a team of architects and town-planners with instructions to create a modern city. The all-star team included Le Corbusier of France, Albert Mayer of New York, and the Maxwell Frys (a husband-and-wife partnership) of England. The chief challenge to the experts was that their city, when completed, would have as backdrop the 92 visible peaks of the Himalayas, all of them over 24,000 feet high. The city would be expected to live up to the scenery.

To my mind, the architects' joint efforts were shaping up into a cubist's paradise and an ordinary man's nightmare. The sharp-angled buildings, all squares, boxes, and oblongs, recalled the submarine turrets that were sprouting along the highway into Karachi. There was a great emphasis on "sun-breakers," projecting bricks and concrete fins set at angles in the walls. Turrets with knobs on. "You will find here no gorgeous towers, no gigantic domes, no cupolas or ornate lattices," said an enthusiast. "The planners have avoided the expressionist luxuries of traditional Indian architecture." That they had. So do the people who design prisons.

But somehow caste had crept in. We were taken to see a house in Sector 16. It looked like a large apartment house that had been miraculously shrunk to the proportions of a single home, but without losing any of its suggestion of communal cubicle living. A flat-top, it had two walls of brick, but the rest was white concrete. "It is an upper-category house," our guide explained. "It is reserved for a higher-grade government servant." Then he took us to see some boxlike apartments, built in two stories in a crouching row and faced with brick screens pierced with round holes for ventilation. They looked to me like a row of Indian sweepers bent double. "These are for personnel of a lower category," he explained.

Some children were playing in a scrubby park. They were clambering up and down a concrete object that resembled the twisted bleached branches one finds cast by the sea on a shore. "It is a sculpture," said the guide. "It symbolizes the uplifted caressing arms of a mother."

We inspected the nine-story Secretariat, oblong and very knobby, then passed to the highlight of Chandigarh, the squat square High Court building. A turbaned sentinel, complete with rifle, stood on guard between the massive pillars flanked by concave vaulted walls. In the Hall of Justice, which had bright yellow chairs, the Chief Justice sat with his back to an enormous abstract tapestry which would have provoked controversy if placed in the Museum of Modern Art.

The official residences provided for Punjab Ministers had sharp-angled snakes wriggling across the outside walls. "They are zigzags," said the guide, "to break the monotony."

We visited the white-pinnacled temple of the goddess Chandi, slayer of demons, and departed from Chandigarh with mixed feelings.

All things must be shared. THE *Mahabharata*

IN AN upland valley not far from Tanakpur, on the Nepal border, a sixteen-year-old girl was spiritedly contesting the valley custom whereby all the younger sons share the elder son's wife.

The hill slopes were covered with tiny terraced fields and the people, who looked Mongolian, lived in tall and rather splendidly carved wooden houses. On the veranda of her home the girl went on determinedly spinning wool and paying no attention while her five husbands and the village elders pleaded with her.

"I married only Gulab Singh," she said. "I will have nothing to do with his four brothers." She cast the discomfited young men a scornful look. "If I cannot have one husband, then I will divorce all five." Gulab Singh, the elder brother, a handsomely built man, looked both pleased and appalled.

The valley folk had devised the custom to prevent the little farms from being subdivided. "If each son had his own wife," a village elder explained, "he would naturally want his own farm." The Indian Government had taken note of the custom and had dispatched a team of social workers to investigate. "They go around with notebooks asking us indecent questions," said the elder indignantly. It did not seem to me that the custom was going to be easily changed, for, apart from the question of land, there was a great shortage of women, who were outnumbered by the men by four to one. "The men are very sporting about each other's rights," a local politician told me. But the women were evidently getting different ideas.

I had to leave this interesting experiment in polyandry, for at Tanakpur I got news of two missing Welsh mountaineers. Sydney Wignall and John Harrop had set out to climb a mountain in western Nepal and had been seized and taken into Tibet by the Chinese Communists. They had finally been released but had been compelled to walk back over dangerous passes, with no equipment and little food, and had turned up at Pithoragarh.

Beyond Tanakpur the road wound steeply upwards toward snowy peaks, while below the plain of the Terai tilted dizzily: it was like seeing the earth from a high-altitude rocket. I left Singh and the Studebaker at Ghatt, for there was no motor bridge across the river, and walked two miles to catch a bus to Pithoragarh, twenty miles farther on. It was dark long before the bus reach Pithoragarh, but the driver preferred feeling his way to using his headlights. He also had a fearful habit of taking both hands off the steering wheel to make an obeisance when the bus passed wayside shrines to Shiva. As the road was excessively narrow as well as precipitous, so that the offside wheels continually teetered over a dizzy drop, I found this practice somewhat unnerving.

But we reached Pithoragarh without mishap, and I stumbled up a steep pitch-dark street to a dark bungalow, to be enthusiastically greeted by two heavily bearded young men and a smooth-faced one. The bearded men were Wignall and Harrop, and the smooth-faced one was their Nepalese guide, Damodar Suwal, who had shared their adventure. He was an eighteen-year-old student with a humorous eye and a plume of black hair falling over his temple.

I had brought with me quantities of canned salmon, corned mutton, cheese, sausages, ham, and beer, and the mountaineers fell on the food voraciously. They had been kept locked up in Tibet for a long time, and their diet there had left much to be desired. When they were at last released they had been forced to return over a hideously dangerous route, and they had an angry suspicion that their captors had not expected them to survive the march to tell their tale.

We went down the mountain in the morning and crossed the river to Ghatt, where Singh and the Studebaker awaited us. When we got back to Delhi the story had two odd sequels.

XX

DELHI: THE NEW LOOK

We are a more efficient and a cleaner nation than most nations of the world. NEHRU

IN NEW DELHI they were busy building new apartments— with servants' quarters—for government bureaucrats. The apartments were going up south of the Diplomatic Enclave, an area set aside for foreign embassies. In the Diplomatic Enclave the United States was planning to build an imposing new embassy to resemble the Taj Mahal. I had my doubts if this would endear the United States to the starving Indian masses.

Meanwhile in New Delhi's Connaught Circle the carpenters' shops and printing presses and metal workshops had overflowed on to the sidewalks, where they competed for *Lebensraum* with the city's beggars and its 20,000 lepers. In Old Delhi sewage overflowed the main streets, and the "markets" were still piled high with junk and filth. In both New and Old Delhi the drains were choked, and the goat carcases in the butchers' shops were blanketed thickly with flies. The newspapers were filled with an indignant clamor about those conditions, and the Health Minister was finally prevailed on to send round inspectors.

But the inspectors were withdrawn when a number of them got stabbed, by people who protested that the inspectors were trying to take away their livelihood and so add to the millions of India's jobless. A wit explained: "The hawkers of Delhi hold it as their fundamental right to poison the citizens, under the umbrella of full employment."

There was an epidemic of jaundice, which was finally traced to the fact that sewage had got into the city's drinking water.

Nehru gave a reception for the Shah of Iran in the Red Fort. Officially it was a civic reception, and Nehru modestly declined a front seat, contenting himself with a chair placed behind the Delhi Chief Minister. There was a sycophantic roar of laughter from the gathering over the Pandit's modesty, but in fact his move proved a wise one. When the Shah turned up the crowd stampeded in order to get a better view of him, and pandemonium ensued. The members of the diplomatic corps, whom I had last seen being trampled underfoot at the airport when Nehru returned from Russia, this time scrambled to safety by climbing up on top of the Red Fort's marble pavilion. A floodlight came crashing down, narrowly missing the Pakistan High Commissioner. An Indian lay screaming on the floor with his leg caught in the steel bracket of an overturned chair, while the crowd milled over him.

The builders of the new apartments were trying to give Delhi a new look, but it all seemed distressingly familiar to me. This I felt was where I had come in; and it was almost time to go.

I went to see Sett Rao, for I was anxious to learn how he had fared in his attempts to capture Putli, the bandit queen. "Oh, she is still at large," he said cheerfully. "The other day she led her men into a village, on horseback, and had them tie up fourteen villagers whom the dacoits suspected of being police informers. She had them all shot, and then she rode away." When I asked Sett Rao what he proposed to do, he shrugged. "It is out of my hands; the government is sending me to Peking."

I was busy with my own departure plans. Jane and the children were leaving first, by sea: I would follow them later. The wicker shield and Picasso's portrait of Gertrude Stein were packed away, to the distress of the lizards who had lurked behind them while digesting flies. All our books were crated, and

327

a list in triplicate duly delivered to the Indian customs, lest we might be trying to smuggle pernicious literature out of India. At last I was left alone in the white bungalow.

The Welsh mountaineers had told their story, and the Nepalese Embassy issued an indignant denial. Under pressure the Embassy agreed to hold a press conference. The Welsh mountaineers were not invited, but the Embassy's star witness was Damodar Suwal. He was an honest young man. When an Indian reporter asked if it were true that the mountaineers had been ill-treated by the Chinese Communists, Suwal answered cheerfully: "Oh, yes: they also beat me, with rifle butts." The Nepalese Embassy officials were anxious not to offend Red China, Nepal's powerful next-door neighbor. An official leaped up, thrust Suwal back in his seat, and said: "Gentlemen, do not pay any attention to our young friend, he has been drinking too much brandy." That terminated the press conference. Suwal was hastily put on board a plane and flown back to Katmandu, the capital of Nepal. I sincerely hoped he would come to no harm for having told the truth.

The other sequel to the episode of the mountaineers was the arrival in Delhi of a policeman from faraway Tanakpur. He brought with him a warrant for Singh's arrest, but he had no notion what the charge was. He simply repeated stolidly that he had been sent by his superior officers to arrest my driver and take him back to Tanakpur. I was appalled. We had not run over as much as a chicken, and I could think of no offense that either Singh or I could have committed. I racked my brains, and thought back over the details of our mountain trip. We had seen no traffic, for the road had wound desolately and precipitously over the mountains. We had passed a few herds of goats, but hardly any people. Singh said gloomily that it would take him at least a week to get to Tanakpur and back. I reluctantly relinquished him to the policeman, and urged him to lose no time in getting a message to me if the charge turned out to be serious.

I went round saying good-by to all our friends, but the farewells were overshadowed by my anxiety about Singh. I myself had to leave soon for Bombay, but I could not go until I knew what was happening to him.

He was away eight days, and when he turned up he was stroking his beard and mustache, and grinning.

"What happened?" I cried.

"Very little. I had to appear in court, but I was only fined five dollars."

"But what was the charge?"

Singh's grin broadened. "Crossing an intersection without halting."

XXI

BOMBAY: CITY IN TUMULT

The wisest foresee a rending and tearing of those kingdoms by division when the king shall pay the debt to nature, and that all parts will be torn and destroyed by a civil war. SIR THOMAS ROE, 1616

IN AMRITSAR Nehru had warned that a continuation of violence in India would lead to civil war. But the Maharashtrians of Bombay were unimpressed by the arguments for national unity, and were in the grip of the demons of provincialism and lingualism.

Truckloads of steel-helmeted police drove round streets littered with debris. The Gujeratis' stores had been looted, and an old man with a white beard lay over the threshold of his shop in a pool of his own blood; the rock that had been used to smash his skull lay beside him. In the alleys between the *chawls*, tenements where the Maharashtrian mill-workers lived, the mobs had hung up crude effigies of Nehru and Gandhi, and had then set them on fire. The mobs smashed every statue of Gandhi they could find, then garlanded the broken statues with festoons of old shoes—the ultimate Hindu insult, for shoes are made of leather. "They have forgotten he was the Father of the Nation," said a tight-lipped city official. "They only remember he was a Gujerati."

Young men in ragged shirts were dragging benches into the middle of streets to serve as barricades. Behind the barricades, which were to halt the police trucks, they heaved up paving-stones with crowbars, then carried the stones indoors and up to the balconies of the tenements, from which they dropped them with a resounding crash. Other young men were collecting the broken chunks to use for throwing at the police.

A truck loaded with police swung round a corner and halted at one of the barricades. It was greeted with a fusillade of stones, and the police opened fire with rifles. A man fell screaming and holding his bloody stomach, which had been ripped across. One of the mob wrenched open the door of my taxi and bundled the wounded man inside at my feet. Then he leaped in beside the driver and ordered him to drive to the nearest hospital. The blood of the wounded man soaked over my shoes, and on the way to the hospital we ran into a barrage of tear gas. I washed my eyes at the hospital fountain while they rushed the wounded man indoors.

The police drew their trucks up in a long line, facing a row of *chawls*. The trucks were suddenly showered with bottles filled with acid, thrown from the upper windows, and the police fired back with their rifles. The windows were hastily closed. A platoon of policemen with their heads lowered raced across the street and battered their way into one of the tenements. There were confused shouts, and shots, and the policemen returned with struggling prisoners.

Sikh soldiers with bayoneted rifles stood by at the Cricket Club. The Sikh captain I had met at Poona had been right: when things got very bad, the Sikhs were called in. "But we shall not interfere unless we have to," an officer told me. "The trouble is that most of the police are themselves Maharashtrians."

I called on one of Nehru's top Ministers at his big house on Malabar Hill overlooking the bay. He was a Gujerati. We sat on his veranda, looking down at the curve of the bay. He sat on a couch, with a telephone close to his hand. Every few minutes the telephone rang and more reports of violence came in. The

Gujeratis were beginning to leave the city; it looked like the Partition all over again.

But he was remarkably calm. He talked patiently of the virtues of nonviolence. It was a hot, sticky day, and there were mosquitoes about. When I slapped one he looked pained.

"You should not have done that," he said severely. "It is very bad to kill any living thing." He was a Gandhian, a teetotaler, a nonsmoker, and a vegetarian. Killing for food and for self-preservation had hitherto been the law of life, he said, but it need not always be so. "Even the caterpillars eat the cabbage leaves. But one day, by pure love, we shall teach them to eat only dead leaves."

I brought the subject back to the killing that was going on between Maharashtrians and Gujeratis, and asked him what he proposed to do about that.

His eyes flashed.

"You must show justice to a wolf; but you need not be kind to it. These Maharashtrians are wolves. If we allow them to have their way, they will destroy Bombay, which we Gujeratis created. We must not give in, for, if we do, democracy will become mobocracy, and all of India will be torn to pieces. I shall restore order in Bombay if I have to shoot every Maharashtrian!"

The rioting died down, flared up again, died down, simmered sullenly with much unrest under the surface. It shifted finally from Bombay to Ahmedabad, the great cotton town, where the Gujeratis in their turn went on the streets to smite the Maharashtrians amid further bloody rioting and police firing. Nehru sped down from Delhi, and addressed a stormy meeting. For the first time in his life, he was booed instead of being cheered. Four thousand students from Gujerat University howled him down. "You are neurotic, frustrated, juvenile delinquents," Nehru told them. "You are Fascists, and the Communists are your brothers." The Pandit was understandably angry, for he had every reason to believe that India's right-wing parties had joined hands in an unholy alliance with the Communists to keep the riots going and bring chaos to India. It was already a far cry from the day when Nehru had smilingly joined Khrushchev in the slogan: "Indians and Russians are brothers!" I was not to know it at the time, but the Hungarian revolt would shortly be adding to Nehru's growing doubts.

And so I left India: a continent, as someone had said, as polyglot and populous as Europe; a land of snowy mountains and rich river valleys, of baking plains and deserts, of thick jungles and palm-fringed coasts. I had not seen all of it, but I had seen a good deal. I had met many of its politicians; but I had fonder memories of the friendly peasants in its 600,000 villages. They had been very kind to me: I could say, with Kipling: "I have eaten your bread and salt." And I recalled what Nehru had said, sadly, in the midst of the riots on the anniversary of Mahatma Gandhi's death: "We are all small men, living in a big country." But there were some big men, too.

INDEX

i

A NOTE ON THE AUTHOR

ALEXANDER CAMPBELL was born in Edinburgh, Scotland, on October 19, 1912, and was educated at Edinburgh University. He worked as an editorial writer on a Scottish newspaper until 1937, when he moved to South Africa, where he lived for seventeen years. *The Heart of Africa* (1954), a thorough survey of that troubled continent, was his first book to be published in this country, although six others had appeared in England and South Africa. In 1954 Mr. Campbell left his post as Johannesburg bureau chief for *Time* and *Life* and moved to the New Delhi bureau. During his two years in India he ranged from Srinagar and Calcutta down to Bombay and Pondicherry, getting the feel of the country by meeting its people face to face. *The Heart of India* is the record of these encounters. Mr. Campbell now heads the Tokyo bureau of *Time* and *Life*. He is married and the father of three children.

A NOTE ON THE TYPE

This book is set in ELECTRA, *a Linotype face designed by* W. A. DWIGGINS *(1880–1956), who was responsible for so much that is good in contemporary book design. Although much of his early work was in advertising and he was the author of the standard volume* Layout in Advertising, *Mr. Dwiggins later devoted his prolific talents to book typography and type design, and worked with great distinction in both fields. In addition to his designs for Electra, he created the Metro, Caledonia, and Eldorado series of type faces, as well as a number of experimental cuttings that have never been issued commercially.*

Electra cannot be classified as either modern or old-style. It is not based on any historical model, nor does it echo a particular period or style. It avoids the extreme contrast between thick and thin elements which marks most modern faces, and attempts to give a feeling of fluidity, power, and speed.

This book was composed, printed, and bound by KINGSPORT PRESS, INC., *Kingsport, Tennessee. The paper was manufactured by* S. D. WARREN COMPANY, *Boston. The typography and binding designs are based on originals by* W. A. DWIGGINS.